Race and the Revolutionary Impulse in THE SPOOK WHO SAT BY THE DOOR

Studies in the Cinema of the Black Diaspora

MICHAEL T. MARTIN AND DAVID C. WALL

Published in cooperation with the Black Film Center/Archive, Indiana University

Indiana University Press

RACE AND THE REVOLUTIONARY IMPULSE IN

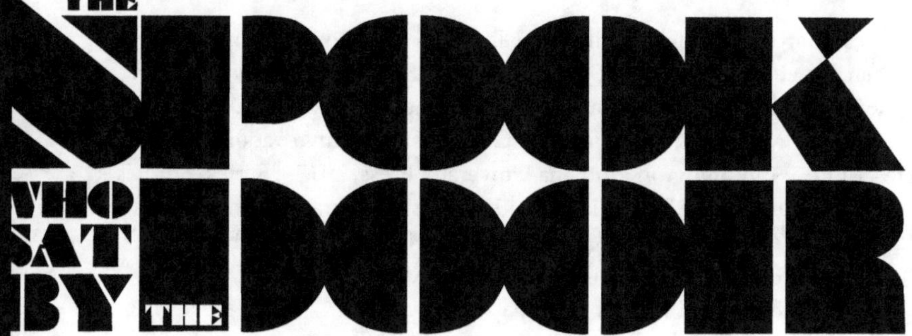

Edited by MICHAEL T. MARTIN,
DAVID C. WALL, and MARILYN YAQUINTO

This book is a publication of

Indiana University Press
Office of Scholarly Publishing
Herman B Wells Library 350
1320 East 10th Street
Bloomington, Indiana 47405 USA

iupress.indiana.edu

This publication supported by funding from the Black Film Center/Archive, Indiana University

The paper used in this publication meets the minimum requirements of the American National Standard for Information Sciences—Permanence of Paper for Printed Library Materials, ANSI Z39.48–1992.

Manufactured in the United States of America

Library of Congress Cataloging-in-Publication Data

Names: Martin, Michael T. editor. | Wall, David C. editor. | Yaquinto, Marilyn editor. | Greenlee, Sam, 1930-2014. Spook who sat by the door.
Title: Race and the revolutionary impulse in The spook who sat by the door / edited by Michael T. Martin, David C. Wall, and Marilyn Yaquinto.
Description: Bloomington : Indiana University Press, 2017. | Series: Studies in the cinema of the black diaspora | Includes bibliographical references and index.
Identifiers: LCCN 2017020635 (print) | LCCN 2017015154 (ebook) | ISBN 9780253031808 (eb) | ISBN 9780253031754 (cl : alk. paper) | ISBN 9780253031792 (pb : alk. paper)
Subjects: LCSH: Spook who sat by the door (Motion picture) | Racism in motion pictures. | Race relations in motion pictures. | African Americans in motion pictures.
Classification: LCC PN1997.S653 (print) | LCC PN1997.S653 R33 2017 (ebook) | DDC 791.43/72—dc23
LC record available at https://lccn.loc.gov/2017020635

1 2 3 4 5 23 22 21 20 19 18

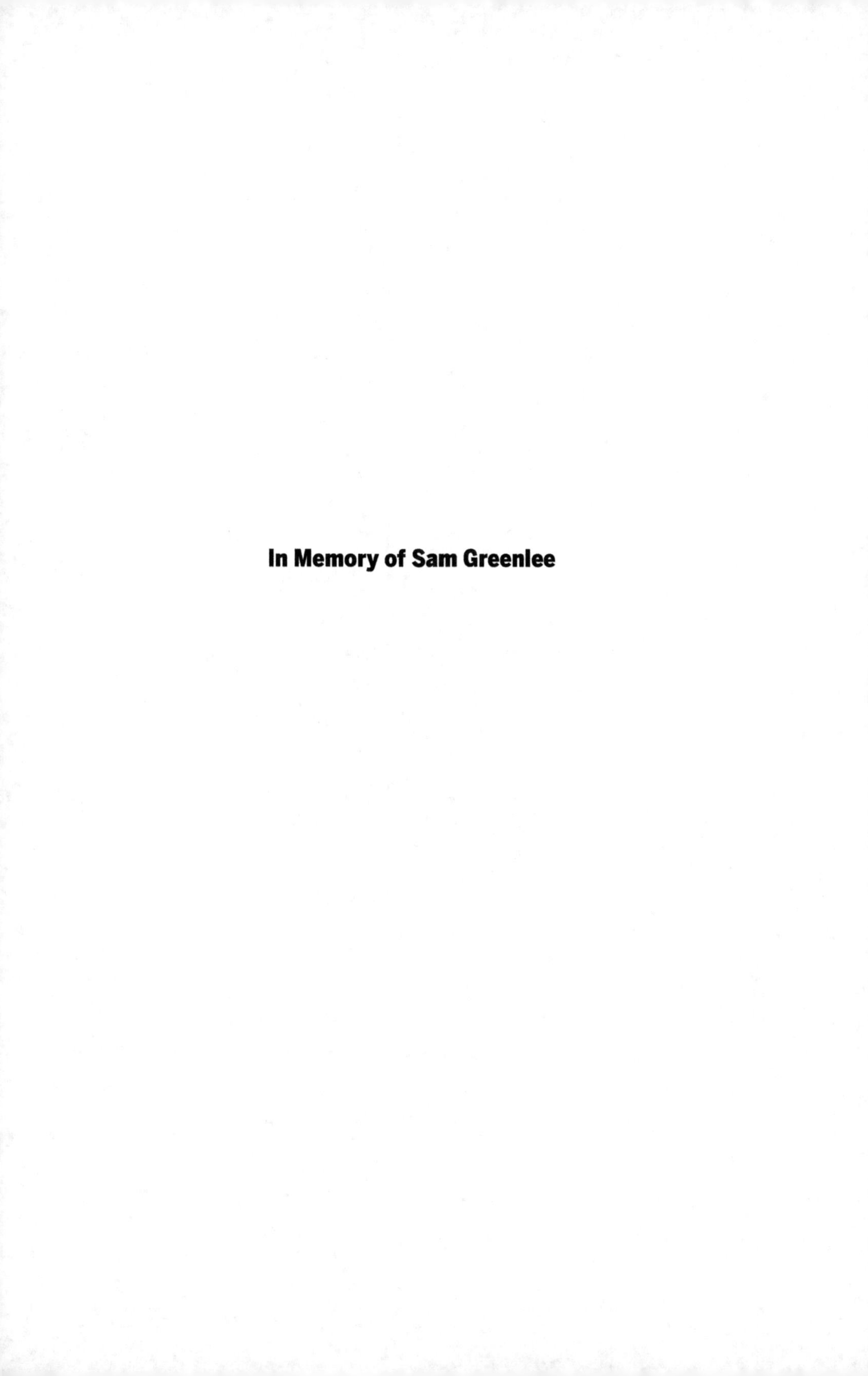
In Memory of Sam Greenlee

CONTENTS

ACKNOWLEDGMENTS

A project such as this is inevitably the work of many more hands than merely those of the editors. It is to all those people we must offer a general thanks for their support, encouragement, and useful and necessary criticism. There are, however, some more specific thanks we would like to offer. Firstly, we must acknowledge the support of the Black Film Center/Archive (BFC/A) at Indiana University, Bloomington, which hosted the *Cinematic Representations of Racial Conflict in Real Time* symposium in the spring of 2010 from which this book derives. Equal thanks must go to Indiana University for their awarding of a New Frontiers grant to the BFC/A without which the symposium itself would not have been possible. As we have gone through the process of putting this collection together many people have committed their time and energy in countless ways in an effort to ensure the quality and relevance of the contributions herein. At Indiana University Press, Janice Frisch and Kate Schramm have given us invaluable support and advice. Their patience with the progress of the book (as well as us!) has been exemplary. We must also extend heartfelt thanks to Rachelle Pavelko of the BFC/A for her constant efforts in dealing so effortlessly and cheerfully with the organizational and technical limitations of the editors! We must also thank the contributors, the range and quality of whose work serves as a testament not only to the importance of the film but also to the ever-burgeoning body of scholarship being undertaken around the subject of black cinema. Lastly, our greatest thanks must go to

Sam Greenlee for his unceasing efforts on behalf of the project. In addition to making contributions in terms of his personal narrative and the lengthy interview contained in the book, both of which give unique insight into the history and context of one the most significant black films of the period, he gave us free access to all the materials at his disposal as well as giving freely of his time over the lengthy process of putting the volume together. It would, of course, be a much lesser volume indeed without his work and involvement. Sadly, Sam passed away in the spring of 2014, and we hope that this book, in however small a way, will serve as a lasting testament to his work.

The Editors

Race and the Revolutionary Impulse in THE SPOOK WHO SAT BY THE DOOR

Introduction

THE SPOOK WHO SAT BY THE DOOR

Michael T. Martin and David C. Wall

A profitable and appropriate beginning for introducing the subject of this book recalls the events that spawned it, and with which it directly engages: a symposium organized and hosted by the Black Film Center/Archive at Indiana University. The two-day event, provocatively titled—*Cinematic Representations of Racial Conflict in Real Time*—addressed two defining American films of the 1960s and 1970s: Michael Roemer and Robert Young's *Nothing But a Man* (1964) and Ivan Dixon and Sam Greenlee's *The Spook Who Sat by the Door* (1973). Each film, having utility for ideological accounts of historical activity, renders a distinct and compelling mode of political address in real time and during a particularly intense moment of racial conflict in the United States. Indeed, both films foreground the mobilizing strategies of black militants and civil rights activists at the time of their release and similarly share several thematic concerns, from the moral and physical decay of black life in urban America and the challenges of gender and the black underclass to inequality and political oppression.

At a conceptual level, the symposium engaged two concerns: first, the representational strategies deployed in film to signify modes of political address, and second, assessing whether such films contribute to the intelligibility of the present. Do they suggest alternative constructs of agency and social change? Do they contribute to the project of world making? And comprising *cine-memories*, do they mediate between historical moments and infer a futurity?

Of the two films studied in the symposium, *Nothing But a Man* led to the publication of a "close-up" in the film journal *Black Camera*, followed recently by the publication of a volume, expanding the close-up to include several essays, the script, the director's (Roemer) statement, and official press kit.[1] It marked the first sustained book-length interrogation of the film. Similarly, this volume, devoted to the second film in the symposium, *The Spook Who Sat by the Door*, constitutes the first comprehensive book-length project of its kind on this subject. As the materials we have selected for this volume demonstrate, *Spook* has had a dramatic life. At one point all copies of the film had been destroyed other than the one retained in a vault by Ivan Dixon, which then found an underground life on pirated VHS copies until its eventual rerelease on DVD in 2004.

A final fascinating chapter in the story of *The Spook Who Sat by the Door* came in 2015 when it was placed on the US government's National Film Registry. Established in 1989, the registry was designed to preserve those American films considered to be of profound "cultural, historical, or aesthetic significance."[2] Of the 675 films currently on the registry, arguably none have had a more contentious history than *Spook*, and none might have seemed less likely to be included. But its inclusion points squarely to a recognition of the film's significance not only as an extraordinary piece of American filmmaking but also its much wider life as a political document of unique historical importance.

* *

Few American films can have had the contentious and troubled history of *The Spook Who Sat by the Door*. Based on Sam Greenlee's novel of the same title and directed by Ivan Dixon, and while subject to the predictable and usual difficulties of any small independent film project, it was *Spook*'s timely and provocative subject matter that became one of several major hurdles to overcome. The story of Dan Freeman, the first African American recruited by the Central Intelligence Agency (CIA) who subsequently leaves the agency to foment what the editors of this volume characterize as a neo-Marxist revolution among the street gangs of Chicago, *Spook*'s radical vision was unlikely to garner sympathetic supporters in Hollywood. Greenlee and Dixon eventually secured funding through a number of wealthy black investors, produced the film independently through Bokari Ltd., and agreed

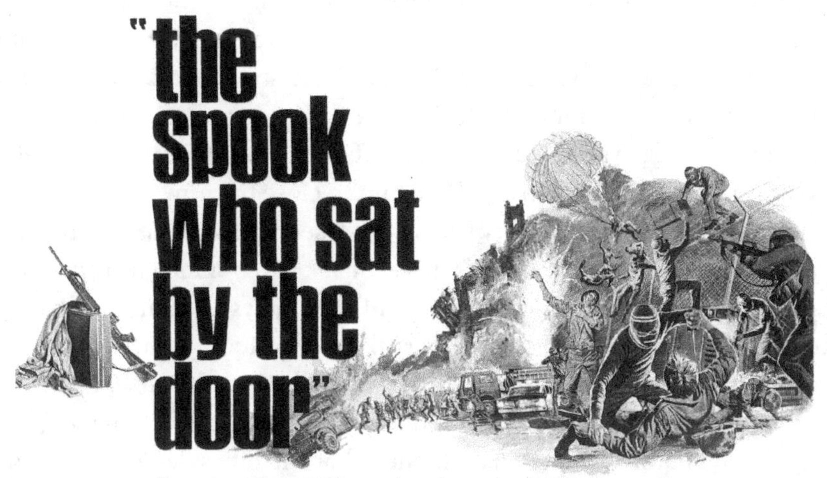

Fig. 0.1 United Artist's original theatrical release poster for *The Spook Who Sat by the Door* (1973).

to a distribution deal with United Artists (UA), which apparently assumed that *Spook* was just another blaxploitation movie. However, in a telling marketing move, UA decided that the original theatrical release poster, though featuring violent clashes between the Cobras and the National Guard as it does, should have no black characters visible at all. With the Cobras all heavily masked, the only faces we see are those of white soldiers, a complete elision of race that is surely reflective of UA's deep ambivalence about the project.

The day-to-day production itself was also beset by problems, with successive interruptions to filming because of financing problems and Mayor Richard Daley's refusal of permission to film anywhere inside the city limits of Chicago. The most notorious event, however, took place once the film was released when, after just a few weeks of being shown, it was pulled from some theaters by UA. Greenlee and Dixon believed that this was because of direct intervention by the Federal Bureau of Investigation (FBI).

As Greenlee asserts in the interview in this volume: "The film opened on Labor Day and, just as it was about to become profitable, they pulled it off the market at the behest of the FBI. . . . [W]hen it opened on a second run at the McVickers Theater on State Street, I went down there and spoke with the manager. . . . He sat me down in his office and said that the week before, two FBI agents had come in to advise him to close the film."

From the hindsight of forty years, it may seem silly to imagine that such a film could pose a terrifying threat. Yet *Spook* is very much a product of its historical moment as it remarks upon and anticipates all manner of national political tumult and global crises in real time, including the nexus that so powerfully resonated between Third World independence struggles and the long history of black insurrection beginning with the colonial period in America. It is quite understandable then that the film's depiction of armed resistance and revolution was threatening to some audiences, the state, and local enforcement agencies.

Spook in the White Imaginary

But *Spook* was no less threatening in other, perhaps less obvious, ways. In his 1973 review of *The Spook Who Sat by the Door,* Kevin Thomas called it "one of the most terrifying movies ever made."[3] This is a fascinating claim to make for a film that *Variety* described much more prosaically as just another "entry into the Blaxploitation sweepstakes,"[4] but of course Thomas was uttering an underlying yet liminal phobia that the movie evokes about America itself. Most apparent, his comment begs the question: terrifying for whom? As Sam Greenlee explains, he first titled his novel (upon which the movie is based) *The Nigger Who Sat by the Door.*[5] But this title would carry none of the nuanced subtleties of "spook." As Samantha Sheppard points out in her essay, the "spook" of the title is intended be read in different ways. It refers, of course, to the term given to spies, to the fact also that blacks were stereotypically characterized as superstitious and fearful, and "because of their skin tone, look like ghosts in the dark."[6] But beyond this she suggests that the term embodies "the psychological fears of an armed Black resistance that haunts white America's consciousness."[7] It is this specter that in part assumes such a terrifying form for Thomas, as the Black Lives Matter movement evokes today, a troubling challenge and preoccupation. However, more than this, while the horror of *Spook*'s meaning certainly renders a vision of an American society unmoored by upheaval and poised on the brink of insurrection, the real existential threat—the phobic haunting—goes beyond the fear of revolt and directly to the terror itself: the ghost—the specter, the ghoul, the spook—lives in that most feverish and potent of spaces, the white imaginary.

This ever omnipresent ghost that *Spook* invokes was first evinced most effectively in *The Birth of a Nation* by the Ku Klux Klan, assuming the garb of the ghostly, as it terrified and brutally forced dominion over the emancipated black citizenry. As such, we are witnessing, in *Spook*'s evocation, the dizzying and futile effort to repel and repress the ghosts of blackness as they sit balefully in the white imagination. And it is to this phobic obsession that the very existence (both literal as well as metaphorical) of whiteness depends. The terrifying reality of the spook, then, is its very phantom presence—the simultaneously here and not-here—and thus that which can only ever be chased, hunted, denied, refused, and contained, but never destroyed. Consider the fundamental paradox at the heart of white America's racial fear and fascination that reveals the porousness of the boundaries that purportedly exist in order to maintain the purity of racial distinctions and supremacy. And while those boundaries between racial, social, and political categories and domains are literal, figurative, and discursive, their porousness invites constant transgression. Moreover, whatever else *The Spook Who Sat by the Door* is, its transgressions sit troublingly on the boundary between the binaries of presence and absence, reality and fantasy, white and black, a constant reminder not only of the ubiquity of blackness in the white imaginary, but also that it is the very thing upon which the white subject depends and rationalizes for its own ontological coherence. As Ralph Ellison explains so potently and poetically in *Invisible Man*, whiteness can exist only in terms of its relationship to blackness. And so, as what is socially marginal assumes a symbolic centrality across the landscape of culture and race (Why else would white America anxiously garland itself in representations of blackness from the pepper pots, money boxes, and lawn jockeys of the early twentieth century to white appropriation of hip-hip fashions in the early twenty-first century?), all representations of blackness in the context of America are girded by those roiling mutually constitutive extremes of fear, fascination, and desire. This is a terrifying film to Thomas because he—no less than Sam Greenlee himself—understood the fact that blackness has haunted the white imaginary since slavery.

Context and Genre

The backstory to *Spook*'s incarnation is derived from Greenlee's experience in the US Information Agency during the 1950s and 1960s, and while he was living in Mykonos, Greece, in the summer of 1965. In response to independence struggles in the Middle East, Africa, and Asia, as well as the increasingly fraught and fractious trajectories of the civil rights movement in the United States, Greenlee determined that the Watts uprising in 1965 was "a forerunner of anti-colonial rebellions, so I went back to Greece to write about how and why an armed rebellion could develop in the U.S."[8] By the time the novel was published in 1969, the rhetoric of nonviolent protest as embodied in King's Southern Christian Leadership Conference (SCLC) had been rivaled by the more militant voices mobilized under the broad umbrella of "Black Power," most notably of the ilk of SNCC (Student Nonviolent Coordinating Committee) and the Black Panther Party. This in turn reflected a more general radicalization of countercultural protest seen in the emergence of increasingly disparate revolutionary organizations, such as the White Panthers, the Black Liberation Army, the Symbionese Liberation Army, and the Weather Underground. Further, events such as the police riot at the 1968 Democratic Convention in Chicago and the subsequent show trials of the Chicago Seven, the 1968 assassinations of Martin Luther King Jr. and Robert F. Kennedy, the 1969 assassination of Chicago Black Panther organizer Fred Hampton, the Kent State and Jackson State shootings, along with the Vietnam antiwar movement, all attest to the volatility of American society in the years leading up to the release of *The Spook Who Sat by the Door* in 1973. Reflecting and refracting these volatile political and racial contexts, the film itself was no less incendiary in its revolutionary project.

While the broader global and domestic political contexts are critically important in making sense of *Spook*, and while *Variety*'s comment quoted above may seem curtly dismissive, the issue of blaxploitation is no less critically important than the broader political landscape of the 1960s and early 1970s. The kind of boundary anxiety we see embodied in the presence of the spook is mirrored in the confusion and contestations over *Spook*'s genre and status. Identifying the particular genre of a film may seem a trivial matter, and perhaps in some ways it is. However, not only is genre the central element in the marketing of all American cinema—mainstream and otherwise—it is also connected intimately to the politics of race. As George Lipsitz puts it in his discussion of genre anxiety and race in 1970s cinema, "generic codes . . . connect activity to identity, reserving clearly defined roles for distinctly gendered, classed, and raced characters."[9] More than this, however, the discourses of cinema inevitably reveal much deeper social and political concerns.

So what genre is *The Spook Who Sat by the Door* and why does it matter? If we accept or assert that *Spook* is an example of blaxploitation, we are immediately situating it within a critical framework that draws upon those negative responses that perceived blaxploitation as essentially apolitical or that, at best, promotes individual over collective agency. And in making any kind of assertion of genre in this way, we are always and immediately limiting and demarcating its significations. But, interestingly, *Spook* deliberately and consciously plays with, up-ends, and subverts these efforts. Multivalence is of course a constitutive feature of all cinematic texts and, released the same year as such now notable blaxploitation films as *Black Caesar* and *Shaft in Africa*, the cinematic as well as cultural status of *The Spook Who Sat by the Door* is profoundly equivocal. As noted earlier, though pitched as blaxploitation to UA by Dixon and Greenlee in order to convince the studio to distribute the movie, it bears little more than superficial similarities to such classics of the genre as *Shaft* (1971), *Superfly* (1972), and *The Mack* (1973). Greenlee and Melvin Clay (co-author of the screenplay) quite intentionally played with the notion of genre as a deliberately articulated political strategy to generate funding for the film. It is a strategy that echoes much of the politics of invisibility that Greenlee employs in the narrative of the film and, as it is built into the very material history and structure of the film, suggests *Spook*'s profound generic instability and unreliability. Indeed, *Spook* is in fact its own spook, moving beyond the attenuated gestures of resistance bound up in materialism and hyper-masculinity of such films as *The Mack*—enough to prompt Ed Guerrero to describe *Spook* as "transcending the boundaries of formula and dominant ideology to explore revolutionary impulses."[10]

Spook as Primer for Revolutionary Praxis

Whatever else it is, and no matter how complicated and unreliable its textual status or how slippery its genre, *The Spook Who Sat by the Door* is a film about black liberation; it is also a primer for urban armed insurrection. But what are those revolutionary impulses? How might we think through *Spook* as a profoundly radical political-cultural text that not only articulates a set of revolutionary strategies, but also presents an example of agitprop, a form of cine-memory that "serves to inspire activism in real time in the real world," "transform consciousness and . . . contribute to the project of world-making."[11] As Marilyn Yaquinto explains at some length in her essay "Cinema as Political Activism," *Spook* is a seminal rendition of Third Cinema. In this sense the film is both descriptive and prescriptive, combining as it does a radical critique that defines black America as an internal colony, while at the same time laying out a programmatic response rooted in time-tested and durable strategies and methods deployed by independence movements to this day in the Third World. *Spook* is unequivocal on this point, asserting that the historical telos of armed response is with the movement. And as Sheppard puts it: "Illustrating the possibilities of a deliberately fomented rebellion, *Spook* dramatizes, as revolutionary, the theme of African American freedom and equality being gained through a political consciousness of armed resistance."[12]

So even though in terms of its cinematic and narrative structure, *Spook* offers little more than a conventional action movie, it is in its mobilizing and prescriptive politics that the truly radical nature of the film (as well as its greatest threat) resides. The argument that radicalism must always be expressed through a dismantling and disruption of the formal qualities of film belies an institutionally racist history approach to film studies and analysis. As David E. James suggests, frequently black cultural production of the period for the most part quite deliberately eschewed any kind of radical formal or aesthetic experimentation because the need was to "stress a populist functionalism."[13] This populist functionalism is where we see those "revolutionary impulses" to which Ed Guerrero makes reference. Eschewing the kind of formal radicalisms championed by European and Latin American directors such as Godard and Solanos, then, Greenlee was explicit that *Spook* should perform its cultural and political labor in this populist way. There is an instructive scene nearly halfway through the film when the protagonist Freeman is in discussion with Pretty Willie, the light-skinned member of the insurgency.

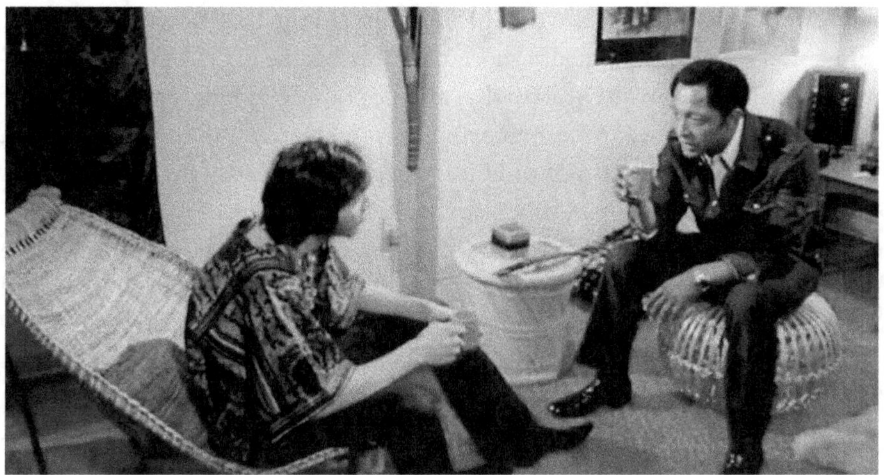

Fig. 0.2 Freeman (Lawrence Cook) discusses the production and use of propaganda with Pretty Willie.

FREEMAN	I wanna talk to you, Willie. The brothers tell me you write.
PRETTY WILLIE	Yeah.
FREEMAN	Good. We need a propagandist. So you are the Minister of Information. I want you to set up a group and use whoever you want.
PRETTY WILLIE	What you want? Like some posters, music, poetry?
FREEMAN	Anything. Just so long as you talk to the people in a language that they understand.

The critical point is not the form—it can be posters, poetry, or whatever Willie decides—but that it be in the language that "the people" understand. This same strategy serves as the foundation for *Spook* as a cinematic text as it did for Gillo Pontecorvo's meditation on the North/South antinomy in *Burn!* (*Queimada!*, 1969).[14] Thus the film is designed never to lose a radical sensibility—rooted in a notion of "the people" that returns us again to the status of this film as an exemplar of Third Cinema—and as it "embraces Third Cinema's goal to use film as a revolutionary tool."[15]

But the drive to be populist and understood by as wide an audience as possible belies the films profound complexity. With *Spook*'s radicalism inhering in its political critique rather than formal structure, there are nuances and complexities in the film that draw us toward the tradition of earlier race movies and more specifically those of Oscar Micheaux. As such *Spook* offers a traditional narrative form that also contains challenging and counter-historical discourses around race and representation. Film critic Jonathan Rosenbaum argues that not only was *Spook* "the most radical of the 'blaxploitation' films of the '70s," but also that it "remains one of the great missing (or at least unwritten) chapters in black political filmmaking."[16] And, like Oscar Micheaux's *Within Our Gates* (1919), Spook too foregrounds "racial issues and social conflicts in powerfully graphic ways that aroused anger and anxiety among both blacks and whites."[17] Notwithstanding its narrative and structural conventionality, this "sobering and angry film" that was "not likely to please either white or black liberal audiences" was indeed, as Michael Ryan and Douglas Kellner contend, "one of the most radical film statements of the era."[18] For Ryan and Kellner it was the film's rejection of the liberal impulses behind the early-modern civil rights movement that assumed equality through integration as a political and social possibility. *Spook* rejects this operative assumption, asserting that racial (as well as gender and class) equality is simply not possible under liberal capitalist democracy, no matter how well-meaning progressive blacks and whites may be. As Ryan and Kellner note, "*Spook* thus places itself far beyond the scope of liberalism, the belief that oppression can be lifted through a negotiated harmony of interests. By dramatizing (indeed merely documenting) the violent nature of white oppression, the film argues for the necessity of much more radical forms of structural change."[19]

While acknowledging the "populist functionalism" of a text such as *Spook*, James goes on to argue that late-60s and early-70s cinema offered a singularly unproductive medium within black cultural production largely because "the contribution of [film's] narrative and formal codes to bourgeois ideological reproduction . . . allowed only one role for the proletariat, that of consumer."[20] But his reading fails to take into account two critically important issues: first, the spectator never engages the text passively. Our relationship to it is always an ongoing process of active engagement rather than passive consumption. And just as individual characters in the films are socially and cinematically constituted subjects, we as viewers are also socially and cinematically constituted subjects. However, while accepting that we make meaning of the text as much as we take meaning from it, we find ourselves on ground that is always contestable and indeed always contested; thus, no film is simply an inchoate or empty eruption waiting for us to pour meaning into. Indeed, every text asserts a claim as to an "official" reading and, in *Spook*'s case, it is the assertion of a clearly delineated program of resistance and revolution. Again, it is one of the intentions of the film that, in its focus on how the characters generate meaningful and revolutionary interactions with and from the social, material, and ideological conditions of their existence, *Spook* encourages the spectators to see in themselves the processes and possibility of making meaning (perhaps even history!) not only within the film but also from their own social conditions. There is a fundamental and inseparable relationship between the discursive and the material—between the social imaginary and the social reality—as the ideological assumes material form in real time. We know that the structures of race are fictions and yet cannot discount the social reality of the lived experience of race. Further, in asserting that consciousness can be raised through political education, *Spook* inserts itself into the materialist functioning of history as an active agent of change. And in its commitment to change coming from the lumpenproletariat—a social class largely dismissed for revolutionary purposes by Marxist orthodoxy—in its asserting the possibility of revolution as a consequence of history, the film demands an acknowledgment that individuals are anything but passive consumers to be simply molded and determined by the bourgeois-inflected narratives of popular cinema.

Second, the apparent simplicity and straightforward linearity of *Spook*'s narrative structure actually belies the profound complexity of the ideological and discursive alignments and allusions to which not only the story and character, but also the spectator, are then made subject. We see this not only through the ways in which Freeman shapes the Cobras into an effective and disciplined guerilla unit but also, and perhaps more importantly, by the way in which the film constantly engages with race as a form of structural discursive performance.

In its implicit reference to thinkers such as Frantz Fanon, *Spook* acknowledges the constructed nature of the racial subject, that race functions as a performative discourse through which characters literally enact the ideological processes through which they are individuated as racial subjects. Indeed, we might argue that from one perspective the film is largely

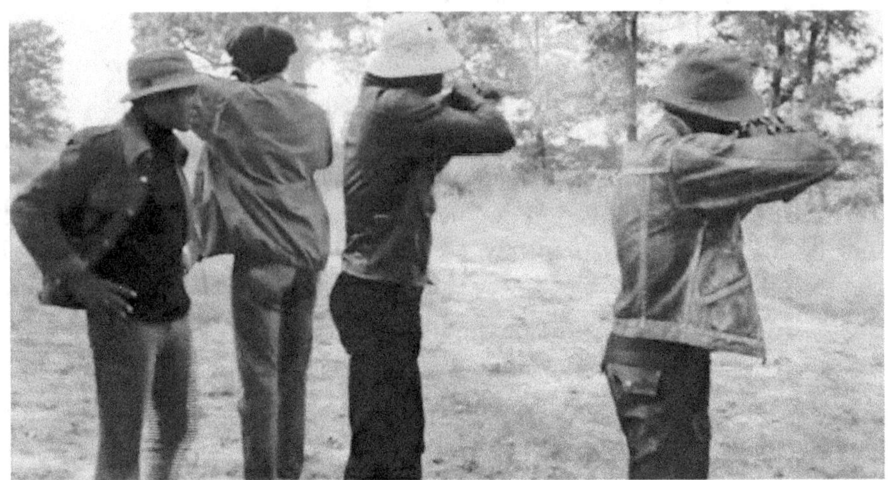

Fig. 0.3 Freeman instructs the Cobras in guerilla training.

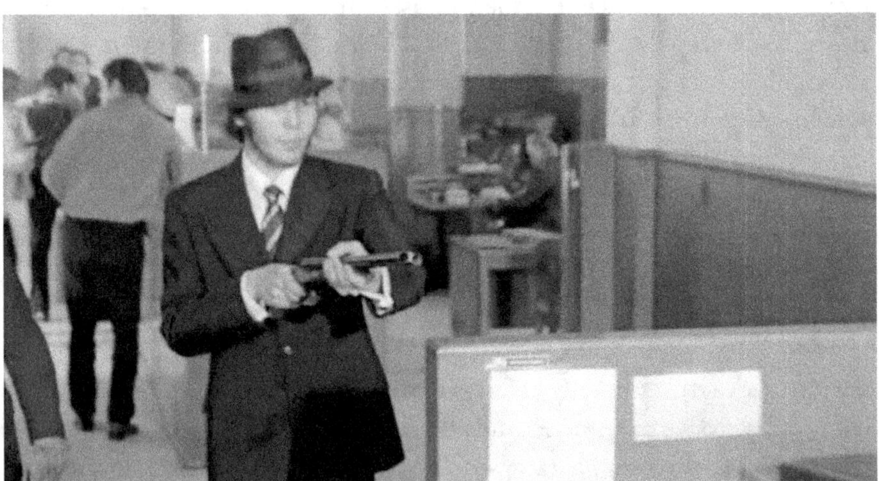

Fig. 0.4 Pretty Willie (David Lemieux) leads the Cobra gang in their armed robbery of the bank.

constituted by the suturing of multiple performances of race, each offering not only a materialist analysis of the kind of coded strategies necessary for survival in the real world, but also the potential pleasures of a conscious ludic engagement with race as performance.

The film is replete with examples, from Freeman's pretense at the CIA to the light-skinned Cobras' tactical role in the bank robbery to Joy's wig

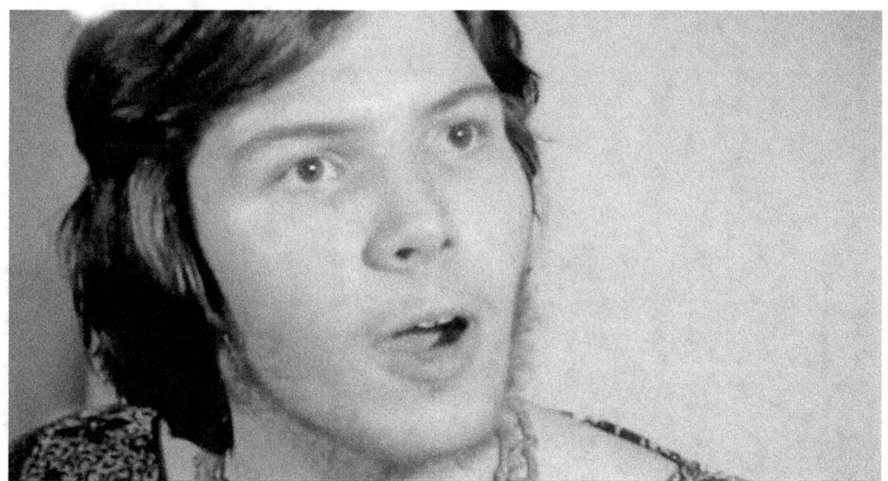

Fig. 0.5 Pretty Willie passionately asserts his blackness to Dan Freeman.

and Pretty Willie's impassioned delineation of blackness as performance when he declares to Freeman that, notwithstanding his light skin, he is always seen as "black": "I am not passing. I am black. Do you hear me, man? Do you understand? I am black! I am a nigger! Do you understand me? I was born black, I live black, and I'm gonna die probably because I'm black. Because some cracker that knows I'm black better than you, nigger, is probably gonna put a bullet in the back of my head."

But of the many examples offered by the film, perhaps none is more telling than when Stud, disguised as a janitor, is sent into the office of Chicago Edison's president to steal a prized collection of pipes literally from under his nose. In setting up the operation, Freeman explains: "Remember, a black man with a mop, tray, or broom in his hand can go damn near anywhere in this country. And a smiling black man is invisible." In articulating the social and material reality of the black subject in white America, this scene simultaneously demonstrates the fluid strategies of pretense necessary for survival and the ways in which that might then further be redeployed tactically by insurgents. But the scene is designed to be as comic as it is serious. And it is in that very redeployment that the pleasures of performance and play are made available to an intended black spectator who will see an identification with and profound investment in the characters and representational strategies on the screen. But this is not an exercise in a kind of theoretical

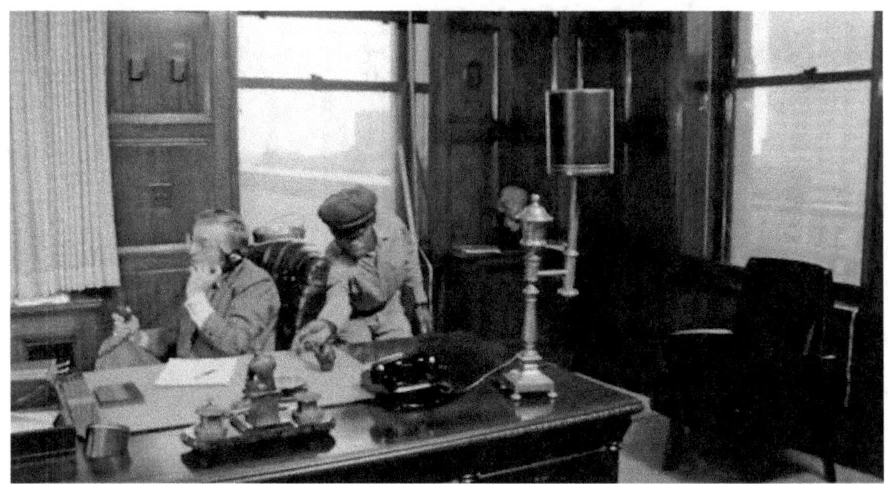

Fig. 0.6 Stud stealing pipes literally from under the nose of the president of Chicago Edison.

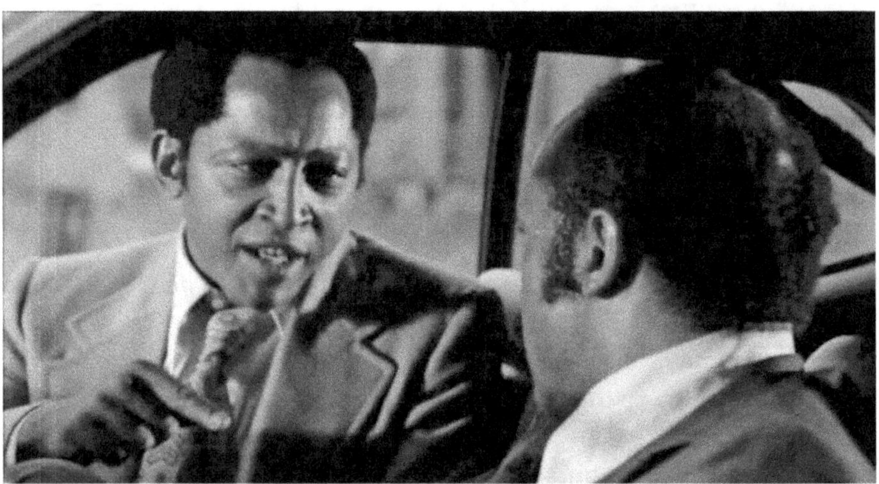

Fig. 0.7 The morning after the violent unrest, Freeman angrily reacts when Dawson (J. A. Preston) criticizes the rioters.

play of significations of race. It is about the material reality and negotiation of lived experience in history. Indeed, as the film demonstrates, it is about understanding the realities of race in late-twentieth century America as a matter of literal survival. It is in that critical moment when Freeman is on the brink of recruiting Dawson that he articulates perhaps the film's deepest truth: "Listen, you think because you got a badge and I got a couple of degrees that makes a difference? Do you know what white folks call people like you and me in private? Niggers, Daws, niggers!" Whiteness sees only the blackness it expects to see. The brilliance of Freeman's (and Greenlee's) strategy is to redeploy that performance and, in its confirming of the assumptions and prejudices of whiteness, to subvert the social and political discourses so that the deeper boundary transgressions (those of liberal democracy) might be undertaken—with the inevitable consequent structural social and political change. In short, the film tells us that history is determinate and the revolution imminent.

As well as the expression of revolutionary politics within the narrative, the material history of the film's own production can lay claim to the radical practice of guerilla filmmaking that corresponds with the finest tradition of Third Cinema. As both Sheppard and Yaquinto illustrate, and as Greenlee repeatedly confirms, if the production of *Spook* was difficult at best, its subsequent release and distribution (as noted earlier) was troubled to say the least by the FBI's intervention. In view of this, it is often difficult to look beyond the issues surrounding the film's generic status, its radicalism, and the controversy surrounding its release. Furthermore, and as a consequence of the nature of the film as agitprop, not much critical analysis has focused on character. But we might argue that that is at least in part because the political impulse of the film as a revolutionary text inevitably situates many of the characters as archetypes or stock characters, upon which the narrative depends, within a populist frame. But there are three critically important characters through which we can discern a key triangulated relationship. Freeman, Dahomey Queen, and Dawson each occupy a fascinating subject position, not only in relation to each other as characters within the narrative, but also as embodiments of the logic of the historical telos; each speaking to the history of and for race in the real time of a counter-hegemonic moment. Thus they represent a profoundly significant expression of Greenlee's sense of black America as an internal colony much like Haile Gerima evokes later in *Bush Mama* (1975), situating the black community's malaise and underdevelopment within global and colonizing formations. As Freeman, without equivocating, explains to the Cobras: "What we got now is a colony. What we want to create is a new nation. In order to do that, we gotta pay a different kind of dues. Freedom dues."

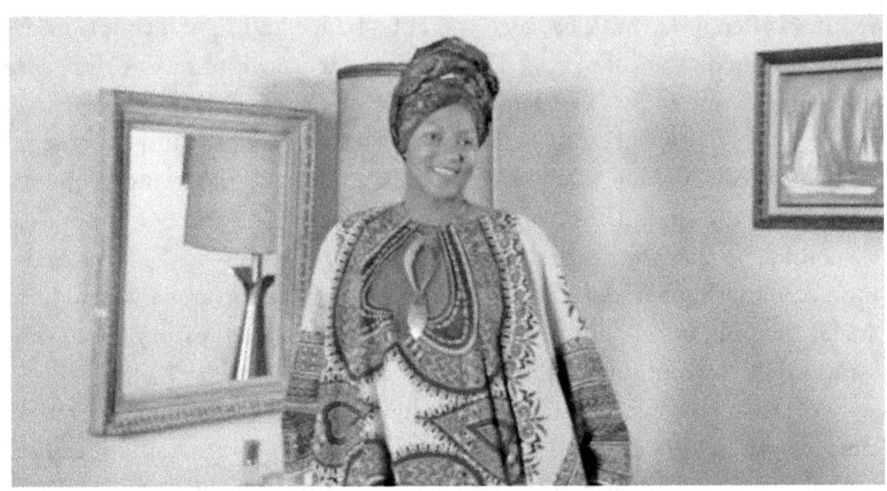

Fig. 0.8 Her political consciousness having been raised by Freeman in the first part of the movie, the Dahomey Queen (Paula Kelly) reappears later in the film in African dress.

While Stephanie Dunn argues (not unconvincingly) that, from one perspective, Dahomey Queen functions as the focus for a "heterosexist black masculinity"[21] at the core of the Black Power movement, we might equally well-read her as an image of political empowerment. Arguably the most significant character in the film after Freeman, it is Dahomey Queen alone who literally embodies the move toward full and radical political and cultural enlightenment. As Dunn says, her late appearance in the film wearing "full African regalia . . . symbolizes her evolution into the Afrocentric consciousness that Freeman introduced her to."[22] But again, while Dunn argues that she functions as an "exotic sexual primitive,"[23] we can see that her gaining an understanding of her own history in this way allows her to see herself as connected much more broadly and purposefully to the community. This has deeply radical implications. In introducing her to the Dahomey peoples, Freeman is actually introducing her to an entire history of Africa that had been systematically discredited and denied, and of which she was completely unaware. Though she appears on screen for a relatively short time, Dahomey Queen signals a profound shift in both political and racial consciousness, moving as she does from prostitute to guerilla operative—yet another spook—working from the inside and supplying Freeman with information that is critical to the success of the insurgency. It is telling also that Freeman is able to trust Dahomey Queen with the truth of his identity in a way that he cannot with his oldest friend, Dawson, or his ex-girlfriend Joy, whose bourgeois commitment to the social and racial status quo is informed by her inability to think outside of the dominant structures of race. Defined wholly by her false consciousness, Joy has too much to lose to be able to think of herself as black rather than middle class.

As the central protagonist, Freeman sits in relation to the characters by whom he is surrounded. Mirroring the febrile instability of the modern subject, his identity is in some ways floating and unfixed. This ambivalence speaks to the ontological instability of the racial subject within a set of cultural and historical discourses that have consistently refuted the humanity of blackness. We might even link this ontology of blackness back to DuBois's double consciousness, as Freeman embraces the tension of visibility/invisibility and employs the veil as a political and military tactic. It would appear that nobody—from his fellow agency recruits to the CIA top brass to Dawson to Joy—knows the real Dan Freeman. But of course rooted in the material as this Marxist analysis of society is, there must be a real Dan Freeman and indeed, as he reveals to Dahomey Queen, there is. However, employing race as he does—quite deliberately as a "floating signifier" with multiple referents—it is a deep reality and a truth that Freeman reveals only at those moments and to those people he decides can be trusted. This serves to both reject any sense of victimhood while underscoring the importance of masking as a visual, rhetorical, and political strategy employed in the service of the revolution. Freeman's dress acts as potent signifier of his shifting identity, indeed it is the most obvious form of masking. Switching from sober suit, white shirt, and tie at the CIA to dressing casually but fashionably as simply another member of the black, educated middle class in Chicago, or wearing guerilla gear combat gear when fighting with the Cobras, Freeman's shifts and changes are another element in the constant process of tactical and political engagement.

In some ways Freeman's most significant relationship is with his oldest friend and erstwhile fellow gang-member, Dawson. Though they have each escaped the street life of their youth and apparently become respectable members of the black middle class, their lives are then drawn across the vectors of history in very different ways. In a narrative relationship that echoes films such as *The Public Enemy* (1931), Dawson and Freeman find themselves

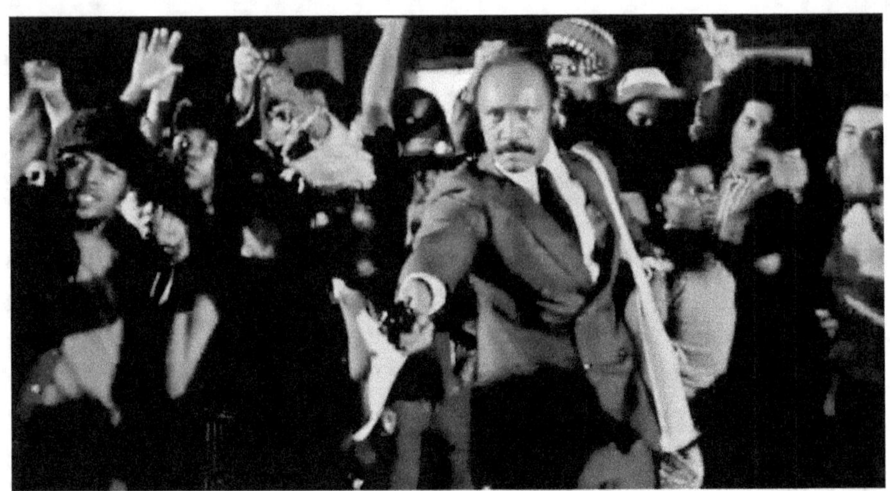

Fig. 0.9 Against Dawson's orders, police dogs are brought out in an effort to disperse the demonstrators.

on opposite sides of the law. But what might at first appear to be a retelling of a Hollywood cliché is actually a much more nuanced and complicated effort to understand the complexity of a character such as Dawson. It is too much of a simplification to suggest that like Joy he has simply bought an investment in the status quo that he is unwilling to cede. Rather, Dawson is all too well aware of the tensions and pressures to which African Americans of all classes are subject. A case in point occurs during the riot when he reacts violently to the sudden presence of police dogs threatening demonstrators. Similarly, as he and Freeman discuss the violence that has taken place over the previous few days, he makes an implicit connection to the notion of black America as an internal colony when, in his own invocation of "the people," he acknowledges the racial structures of the oppressive state:

FREEMAN	When did the National Guard come in?
DAWSON	Late last night. All white.
FREEMAN	I noticed.
DAWSON	Yeah, the people didn't dig it when they woke up this morning and, uh, found the troops were here.

Further, he then also accepts that what had taken place was not a "riot" in the normative sense of that term: "There were some good people out there on the streets the last few nights. Not just hoodlums like they say in the newspapers." As Greenlee asserts in the interview: "It would be easy to dismiss [Dawson] as being one more bourgeois sell-out. He's not, you know. He's on a tightrope. He knows, like Freeman, the kind of pressures he's under. But he has been brought up to try to make things happen. Freeman has rejected that premise; he knows it ain't gonna work." Dawson makes a different choice to Freeman for motives unlike that of Joy's, which ultimately costs him his life. It is part of the film's subtlety that both Dawson and Freeman are seen to make perfectly understandable choices within the logic of their own characters and circumstances; Freeman comes down clearly on the side of revolution, and Dawson, the status quo. For Greenlee, in Dawson's case it was simply and historically the wrong one. More revealing of the Freeman-Dawson duality (binary), we discern a historically important counterpoint: that social class standing is not always an accurate determinant and predictor of political affiliation.

Spook's Audiences

Gesturing as it does to a critical social engagement with the material and political conditions of lived experience, a consideration of the film's audience is particularly important. Though *Spook* was not made with a white audience in mind, contends Greenlee in the interview, we need to consider how varied subject positions might bring multiple and contingent meanings to the text. In other words, the complexity of character within the frame, we argue, is reflected in the complexity of spectatorship because the multiplicity of subject positions within any given audience (whether of race, gender, age, class, nationality, ethnicity, etc.) will invariably render an equally diverse set of responses by audiences. The reality of race as a floating signifier demands that we acknowledge the potential multiplicity of readings of race within any given text. But in acknowledging the multivalence of the text, we also need to keep in mind that there is a clearly articulated set of intentions—an official reading, as it were, that is in constant tension with the film's own assertions, aggressions, elision, and erasures. Greenlee is quite explicit about what that official reading should be. The purpose of the film, as he explains in the interview, is to be a "handbook" for armed struggle and written explicitly for "the brothers and sisters on the block."

There were other radical independent films of the period dealing with similar themes, not least of which was the vision of white director

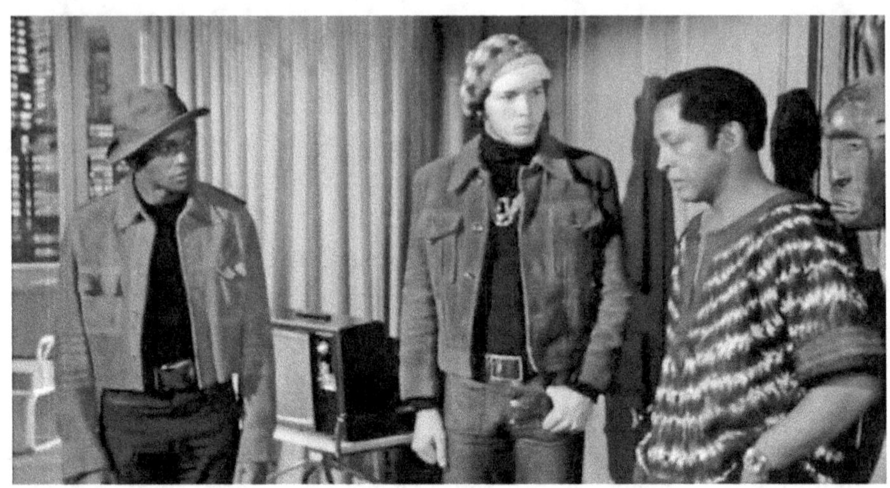

Fig. 0.10 Stud (Don Blakely) and Do-Daddy (Paul Butler) arrive at the apartment to discover that Dawson has been killed by Freeman.

Robert Kramer's *Ice* (1970), which imagined a multiracial insurgency in urban America. But of those films made specifically for a black audience, we need to mention John Coney's *Space Is the Place* (1974.) Indeed, there is a credible argument to be made that *Spook* and *Space* are perhaps the two most genuinely radical American films of the early 1970s. Though different in style, theme, narrative, and genre, they share an uncompromising belief in an imminent black liberation fueled by a transformation in social, economic, political, and cultural life. In short, each film demands an intervention in the processes of history that will lead to black liberation. In *Space Is the Place,* Sun Ra's conclusion is to exit planet earth and migrate to the stars to establish a black world elsewhere; for Greenlee, it is to reconstitute the black subject and transform the material conditions of life under capitalism.

But while offering two profoundly different responses to the crisis of black America with each intended to empower black people, we might consider also how *Spook* speaks beyond the black audience. Consider that Greenlee's address and analysis goes far beyond the limitations of race to encompass class as a similarly key analytical category. For example, when Pretty Willie asserts his hatred of "white folks," Freeman angrily corrects him: "Hate white folks? This is not about hate white folks. It's about loving freedom enough to die or kill for it if necessary." Freeman of course has to make that choice himself when he kills Dawson at the close of the film. It is not that race is not of primary importance but that the efficacy of the insurgency and, therefore, revolution will depend on class solidarity. As Freeman explains to Stud and Do-Daddy when they arrive at his apartment to remove Dawson's body:

> You think we're playing games, killing white strangers? There are a lot of Dawsons out there, and some of them will try to stop us. But anybody who gets between us and freedom has got to go. Now that's anybody. You got the Airborne out there now, and forty percent of those troops are black. Maybe they'll help us, and maybe they won't. But in the meantime, if you hesitate with any one of them because he's black—just once—you'll be one dead Cobra.

It is the blandishments of bourgeois ideology—whether through the likes of Joy who has bought into the entire apparatus of middle-class materialism or the kind of intellectuals who, as Greenlee puts it, "don't make revolutions [but] co-opt revolutions"—that *Spook* is designed to counter. In seeing the film as a critical commentary on America of the 1960s and early 1970s, as well as a "primer for revolution," Greenlee insists that the film is designed to engage, connect with, and inspire the lumpenproletariat. He asserts that the lumpen "are always the center," and as such *Spook* was made for the people "down on the block." And while acknowledging that the revolutionary cause can transcend race and that "there was a cult following among revolutionaries and left-wing whites," the film's "core audience has always been the brother and sister on the block."

Though over forty years have passed, *Spook*'s complex articulation of the intersection of race and class is no less relevant now than when it was first released in 1973. Watching with the benefit of four decades hindsight, it is easy to dismiss its vision of revolution as either fantastical or inevitably doomed to failure. When asked why the revolution he envisioned hadn't taken place, Greenlee argued that it had been sold out by what he called "the bourgeois leadership," as has been the case with "every social revolution in the twentieth century." Whether that is historically the case or not demands a different arena for discussion, but it is doubtless true that, as Greenlee says himself, "revolution is always relevant!" In that sense, in its assured and undeterred vision of an America in which black people are systematically denied equal rights and subject to state sanctioned violence, *Spook* speaks presciently to the contemporary moment. It is a sobering thought that the emergence of the Black Lives Matter movement is the consequence of these historical facts and reality of life. As we turned the corner of the late-twentieth century and stumbled into the twenty-first, a startlingly similar condition of black social life remains the same to that of the early 1970s. Ostensibly in response to the acquittal of George Zimmerman in the shooting death of the black teenager Trayvon Martin in 2013, we suggest that Black Lives Matter is the most recent formation in the long history of black resistance since emancipation.

From this context and perspective, though out of circulation for many years and with a narrative rooted in the tumultuous specificities of the mid-to-late 1960 and early 1970s American society, *Spook* resonates far beyond the confines of its own place and history. As becomes apparent through the collection of materials contained in this volume, the film's dynamic engagement with the politics of race is prescient, anticipating raced political events that continue to play out to this day. As the materials collected in this volume clearly illustrate, the cinematic text is inescapably linked to the broader historical and political contexts from which it emerges. Though much of American film is dismissed as "mindless entertainment," they each demonstrate the fallacy of that argument in relation to *The Spook Who Sat by the Door*. Situating its agitprop Third Cinema impulse in the contemporary moment, Marilyn Yaquinto persuasively argues for the film's endurance as "a historical text about black militancy in the early 1970s, but also as a study of the revolutionary potential of oppressed peoples anywhere and the use of the cinema as a potential tool of liberation." In her detailed analysis of the history of *Spook*'s production and exhibition, Samantha Sheppard examines the way that the film engages with a range of black cultural production, not least the plethora of documentary work of the late 1960s and early 1970s that sought to understand black America. Further, she analyzes what she sees as the "interrelated histories" of gangs and social resistance asserting the utopian impulse that lay behind the film's visionary efforts to historically resituate and purposefully redeploy the black underclass and disaffected youth from hoodlums to revolutionaries. In doing so, and reiterating arguments around the nature of the text itself, Sheppard suggests that "*Spook*'s complex relationship to the past, present, and future can be and should be contextualized within the rebellious and radical narrative of the film itself." These two essays are complemented appropriately by the screenplay and press kit for the film, and a lengthy interview conducted by the editors with Greenlee, in which he outlines in great detail not only the genesis of the novel, but also the subsequent history of the movie and its relationship to the novel. In elucidating and expanding upon the storyline, characters, and production itself, Greenlee fleshes out his political vision at the heart of the film, which still resonates nearly fifty years later. Throughout the interview he returns again and again to the idea of class struggle as the key analytic in understanding the social reality and mobilizing imperative of race in America; he refuses to accept the neo-liberal assertion that Fukiyama's "end of history" is upon us. Asked whether he really saw the film as a primer for revolution, he assents: "Yeah, it could have happened exactly the way I wrote it and should have!"

NOTES

1. See *Black Camera*, vol. 3, no. 2 (Spring 2012): 85–204; and David C. Wall and Michael T. Martin, eds., *The Politics & Poetics of Black Film* (Bloomington: Indiana University Press, 2015).

2. "National Film Preservation Board," Library of Congress, https://loc.gov/programs/national-film-preservation-board/about-this-program/.

3. Kevin Thomas, "Melodrama with Powerful Message," *Los Angeles Times*, December 19, 1973.

4. Sege, "*The Spook Who Sat by the Door*," *Variety*, October 2, 1973.

5. See interview with Greenlee.

6. Samantha Sheppard, "Persistently Displaced: Situated Knowledges and Interrelated Histories in *The Spook Who Sat by the Door*," *Cinema Journal*, 52.2 (Winter 2012): 71–92.

7. Ibid.

8. See interview with Greenlee.

9. George Lipsitz, *American Studies in a Moment of Danger* (Minneapolis: University of Minnesota Press, 2001), 186.

10. Ed Guerrero, *Framing Blackness: The African American Image in Film* (Philadelphia: Temple University Press, 1993), 103.

11. We define this particular form of cine-memory in the following way: "*Cine-memory* of this kind works in a film's narration to transform consciousness and, in the best tradition of Third Cinema, invites audiences to consider their own outcomes for historical struggles. In this sense, such *cine-memory* contributes to the project of world making. Further, the use of Class 3 *cine-memory* projects alternative modes of human conduct, alludes to both preexisting and potential social formations, suggests new and alternative social and political concepts, and foregrounds the future as indeterminate. Accordingly, in theory, Class 3 *cine-memory* is transformative and emancipatory. It proffers an enlightened and optimistic view of the human condition, illuminating a path towards the future." For a fuller discussion and explication of the theory of "cine-memory" and its political function within narrative cinema, see Michael T. Martin and David C. Wall, "The Politics of *Cine-Memory*: Signifying Slavery in the History

Film," in *A Companion to the Historical Film*, eds. Robert A. Rosenstone and Constantin Parvulescu (New York: John Wiley & Sons, 2013), 445–467.

12. Sheppard, "Persistently Displaced," 71.

13. David E. James, *Allegories of Cinema: American Film in the Sixties* (Princeton: Princeton University Press, 1989), 177.

14. Deploying conventions of the action genre, *Burn!* takes up the transition from slavery and colonialism to neocolonialism on a Caribbean island, signifying the global struggle between capital and labor. It is also the late director's critique of the war waged by the United States in Vietnam and in recent years the subject of renewed interest because of the Anglo-American war in Iraq.

15. Marilyn Yaquinto, "Cinema as Political Activism: Contemporary Meanings in *The Spook Who Sat by the Door*," *Black Camera*, vol. 6. no. 1 (Fall 2014): 5–33, 7.

16. Jonathan Rosenbaum, "The Spook Who Sat by the Door," http://www.jonathanrosenbaum.net/1988/07/the-spook-who-sat-by-the-door-2/.

17. Robert Henry Stanley, *Making Sense of Movies: Filmmaking in the Hollywood Style* (New York: McGraw-Hill, 2003), 319.

18. Michael Ryan and Douglas Kellner, *Camera Politica: The Politics and Ideology of Contemporary Hollywood Film* (Bloomington: Indiana University Press, 1988), 32.

19. Ibid., 33.

20. James, *Allegories of Cinema*, 178.

21. Stephane Dunn, *"Baad Bitches" and Sassy Supermamas: Black Power Action Films* (Chicago: University of Illinois Press, 2008), 82.

22. Ibid.

23. Ibid.

1. Writer/Producer's Statement

THE MAKING OF *THE SPOOK WHO SAT BY THE DOOR*

Sam Greenlee

The idea that eventually produced my first novel, *The Spook Who Sat by the Door,* first occurred during a visit to Chicago from my home at the time on the island of Mykonos in 1965. It was the summer of the Watts rebellion, and I was convinced that it was only the harbinger of numerous other "riots." It was at the time of severe unrest among the black community: King-led demonstrators were on the march, and there was anti-racist activity throughout the nation. Armed struggle had not yet begun, but I felt it inevitable in reaction to mounting police abuse.

Returning to Greece, I gave serious thought concerning the possibility of an organized black revolution in the United States, and several months after my return to Mykonos, I abandoned the book I was writing at the time to begin the manuscript of *The Spook Who Sat by the Door.* I finished the book in early September 1966, and before the end of that year, I'd received the first of more than forty rejections of the manuscript in the US prior to its eventual first publication in London by a brand new publishing firm founded by two twenty-three-year-old former classmates: Englishman Clive Allison and Ghanaian-born Margaret Busby. An instant best seller that was excerpted in the *London Observer,* receiving three book-of-the-year mentions in the *London Times, Telegraph,* and *Irish Times,* the book was bought by Bantam Books and published in the States in January 1969 and eventually translated into German, Dutch, Finnish, Swedish, Italian, and Japanese.

In writing the book, I drew on my experiences in Third World postcolonial nations in which I'd served as a Foreign Service Officer of the United States Information Agency in Iraq, East Pakistan, and Indonesia, as well as my personal and vicarious experience with armed revolution and guerilla warfare; my master's thesis concerned the Soviet revolution of 1917. My experiences in postcolonial nations had convinced me that many of the same instruments of control during the centuries of imperialist domination (segregation, discrimination, the assault on indigenous languages and culture) were identical to those same measures utilized in the oppression of black America; therefore, I determined to write the story of a Third World colonial revolution as it might happen in the United States. Furthermore, I was determined not to write a "protest novel" wherein the protagonist would be physically or spiritually destroyed in a futile effort to confront American racism; on the contrary, I would write a novel of defiance that featured a protagonist without illusion concerning the futility of appealing to the nonexistent conscience of white America and who would meet racism on its own military terms.

Although the book would be a conscious departure from classic works such as Wright's *Native Son*; Himes's *If He Hollers, Let Him Go*; and Ellison's *Invisible Man,* I was determined to use what I'd learned from those literary masters. I would attempt to capture Wright's fiery defiance; Himes's gritty, blues-based ironic humor, and Ellison's quiet lyricism.

In contrast to more than one hundred reviews in Britain, most of them favorable, my novel was all but ignored by the American literary establishment. That is still true more than three decades later; in short, I am the *Invisible Man* of African American literature. Nevertheless, I felt I'd scored a victory in finally obtaining publication of a book that remains controversial among blacks and anathema among most whites in the United States.

The making of the film proved an even more intriguing adventure. I met actor Ivan Dixon, in Los Angeles in 1970, who indicated an interest in directing the movie version of the novel; we became full partners on a handshake and two years later were shooting the film on location in Gary, Indiana, as the city of Chicago had refused to issue permits to shoot in Chicago; the scenes of Chicago were stolen with a handheld camera.

After the film script had been rejected by every major studio in Hollywood, Ivan and I began raising independent funds from predominately black investors. With only two weeks of production left, a consortium of wealthy black investors in Washington, DC, expressed interest in providing the funds necessary to complete the film; however, Jesse Jackson intervened, invoking the name of Martin Luther King, and the DC investors backed off. King, of course, was dead and, ironically, I met his daughter, Yolanda, last year, and she indicated that her father had read my book in manuscript form and admired it.

We then cut the action scenes into a ten minute trailer, screened it for the major studios, and it was finally picked up by United Artists, thinking they had a blaxploitation shoot-em-up. That provided the final $150,000 to complete the film that was released in Chicago on Labor Day, 1973. After sixteen straight weeks on *Variety's* list of the fifty top-grossing films, *The Spook Who Sat by the Door* was withdrawn from theaters at the behest of the FBI!

I have been the target of phone taps, mail interception, character assassination, and at least one intervention by the CIA that prevented me from attaining a government position. The FBI admits they have a dossier on me but refuse to relinquish it on the grounds of "national security." In addition, I have not published a novel since 1976, nor had a stage production of my work since 1970. In short, I have been designated a "non-person" in the Soviet sense. Were I an African political exile, I could probably command a fat salary at a leading white university, and I am not unaware of that irony.

My academic credentials notwithstanding, I have found it impossible to attain a position at a college or university and, most recently, was turned down as artist-in-residence by the Black Studies ghetto at the University of Chicago, at which I am an alumnus, as well as Chicago State, the Center for Inner City Studies, Columbia College, and Northwestern University. Since my return from voluntary exile in the south of Spain and Ghana, I have [been] turned down as a teacher on a college level thirteen times, and eleven of that thirteen by "black" faculty!

Nevertheless, I have few, if any regrets, because I got in their face and didn't blink. Sing no blues for me because I sing my own, and for me, the blues are freedom songs!

2. "Duality is a survival tool. It's not a disease"

INTERVIEW WITH SAM GREENLEE ON *THE SPOOK WHO SAT BY THE DOOR*

Michael T. Martin and David C. Wall

MICHAEL T. MARTIN: *Thank you, Mr. Sam Greenlee, for agreeing to this interview during the occasion of the screening of* The Spook Who Sat by the Door *at Indiana University Cinema. Let's begin by talking about your political formation. After you completed a bachelor's degree in political science at the University of Wisconsin at Madison, you served as an officer in the army and studied international relations at U. Chicago. Following that you entered the US Foreign Service and worked for the US Information Agency* [USIA] *for several years. Did the Foreign Service experience affect your worldview?*
SAM GREENLEE: It solidified it. I intellectually grew up in the Third World. My first post was in Baghdad. I was hoping to go to Africa, but when I found out what Americans were doing abroad, I didn't want to be a part of it in Africa. I was rubbing shoulders with successful revolutionaries, people who had fought either as armed rebels or as nonviolent protestors to rid themselves of European occupation.

MM: *When were you stationed in Baghdad?*
SG: When the Anglo-American puppet government of King Faysal II and Prime Minister Nuri as-Said was overthrown on July 14, 1958. Most reports claimed it was a Baathist revolution; it wasn't. Qasim's second in command was a Baathist, and he eventually overthrew Qasim, who was an Iraqi nationalist and wanted to improve conditions for his citizens. Because of the pressure against him, he became more and more involved with the communist

party. His second in command I think was Salam, who later ousted him. This occurred after I left Iraq.[1]

MM: *In what capacity were you in Baghdad?*
SG: I was in what they call the Junior Officer Training program [JOT]. It was designed to bring in young people like myself, fresh out of school, and train them as propagandists. For the first two years, I was on probation. I found out after I had left Baghdad that the staff—predominantly white—voted to end my service. Most Americans lived within walking distance or a short distance from the embassy, but there was one family on the opposite side of town who resided there because they wanted to know Iraqis. I was asked to go and escort them back to the embassy under fire and was recommended for a citation. That one act saved me that time because you can't fire a hero.

MM: *Why did they want to end your service?*
SG: I wasn't that kind of nigger that white folks were comfortable around. I ain't Spike Lee. You know, I'm just me, the same in here [BFC/A offices] as I am on Sixty-Third Street.

David Wall: *Were you the only black person there?*
SG: There were three of us among the embassy staff: one in USIA and another in AID [Agency for International Development]. They were just beginning then to recruit blacks into the Foreign Service. I was the third to come in under the JOT program, and when I left eight years later, there were still only three. After I left, one more came after me.

MM: *In* The Spook Who Sat by the Door, *the protagonist Dan Freeman, when speaking to fellow insurgents, cites Algeria as an example of a successful armed struggle against French colonialism. In 1958, when you were stationed in Iraq, the Algerian War of Independence had begun nearly a year earlier.*[2]
SG: Right!

MM: *Did the Algerians' struggle influence you?*
SG: Definitely. The Iraqis I befriended talked about Algeria and about their own circumstance. I knew a revolution was brewing, and I casually

mentioned that to the executive officer and was chewed out. At the time Iraq had the most stable government in the area and was a cornerstone of the Baghdad Pact,[3] but only a matter of months after that, the revolution jumped off. I found out then how deeply American Foreign Service people had put their heads in the sand. They just didn't want to know—"It's not on my watch"—because if an anti-American regime came, then heads got to roll.

MM: *Was your circle familiar with* [Frantz] *Fanon's writings in '58?*
SG: No. I don't think he published until sometime in the '60s.[4] One person asked me if I had been influenced by Fanon. No. I spent more time in a wider variety of Third World countries than Fanon did. I didn't need him to tell me about what was going on out there. I never could have written *Spook* if I hadn't been in the Foreign Service because it's based on my personal and vicarious experiences.

MM: *Was the Foreign Service* [State Department] *concerned about him?*
SG: Not at that time. He came on stage later.

MM: *After Iraq?*
SG: I went to East Pakistan, which is now Bangladesh.

MM: *In the same capacity as you did in Iraq?*
SG: Yeah. It was the final year of my JOT.

DW: *What was your responsibility in Baghdad and East Pakistan?*
SG: I trained and worked in all aspects of the USIA. It no longer exists; it was folded back into the State Department. It was divided into two sections: the information section, which puts [the] word out through press releases, magazines, interviews, and film; and the cultural section supervised the Fulbright Exchange Program. It hosted American artists and scholars who research and teach abroad. In effect, it tries to put a good face on American policy.

DW: *When stuff was disseminated in magazines, for instance, was it attributed to USIA?*
SG: Sometimes yes, sometimes no. For example, USIA made a weekly newsreel that played all over the country and pretended that it was the [Iraqi]

government's. They didn't fool anybody; I'm sure the shoeshine boy knew what they were doing. In Iran, across the border, USIA was openly producing films to support the Shah when I was there in '58.

MM: *What are the most important realizations you came to from your eight-year experience in the Foreign Service?*
SG: That being the parallel history and correspondence of Third World people to African Americans—first as slaves and later as a target for manipulation and oppression. The same tactics were used, the same kind of propaganda, the same methods of hiring flunkies to control people. And I came to recognize that the South Side of Chicago was a Third World country.

MM: *Do you mean that the colonial experience of peoples in the Third World was similar to African Americans in the United States?*
SG: It was almost identical in every way. I saw the same things going down there that I had observed at home. And I also saw the same forms of resistance that we as a people developed over the years. So, I felt quite at home with Arabs and Asians. They accepted me like a brother.

MM: *Did it give you pause knowing what the State Department was doing in the Third World and your complicity in that process?*
SG: I understood exactly what was going on. I stayed on with some reluctance because I felt I was learning so much. In fact, I considered quitting after a year or two, but it would've been counterproductive. It wasn't until I went to Greece that no longer justified my being in the Foreign Service.

MM: *What was happening in Greece?*
SG: I was sent to a Greek university to study and probably would have had a lengthy career spent in Corfu. I was trained in Greek; it's my most fluent language. When I realized that there was no real justification for my being in the Foreign Service, I resigned. In '67, when the CIA backed the colonels' coup d'état, several of my close friends were incarcerated.[5] Because of that, when I asked for an extension on my visa—which I usually got for a year—I was given three months, so I got the message: "Get out of Dodge." I left Greece in three or four weeks. It was there on the island of Mykonos that I

wrote *The Spook Who Sat by the Door.* I came back briefly in '65 to the United States and that's when the Watts rebellion jumped off. I saw that as a forerunner of anticolonial rebellions, so I went back to Greece to write about how and why an armed rebellion could develop in the US.

The problem is that revolutionaries were more rhetoric than actionists. Not many of them had military experience. Geronimo Pratt is one exception; there were others, but the [Black] Panthers weren't really revolutionaries.[6] Had they divided into an unarmed propagandist wing like Sinn Féin,[7] and developed an underground wing, they might still be around today. But they called themselves armed propagandists. That's an oxymoron.

MM: *What was your project in writing* The Spook Who Sat by the Door?
SG: It's a handbook. This is how you do it [make armed struggle]. You can set up underground cells tomorrow based on much of the information I provide in *The Spook Who Sat by the Door.*

MM: *It reads like a primer.*
SG: That's what it is. I didn't have artistic ambitions. I wasn't trying to win a Nobel Prize. I was trying to tell people who were making targets of themselves, "Look man, you gotta be underground. You can't let them know who you are and what you're doing unless you get captured or killed." But they got caught up in the romance of the film, being on television and newspapers. They doomed themselves.

MM: *Why use the novel as the means of inspiring insurrection?*
SG: Because people understand metaphor; our folklore, our comedians make political and social points in telling a story. You know, we're not as didactic as white Americans, so it seemed to me that a nonfiction book would not be as well and widely read as a rousing good tale.

MM: *I hear you.*
SG: Yeah, that's why.

MM: *Who was/is your audience for* Spook?
SG: The brothers and sisters on the block. I don't write for intellectuals. And many black intellectuals resent that.

MM: *Why?*

SG: Because I don't give a damn about them! I don't respect them. They're puppy dogs. This is the first time in our history when our intellectuals are outright hos![8] You know, people like [W.E.B.] DuBois, E. Franklin Frasier, and Lorraine Hansberry . . . giants! There's nobody out there who claims to be a black intellectual who's even remotely in that class. So, I'm contemptuous of them, and they know it.

DW: *With this primer for revolution, did you imagine a publisher was going to snatch it up?*[9]

SG: No.

DW: *Did you consider who might publish it and what its shelf life would be?*

SG: No, I just made the circles. The way it finally got published was because of a young man named Alexis Lykiard who authored several novels and poetry.[10] His uncle and aunt lived on Mykonos, and he used to return there on breaks when he was at Cambridge. We got together around a mutual love of jazz. I had all my jazz records at the time, and he used to come to listen to the music. I let him read *Spook*, and he offered to give it to his publisher. Well, the publisher wouldn't touch it. He then gave it to three other publishers, and they too turned it down. When he came back to Mykonos in '68, not long before I left, he offered to give the manuscript to a couple of former classmates: co-publishers Clive Allison, who was a white Englishman and Margaret Busby, Ghanaian-born. He said they had been publishing poetry and wanted to get into the mainstream. They read it, raised £15,000, and published it in March 1969. It got many reviews, most of them favorable.

DW: *Wasn't it the* Sunday Times *bestseller for the year or so?*

SG: Yes.

MM: *Was the final version of the book different from earlier drafts?*

SG: Not really; each draft refined and tightened the story.

MM: *But did the story change?*

SG: Only one change: In the first draft, Freeman dies. But in the final draft he's wounded and left to the reader to decide whether or not he dies. And

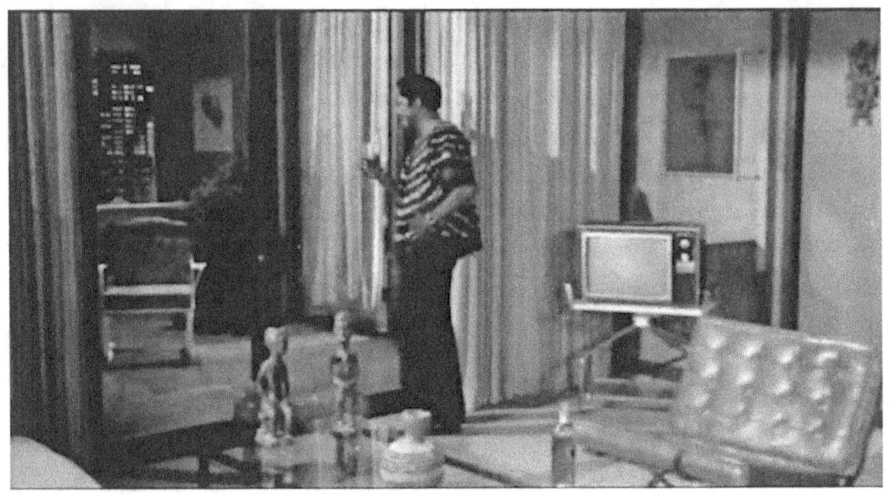

Fig. 2.1 Uncertain of his own future, Freeman (Lawrence Cook) stares out of his apartment window at the uprising taking place in the city streets below.

that was deliberate to make the point that the revolution must not rely on one man. Freeman had established a military chain of command, so it was understood at the end of the book and film that his presence was no longer essential. If he died, they would continue fighting.

MM: *Why did he die in the first draft?*
SG: It was the natural reaction; all of our heroes die. Okay! [laughs]

MM: *This is good.*
SG: A white man brought that to my attention and I said, "No! This cat don't have to die, you know!" [laughs] That was the most significant change I made.

MM: *Mm-hmm.*
SG: How it all came into being is I got tight with a man about my age named Melvin Clay. Mel was a founding member of [The] Living Theatre, which, as you know, was very left wing and anarchist.[11] A jazz buff, he had come to Mykonos to write a film script. One day we were sitting in my workroom listening to music, and at that time I was working on my second novel, *Baghdad Blues*.[12] I told him the idea for the *Spook* book that at the time I called

The Nigger Who Sat by the Door. He said, "Man, what you're going to do is dynamite. You got to do this. It's got to be a film and I can help you write the screenplay." He went to Athens, came back a week later, and I gave him the first chapter of *The Nigger Who Sat by the Door*.

When Dick Gregory published *Nigger*, I decided that "Spook" was a more clever title because it's a play on words.[13] Spooks are black people who allegedly are afraid of ghosts, and CIA undercover agents are called spooks. I finished the first draft in about four months, and then with Mel went right to work on the screenplay and would move back and forth between the two. I would give him the pages of what I thought he should write. He'd bring them back; I'd look at his work, he'd look at mine, and we would discuss it. We didn't know anything about writing screenplays and finished the first draft in about six weeks. We should have gone into a treatment, but the novel itself became the treatment. Our first draft was huge, about two hundred pages.

MM: *Do you have a copy of that first draft?*
SG: The original script? No. We also did a stage version, and that's disappeared, too. I lost a lot of my stuff. It was being stored, and my brother was supposed to pay the storage fees but didn't, so it was sold or thrown out, including my record and art collection. I mourned for two days and then recognized that not having stuff frees you!

MM: *Well, I can tell you that David and I are in mourning right now.* [laughs]
SG: I mean, I could pack up and be on the road in two hours not having to worry about furniture or the rest of that stuff. Well, being broke has a certain freedom. [laughs]

MM: *If not, a certain mobility.*
SG: Yes, it does. I could get up and go wherever I felt like.

MM: *Why did Baron publish* Spook?[14]
SG: For the paperback, the managing editor of Bantam [Books] was in London about the time the hardback was published [1969].[15] People in the publishing industry were talking about *Spook*. When he got to the airport, he bought and read it on the plane and then called and made an offer.

MM: *For the paperback edition?*
SG: Yeah. And then he subcontracted to Richard Baron so that there would be a hardback cover. But Baron didn't publish it until December '69, while Bantam brought it out earlier on January 1. The book has sold more than a million copies. It was translated into six languages: Italian, German, Swedish, Finnish, Dutch, and Japanese. So, it's got an international audience. But I and my work have generally been ignored by the established press. They don't know how to pigeonhole me.

DW: *When did you start working on* Baghdad Blues? *Was that right after* Spook?
SG: I was working on *Baghdad Blues* when I met Mel, did *Spook* and then went back to work on *Baghdad Blues*, which was published in '76.[16] I think it would make a pretty good film because it still offers insights into what we [the United States] were doing in Iraq and what we are attempting to do now. They're trying to replicate the government that was overthrown.

MM: *As a literary form, are there advantages in the novel* [Spook] *unlike other artistic forms?*
SG: Film is one-dimensional. You can't really get into people's heads; you can't deal with their psychological impulses. It's a very primitive art form. But I knew it had to be a film because many of the people I wanted to reach don't read. Not because they *can't* read, it's just there's so little material that's relevant to their lives. So, I wanted to hit both sides of the fence, but the real essence of *Spook* is in the novel.

MM: *What is that essence and how is it distinguished in the novel and not the film?*
SG: Well, the only senses you can provoke in film is sight and sound. But, if I write well about something—a turkey meal—I can have you smelling it. I can make your mouth water. I can have you hearing the sizzle of the meat in the frying pan. A good writer can appeal to all five senses, and that's why I prefer the novel as a medium.

MM: *Using these five senses, what is it that you wanted your reader to taste, smell, feel, see, and imagine in the novel?*

SG: The ghetto. The ghetto as I know it. How black people live. How they laugh. How they drink. What they smoke. What they eat. How they relate to one another, which is totally different once they leave the comfort zone of the ghetto on account of whites. Then they have to put on a mask. As I've recently stated, duality is a survival tool. It's not a disease. You become what will make whites comfortable when you're in their purview. By the time you go home and change your clothes and pour your first drink, you're black again. So, we are gifted actors in the face of whites and when we are around white bigots, we can smell who they are and act in a certain way for safety and protection. But you can only be at home with your blackness among your own people.

MM: *Is that the double consciousness that DuBois observed?*
SG: Yes, and in *The Spook Who Sat by the Door,* Freeman is one thing when he's dealing with whites and somebody else when he's with his troops [insurgents] and with his woman. DuBois decried duality. I've never had any problem with it.

MM: *As a strategic adjustment to white racism?*
SG: Right!

DW: *And as a fact of social experience and existence?*
SG: But I discarded it and am the same everywhere. I don't feel any need to wear a mask anymore.

MM: *You've outgrown it.* [laughs]
SG: Exactly!

MM: *Are there other things you want readers to know about the novel before we move on to the film?*
SG: Actually, the novel is a slave rebellion.

MM: *In real time!*
SG: Freeman is a modern Nat Turner. He was probably closer to Toussaint L'Ouverture or Denmark Vesey, who were far more sophisticated in what they did. Turner just wanted to kill white folks, while Vesey had an elaborate

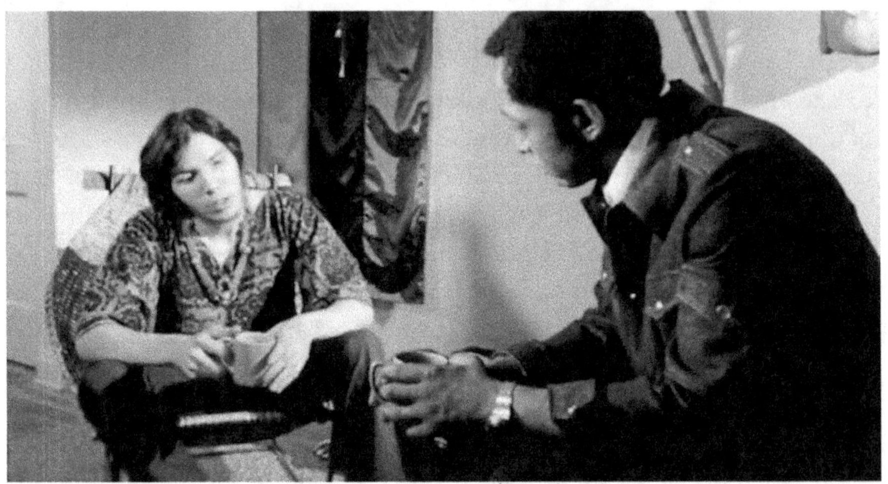

Fig. 2.2 Freeman lectures Pretty Willie (David Lemieux) on the necessity of understanding that the struggle for freedom is not confined only to the issue of race.

plan wherein they would do what John Brown and his supporters hoped to do when they captured the arsenal [at Harpers Ferry, Virginia, and started an armed slave revolt] and moved into the mountains to launch raids from there.

MM: *After Willie—the light-skinned member of the insurgency—rebukes Freeman's push to finish his degree and says he's more motivated by hating "white folks," Freeman comes down on him and declares "This is not about 'hate white folks' . . . you gonna need more than hate to sustain you when this this thing begins." Is that view of the struggle also expressed in the book?*
SG: Yeah.

MM: *Because it lays out the purpose, strategy, and racial dynamics of the insurrection in counterpoint to the criticisms leveled against you, the novel, and film. Clearly, you're not talking a race war here.*
SG: No! We're talking freedom, okay! It just happens that in this case it's color-coded. The same thing that's happening in Libya and earlier in Algeria, in Egypt, Yemen, Bahrain . . . they're all the same color but revolting for the same reasons. They're fed up with being oppressed and dominated by narrow-minded dictators.

MM: *Black or white.*
SG: Black or white. And I find it ridiculous that people on the internet are trying to defend Gaddafi. Why? Because he happens to be black, and he talks nice to black Africans? Fuck that! He ain't black or colored.

MM: *Why do you think critics of* The Spook Who Sat by the Door *frame it as a racist—a black racist—project advocating war against whites when it's not about that; it's about a war of liberation against ruling class oppression?*
SG: They conveniently ignore that because you would have to accept the premise that blacks are not free, okay. They created a whole fiction that the civil rights movement resulted in the liberation of black people, and it didn't any more than white people are liberated. I would say that poor whites are the niggers of white society. They call them "trailer trash" and call us "niggers." But the people who have the most to gain by joining together—poor whites and poor blacks—are at one another's throats. And while we're watching them, and they're watching us, the people who rule this society don't give a damn about color. They've got no problem putting Obama in the White House as long as he takes orders, or Condoleezza Rice or the rest of those colored flunkies. So, yes, the book is about a "war of liberation" and the people who don't deal with that fact don't want to deal with it. And, if they want to call me a racist, be my guest. I always say calling me a racist is like the pot calling the kettle white.

MM: *We're really talking class warfare here and, if I understand you, the African American underclass has a historical and vanguard role in the revolt. I understood that very clearly in the film, and yet critics dismiss this ever important distinction, asserting that race trumps class in the radical project of the film.*
SG: Fuck the critics! I don't write for them. I think the readers understand it. Students are going to see the film this afternoon, and most of them will understand it.

DW: *I think not all of them will, but some will. One of the things that I was thinking about last night looking at the many reviews of the film on different websites, so many of them lazily dismiss* Spook *as just another blaxploitation movie. And that's a very successful way of negating the radical politics, the revolutionary implications of the film.*

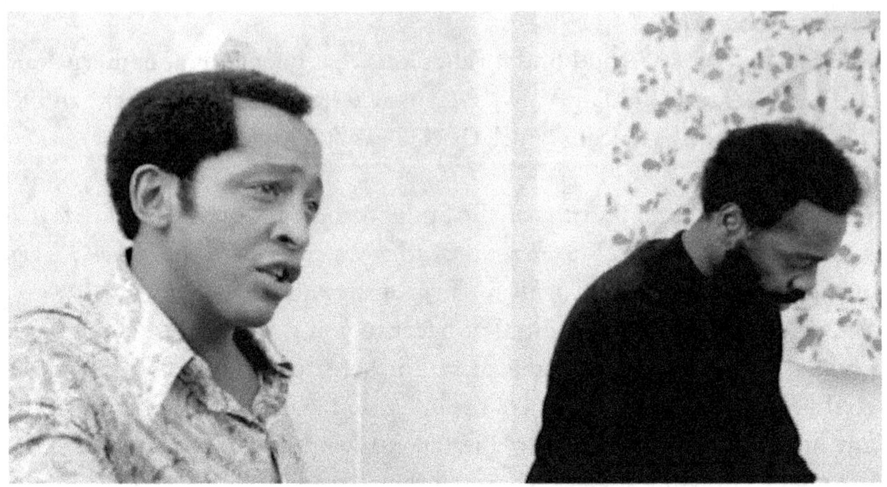

Fig. 2.3 Dan Freeman as the symbolic embodiment of the struggle for justice.

SG: What sends them up the wall is they know I don't give a damn what they think.

DW: *Right!*
SG: Okay. [laughs] Sometimes, face-to-face, I tell them that "I don't give a fuck what you think about that. I didn't write it for you."

DW: *We watched it in my class, just before spring break. We watched also* The Mack *(1973), which was interesting in all sorts of ways, but unquestionably it affirms the legitimacy of capitalism; that you achieve freedom by the acquisition of material.* Spook *is quite the opposite, saying that the system is the problem. So, it comes as no surprise that it would be dismissed because, if you accept that premise, then all the other cards have to fall from there. And the easiest way not to deal with that is to say, "This is another angry black guy with a chip on his shoulder."*
SG: "Hate-filled" is the word critics used most often.

MM: *The protagonist in the book, as in the film, in some respects is privileged by you. He's from the community; gets educated and works through the mainstream, which demystifies the mainstream. He's also the theoretician; Gramsci's organic intellectual. Why is so much invested in him? Is it a narrative device or*

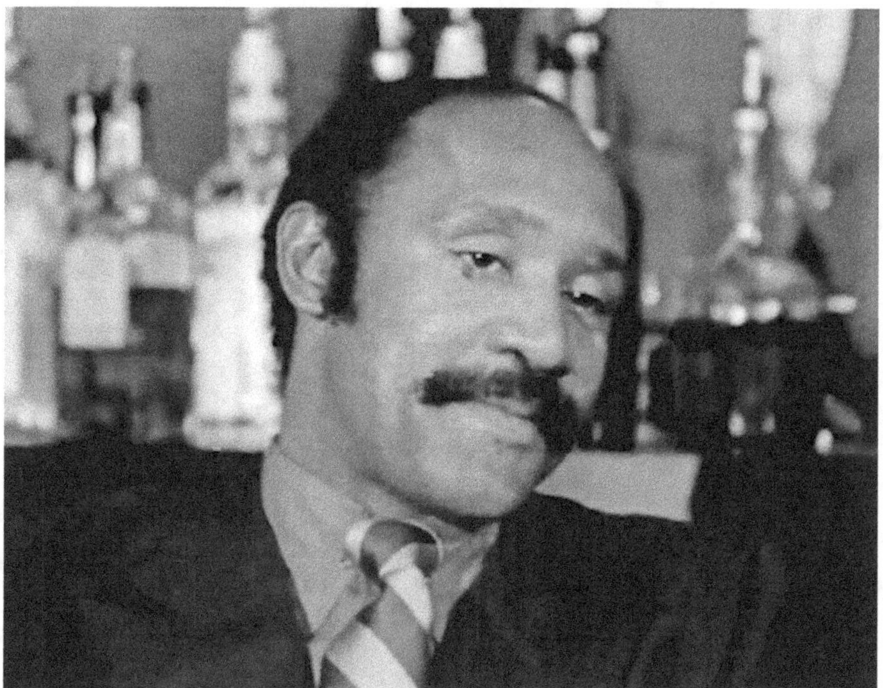

Fig. 2.4 One of the functions of Dawson (J. A. Preston) in the film is to underscore the importance of the black middle class to the revolution.

you're giving him agential authority that enables certain things to happen in the novel and film?

SG: He's symbolic of many people—male and female—in our struggle in the diaspora; in the West Indies, Canada, North America, Central America, South America, and in Africa. They are chosen by the people to give leadership in their struggles for liberation. I was aware of such people, since as a child studying black history, but not as it's taught in most black history courses, which offer more information about whites than they do about blacks.

MM: *But you also do something that's extraordinary, defying orthodoxy: You don't determine your principal characters by their social class standing. That is, because you are class and educated doesn't mean you support or oppose the system. And that exemplified by the divide between Dawson and Freeman who are from the same social environment. Dawson upholds the system, while Freeman*

rejects and opposes it. One goes one way, the other another. If I understand you, you're not foreclosing the revolutionary impulse in the black middle class because their historical role is indeterminate—they can go either way?
SG: Right!

MM: *That, too, is missed by your critics because you're not closing down the possibility for educated and professional African Americans to assert a radical agenda for social change and participate in realizing it . . .*
SG: I thought that concept was important. For example, Dawson is a three-dimensional character. It would be easy to dismiss him as being one more bourgeois sell-out. He's not, you know.

MM: *He's ambivalent!*
SG: He's on a tightrope. He knows, like Freeman, the kind of pressures he's under. But he has been brought up to try to make things happen. Freeman has rejected that premise; he knows it ain't gonna work.

MM: *He spent five years running copies.*
SG: But he was there for a purpose. He went in there with a plan.

MM: *Right! Is that made clear in the book and screen adaptation? Or are you suggesting that he enlisted in the CIA to acquire skills and mobility to then realize that his status as the nigger is unchanged?*
SG: He didn't have a problem with that. He pretended to be a lot dumber than he actually is. He dresses stereotypically; he speaks in a way that doesn't threaten white folks. He is not the man he pretends to be. And he welcomes the bigotry, which becomes his shield. The whites are never able to penetrate his mask because he gives them what they want.

DW: [Ralph] *Ellison's invisibility?*
SG: Yeah.

DW: *That by confirming their expectations, you remain invisible, which is expressed in the scene when the guy goes into the office he's cleaning and steals the pipes and other stuff. As long as you smile, they won't see you, and you can do what you need to do.*

SG: Except Ellison thought of it as a curse. He wanted to be visible. I see it as tactical. It's a tactic that Freeman and any other black person deploys who works in a white purview. You can't afford to be anything that threatens whites because what a lot of people don't want to deal with is the fear that whites have of black people. And for damn good reason—they know what they've done; they know what they continue to do; and they wonder when the shit is going to drop and bring the house down like Samson and the temple.

MM: *So, Freeman has a plan. And his behavior corresponds with that plan.*
SG: Now, let me say this: some people assumed that Freeman became a revolutionary because of his treatment in the CIA. No. He went in there to gain the knowledge he needed. How he was treated rolled off his back like water off a duck. In fact, the treatment was his best shield. Only one brother sat down and asked if he was a fraternity man. Freeman said, "Yeah, I used to be a Kappa." Now that guy was the only one in the group who could possibly have suspected Freeman's motive. And he tried to befriend him, but Freeman couldn't afford to have any friends. So he uses the stereotype to his advantage.

MM: *I'm glad you clarified that his behavior didn't change as a consequence of the CIA experience. And that in fact he joined it knowing fully well his circumstance and the role he would assume there.*
SG: Right.

MM: *Let's transition: You're writing the novel and screenplay with Mel simultaneously. As they evolve, are they different?*
SG: Yeah and I found myself constantly borrowing from each. When I created something in the screenplay that wasn't in the novel, then I'd make that change. But I wanted the screenplay to be as close to the novel as possible, and I think it is.

MM: *In what ways are the narratives different?*
SG: There are no significant differences between the novel and screenplay, but I was able to deal with the main characters in more depth in the novel.

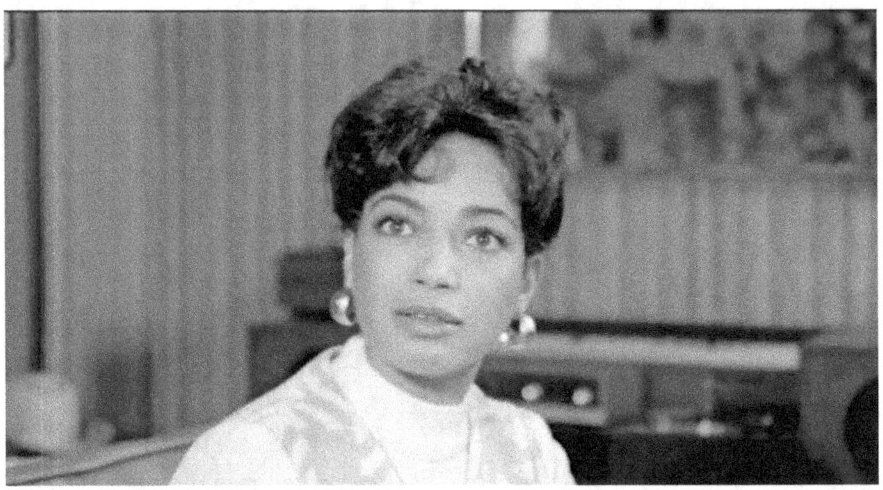

Fig. 2.5 Freeman's girlfriend Joy (Janet League), who appears as the full embodiment of the black bourgeoisie.

Now, there was one change that I didn't make that was very disappointing. In the book, Joy is a product of the same mean streets as the Dahomey Queen, Dawson, and Freeman are. She comes from the projects, she's in school on a church scholarship, she can't dress as well as the bourgeois chicks she's with, and she's desperate never to fall back into where she came from. In a scene from the book, she lashes out and says exactly how she feels about going back to that life in the projects and that she's going to get married for status and money. And she can't deal with Freeman because he's too altruistic and not going to go for the dough. So Joy comes across as a shallow chick who's betrayed Freeman for no real reason. That scene is lost in the film.

MM: *But she alludes to that in the film when she says to Freeman something like "Well, I've lost you," and "I knew this was coming."*

SG: Yeah. But in the book, that scene is spread out. When she comes out of the bath and he asks her, "Don't you remember the way it was when you was coming up?" And she said, "Yes, I do remember. I remember the rats and roaches and the stench of semen and spoiled food and the stairways when the elevator didn't work." She just goes all the way down through the horrors of growing up in the projects, which makes her a much more sympathetic character than she is in the film.

MM: *Why then was that scene left out of the film?*
SG: Because Ivan [Dixon, the director] fell out with the actress.

MM: *For what?*
SG: She was scheduled to re-shoot a scene that Paula Kelly [Dahomey Queen] was in. When there was a cut, Paula had taken off her earrings, and the scene supervisor didn't catch it. So they shot the rest of the scene without the earrings, and it had to be shot over again. For that reason there was no time left for Joy's next scene. And apparently she must have cussed him [Dixon] out in the dressing room because he came out very crestfallen. I believe, in a spirit of revenge. Ivan cut that scene, and it seriously weakened the film.

DW: *So, the scene was originally in the screenplay but cut out during the filming?*
SG: It hadn't been filmed. He cut it out.

MM: *Apart from Joy being a sympathetic character, had the scene been left in, would it have changed the dynamics between the principle characters?*
SG: No, but it would have made Joy, not necessarily more sympathetic, but much more understandable because you would have understood that she was acting out of fear.

MM: *From lived experience.*
SG: Right! The scene is not a strong motivation for action as it is in the book.

MM: *Let's jump ahead of ourselves for a moment: Had you directed the film, would it have been any different?*
SG: I don't think so with the exception of that scene. I thought that Ivan did a superb job, and I deferred to him because I didn't have the experience necessary to direct.

DW: *How did he* [Dixon] *get involved with the project?*
SG: I was in LA talking to Clarence Williams about playing the lead and his wife, Gloria Foster, playing either Joy or Dahomey Queen. Ivan was directing a segment of *Mod Squad* [1968–73] when Clarence mentioned that I was in town. Ivan said at first Clarence didn't want to tell him where I was because he thought he [Ivan] wanted to do the role. Ivan said, "No, man. I'm

not acting anymore, I'm directing. I'd like to direct that piece." So Clarence gave him my number where I was staying at the Sunset Hilton. He called, came by, talked, and said he'd like to direct *The Spook*. He then offered to give me money. When I got back to Chicago, I sent him the script. He said he couldn't afford to put up any money, so I said, "Okay, let's form a partnership, and we'll both own 50 percent of nothing."

DW: *And what year would this have been?*
SG: This was '70 or '71.

DW: *Had the book been published already?*
SG: Yeah, it was.

DW: *Was he familiar with the book?*
SG: Yeah.

MM: *It's ironic that Dixon's working in Hollywood*—Mod Squad—*and here's your project that challenges assumptions about Hollywood, along with a lot of other stuff about race and American society. Was he concerned about how this might jeopardize his future prospects as a director in Hollywood?*
SG: I don't think he anticipated what . . .

MM: *. . . came down.*
SG: Yeah, because he was convinced that the studios would put up the bread [funding]. I knew that wasn't gonna happen. So, while he was shopping around the six major studios, I got together with a former classmate of mine at the University of Chicago who had become a top-flight business consultant. And between the two of us we came up with a proposal and a contract to raise the funds independently.

MM: *For the production.*
SG: And that's what we did. The bulk of the money came from black investors, also with some significant funds from white investors as well; but 85 cents of every dollar that went into that film was raised independently.

One reason we ran out of money was because of Jesse Jackson. A consortium of wealthy business people in Washington, DC, met to discuss putting up the completion funds for the film. To check me out, they called Jesse who invoked the name of Martin Luther King [Jr.] and said that King would disapprove of a film of this nature because it's against his take on nonviolence; that it was a dangerous film and that he didn't think they should invest in it. So, they backed out. Ivan then cut the action footage and shopped it around, and UA [United Artists] thought they had a blaxploitation film.

MM & DW: [laugh]
SG: And that's how UA got involved. When they saw the final cut, man, they were outraged.

MM: *Were you there at the screening?*
SG: Yeah. I said, "Hold on! You required six copies of the script. Don't blame us if y'all can't read! We've got a damn contract. This is the film; put it out there!" So they put it out on a cursory basis, but it jumped off so strong that a few venues realized that they had something hot. They then put me on a twelve-city tour to promote *The Spook*, and for four months it was one of the top-grossing films in Hollywood. The film opened on Labor Day weekend in '73 and, just as it was about to become profitable, they pulled it off the market at the behest of the FBI [US Federal Bureau of Investigation].

MM: *I remember seeing it then and recall that it mysteriously disappeared from the theater showing it.*
SG: That happened. Even though we had a three-week contract, it would open on a Friday and close Sunday. We found out that the FBI visited a number of exhibitors to persuade them to take our film off the market. Up until then it was hearsay, but when it opened on a second run at the McVicker's Theater on State Street [Chicago], I went down there and spoke with the manager who was a close friend of my mother. He sat me down in his office and said that the week before, two FBI agents had come in to advise him to close the film and that he threw them out. So, it was no longer hearsay; I had direct evidence.

MM: *Didn't United Artists have its own exhibition outlets at the time?*
SG: Yeah, but they weren't the producers of the film. A lot of people think they were. Ivan and I were the producers. They were the distributors.

MM: *Didn't they also back out?*
SG: Yeah. They got their chump change back, plus a reasonable profit, and left us waving in the breeze. And we got the rights back when I threatened to sue them.

MM: *Distribution rights?*
SG: Copyright rights. I own the film. Usually when a distributor signs up to distribute a film, they own the rights to it. At this time, I own all the rights to the film.

MM: *One, among several things I admire about you, is your candor when you said earlier in this conversation, "I didn't know enough about that so I relied on that person."*
SG: I went to film school after I made *Spook*. Look, I've been called arrogant, but I'm very humble in the face of my people and my work. I don't share the fears that many people have. I enjoy life. I have a good time. I eat well. I exercise. I'm a good cook.

MM: *For the novel, your audience is black folk. Was it different for the film?*
SG: No, it doesn't change. They remain the core audience, but the film attracted a lot of attention from left-wing whites. I recall Bernadine Dohrn mentioning that she and Bill used to read chapters back and forth to themselves from *The Spook Who Sat by the Door.*[17] So, there was a cult following among revolutionaries and left-wing whites, but the core audience has always been the brother and sister on the block.

MM: *Why did you choose the action genre to frame and mask what is agitprop in* Spook*?*
SG: Because it's the kind of film that appeals to my audience. A documentary wouldn't work because they feel like they're being preached to. And, so, I decided to write an action novel and an action film to get my message across. If I'd been targeting bourgeois intellectuals, I probably would have written a nonfiction diatribe à la *Wretched of the Earth*[18] and my target audience probably would have never even heard of it.

MM: *And, what were the conventions of the action genre that you subverted on behalf of your political project in* Spook?
SG: It was easy. I've been an avid filmgoer until recently. I don't feel any interest in the kind of films that are being made today: comic book adaptations, silly teen romances, superfly, sci-fi and super spy films. I find them a joke. I never met, for example, anyone like Jason Bourne during the time I was in contact with the CIA. Most of them are Midwestern and Southern hicks. The top echelon is often from elite universities; the rest colleges. They are unworldly, unsophisticated. They don't speak foreign languages. They're totally at the mercy of translators and paid informants. And as a result I wouldn't put the CIA among the top intelligence agencies in the world. I would say the Mossad, the French, the British, and the Germans and Russians until recently are all much better.

DW: *Tying to Michael's question about the film as an action movie, I suppose that revolution is never going to be as easily articulated in film as, say, romantic comedy?*
SG: Yeah. It was a challenge passing along complex political ideology in a way that would be easily understood by the people I wrote for. Down on the block, they'd get right into it and know who Freeman is, what he's doing, and why he's doing it, while bourgeois intellectuals nit-pick it to death. They can relate to the women, to the Dahomey Queen, in particular. I've had feminists attack the book and the film for the portrayal of women. I don't worry about that. These are the kind of women who wouldn't approve of anything I did. You know, I'm the kind of black man they despise.

DW: *We talked earlier about, to use the phrase, the novel as a primer for revolution. Did you see the film in the same way for your target audience?*
SG: Yeah! I always thought that film would be a more effective tool for that audience. It's not that they don't read. While many of them are high school dropouts, they are every bit as intelligent as I am. A college degree has nothing to do with native intelligence. Some of the dumbest people I ever met are PhDs.

DW: *You got that right.* [laughter]
SG: And some of the sharpest people I ever met are selling dope on street corners. You know, so, many of them do read and have read the book, but far more have been exposed to the film.

DW: *Can you speak to the transformation of the Dahomey Queen character because she's a prostitute when Freeman first meets her, then she becomes the Dahomey Queen who infiltrates the CIA.*
SG: Exactly! He calls her a queen. He treats her like a queen. And that's how she reacts. When she comes to pull his coat, she pretends she doesn't know what he's doing. She knows he's the man. She says, "I don't know how to get to him, but you do. So put the word out." She knows. And Freeman realizes that she knows, but they never discuss it.

DW: *Is her change in clothes meant to signify a raising of consciousness as a black woman?*
SG: Right.

DW: *And that's signaled by the appropriation of African imagery and African aesthetic?*
SG: Yeah. There would have been no civil rights movement if not for African American women involvement. In some cases they worked in the background as organizers, in others right on the frontlines. In Little Rock, the person who led that movement was a woman, and it was like that throughout the country.[19] You know, there's no white counterpart to Angela Davis—at that time or today.

I've got another screenplay called *Lisa Charter.* It's a modern adaptation of Mrs. Carver—Lisa Charter—a respected ghetto matriarch who organizes the wives and lovers of gang bangers. They go on sexual strike till the gang banging and dope dealing ends.[20]

MM: *And now that we're revisiting black women's portrayals, you do something that works against the negative stereotype of the underclass by rendering it with agential authority, a historical role* [rather] *than footnote in revolutionary transformations. And you do it purposefully by dignifying Dahomey Queen's role as she performs sexual labor on behalf of the struggle ahead and by Freeman's comportment toward her that renders the sense she's more than an object of sexual exchange.*
SG: And she responds to it.

MM: *She responds to it by loyalty to Freeman. When she tells the CIA agent who's doing the background check on Freeman, she says, "If something comes*

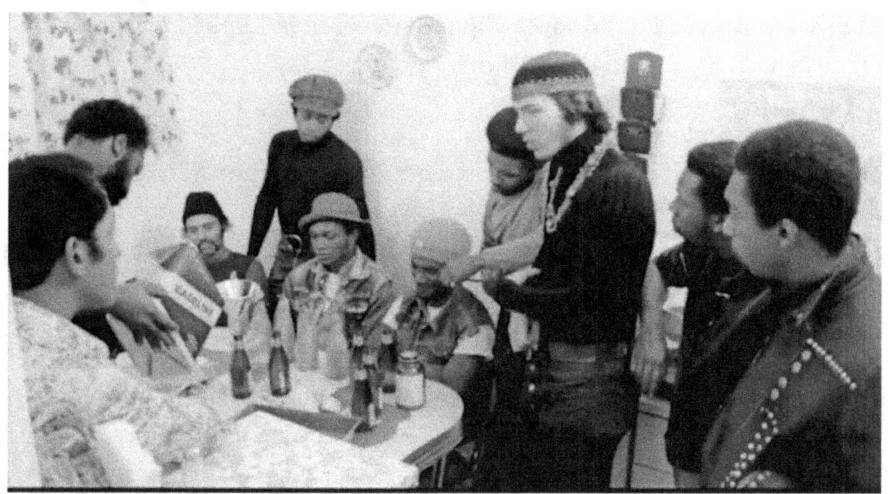

Fig. 2.6 Emerging dynamically from the lumpenproletariat, it is the members of the Cobras who will lead the revolution.

down, I know Dan be in it," recognizing that Freeman would risk his life for her out of conviction than commerce.

And, as noted earlier, you do something that by implication turns normative models of social change upside-down. In Marxist orthodoxy, the revolutionary vanguard is the working class. In Spook*, it's the pimps and the hustlers on the street who become that vanguard.*

SG: Yeah, the lumpenproletariat.

MM: *The lumpenproletariat are written out of revolutionary struggles that like the middle class are indeterminate, but in* Spook *you put them at the epicenter of struggle.*

SG: They're always the center. Bourgeois intellectuals don't make revolutions; they co-opt revolutions. The people in the streets in North Africa are the lumpen, okay!

MM: *Yes, many have nothing to lose.*

SG: They're at the cutting edge, at the vanguard. The bourgeois revolutionaries come in at a later time and take over because they have the organizational benefits [skills]. Doesn't matter whether you're talking about the

Bolshevik Revolution or not—when the revolution jumped off, Lenin and Trotsky weren't even in the country.

MM: *To the Finland Station.*[21]
SG: Lenin was shipped in on an armored railroad train. Trotsky came in from Finland; when he got there, workers had already taken over factories. The lumpen were in the streets fighting the police and army. So I'm saying quite clearly that the intellectual concept of revolution that I've been taught is not true. It's historically erroneous.

MM: *Your assumption is in line, for example, with the Black Panther Party's position about recruiting in the prisons. And Freeman is clear on this point, asserting to his fellow insurgents that if anyone gets caught and is imprisoned they recruit among inmates.*
SG: There you go.

MM: *Algerians did the same in their war of independence* [1954–62] *and so too the Nation of Islam recruits from the underclass. You assert in* Spook *that people living in poverty, imprisoned, street hustlers, et al., constitute a class in society that can make history. And that's powerful stuff!*
SG: Yeah.

MM: *But what gives your assertion historical truth and credibility?*
SG: Because it's already happened. In Algeria and West Africa, uneducated people spearheaded revolutionary activity. They were the lumpen. When the students revolted in Paris [1968] against the state, their demonstrations almost failed until street people got involved.

MM: And the Labor Unions.
SG: No, the Labor Unions were ordered to step back by Moscow. It was the street people who were digging up those cobblestones in the streets and throwing them at the police. Those beautiful cobblestone streets no longer exist. But it wasn't until the lumpen backed the students that the demonstrations were sustained. I mean, students didn't know how to fight cops, you know.

MM: *But by privileging the lumpen in* Spook, *are you saying that there's not much hope among, especially the black middle class to ignite insurrection?*

SG: Yeah. Look, I was not surprised at how the civil rights movement ended. A myth was created that it was destroyed by COINTELPRO.[22] No. It was betrayed by black middle-class leadership. Once they got what they wanted, they abandoned the movement.

MM: *What did they want?*
SG: What they got: integration, affirmative action, the vote. None of these things reached down to the [black] working class, and it was a mass movement. The first demonstrators were entertainers, celebrities, and civil rights workers. But with every fight, there were ordinary working-class black people.

MM: *Yet in* Spook, *in the character of Freeman who becomes middle class is suggested a revolutionary role, unlike Dawson, who* [as] *part of that black middle class, betrays his historical role.*
SG: Well, I want to romanticize the lumpen and not be overly critical of the middle class because there are warriors in both classes. I come from working-class background and attended excellent universities, but I've never lost sight of my roots. I live in the same neighborhood I grew up in to this day. And some of the people on the block know me as a soul dude who walks like he's dancing [laughs], and others know me as the author of *The Spook Who Sat by the Door.* But I'm a respected . . .

MM: *A respected member of the community.*
SG: Yeah, a respected member of the community, which is not true of people like Ishmael Reed and Amiri Baraka who separated themselves from the people. They have an intellectual allegiance, but it's not personal. I see the same people on the bus every day. I eat at the same soul food diner. I buy my black market cigarettes from them, you know. We talk basketball, we talk about the weather, and if somebody jumped on me, they'd be in stone trouble.

MM: *Would it be fair to say that, while your project in* The Spook Who Sat by the Door *challenges orthodox assumptions, it is a theorized meditation on revolution?*
SG: Mm-hmm.

MM: *Apart from your own life experiences, who else informs your ideas about revolutionary praxis, the Black Panthers, Mao Zedong?*

SG: Well, the Panthers didn't come into being until a year after I wrote *The Spook Who Sat by the Door*.[23]

MM: *Were the Panthers influenced by your take on the lumpenproletariat?*
SG: Right. And a lot of people assumed the opposite.

MM: *Me among them.*
SG: I can relate to the people you name, but they didn't influence me. I came to it the same way they did. One woman asked me about Frantz Fanon, and I told her that I hadn't read *The Wretched of the Earth* when I wrote *The Spook Who Sat by the Door*. She gave me a look as if I was telling a lie. Like I said, I was more widely traveled in the Third World than Fanon. He wrote *The Wretched of the Earth* on the Left Bank in Paris!

MM: *I'm glad you clarified this because this sets things in the right time frame.*
SG: I wrote my master's thesis on the Bolshevik Revolution.

MM: *Where did you do graduate studies?*
SG: University of Chicago.

MM: *And undergraduate degree?*
SG: Wisconsin. Madison, at that time it was the only full university.

MM: *You've gone to elite schools.*

DW: *We talked about this last night at dinner. You said Dan Freeman is you, right?*
SG: Yeah. He dressed the way I dressed. He listened to the same kind of music I listen to and ate the same kind of food I do. And I come from working-class background. My father was an activist member of the Brotherhood of Sleeping Car Porters. My grandfather was a skilled welder.

MM: *Did you get your politics from them?*
SG: Mm-hmm.

MM: *How about your mom?*
SG: She was a jazz cabaret super star. She played at the Cotton Club in Harlem and Atlantic City, and all up and down the East Coast. She was gone

for about ten years because that's where the money was. She married a second time and then came back to Chicago when I was ten years old. I was in constant contact with members of what was called "The Sporting Crowd": jazz musicians, hustlers . . . well educated in many cases, totally independent economically of whites. They weren't working nine-to-five gigs with white folks. They were living off the land. And as a result, I'm a pretty good hustler. I've got a pension coming down, but when I run out of money, I know I got to get out in the street and make some. My primary source of income is selling DVDs and books out of my shoulder bag. Gigs like this are great, you know. I could rely on them.

MM: *Skin color has always been noted and a matter of importance in the black community, not to speak of race relations in America. It's a subject you take up in* Spook, *but in a way that politicizes it in progressive ways.*
SG: Mm-hmm.

MM: *It's either a mark against you or a status symbol. How do you understand it?*
SG: Well, I had an upbringing where I saw both sides of the coin. My maternal grandfather and my mother were light enough to pass. And they did from time to time.

MM: *That's an occurrence in most of our families.* [laughs]
SG: Yeah! For instance, my grandfather was what was called at the time a "race man." You know, he was for the race. Saint Luke's Hospital in Chicago didn't accept blacks, and he was determined to break down the color barrier. So, he and my mother went down and signed up for my birth. And imagine the looks on the white folks' faces when I came out! [laughs]

MM: *And took a second look at your mother!* [laughs]
SG: Yeah!

MM: *"Girl, what did you do?"* [laughs]
SG: Yes! And when the family came down to see me, they had to go up the freight elevator.

MM: *Separate but equal.*

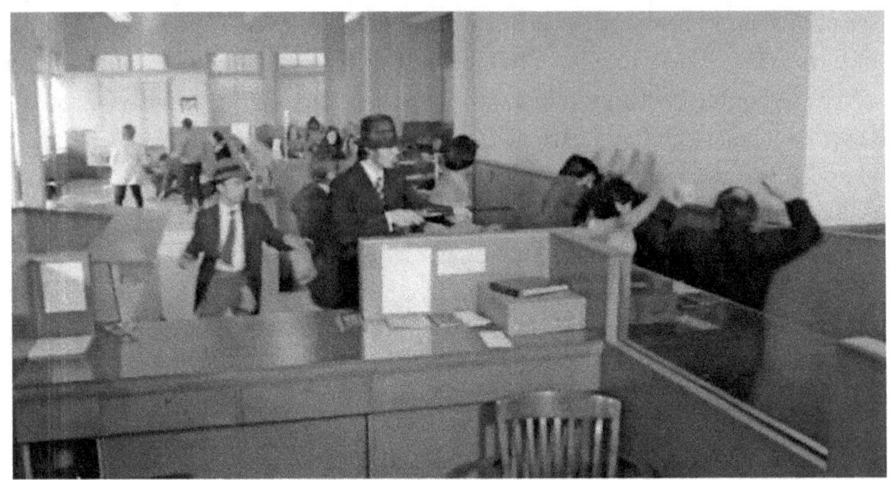

Fig. 2.7 In robbing the bank, Pretty Willie and the other light-skinned members of the Cobras utilize their "whiteness" as a strategic ploy.

SG: Yeah. So I know that the stereotyping of light-skinned blacks has some measure of truth. But it's obvious that among our greatest heroes are people of mixed race or very light in color.

MM: *And you use it to tactical advantage when robbing the bank in the film.*
SG: Right. And Freeman tells Willie that a lack of pigment is not the handicap he thinks it is. It can be used. And that transformed Willie! He came full circle and realized that he didn't have to have a chip on his shoulder. He was just as black as anyone else and confident enough to use his lack of pigment for the community.

MM: *If someone asked me, "How would you characterize Mr. Greenlee's* The Spook Who Sat by the Door,*" I would say, "Yes, it's a theorized work of political importance." But I would also add that "it is imminently practical." Everything that Freeman does—apart from the times he slips up and gives Dawson and Joy pause—is deliberate with the revolution in mind. Everything fits within a model that challenges received notions about race and class. I mean, you're challenging black folk to think about race in different ways. You're challenging the black community to think about those classes of people whom we have dismissed. In this sense, your film is imminently—as a primer should be—practical.*

SG: Mm-hmm. Yeah, it could have happened exactly the way I wrote it, and should have!

DW: *So why didn't the revolution happen?*
SG: As I said, the bourgeois leadership sold out. They stopped the show.

DW: *And was that the moment when the movement was arrested, or the potential of the movement was arrested?*
SG: Yeah. Without exception, the bourgeoisie betrayed every social revolution in the twentieth century. The betrayal is still happening; for example, 80 percent of Cubans are black, yet seeing a photograph of the top echelon, they are white. They don't have any mulattoes in there. They took off one hat and put on another. I don't see any essential difference between Fidel [Castro] and Batista.[24] I think people are probably better off today than they were under Batista, but you still have a color-coded elitist group. The head of the armed forces of Castro's revolution was black and had a mysterious plane accident shortly after they took over. He was the only prominent black person among the leadership. Everyone else is white, yet Cuba is only 10 percent white and 5 percent mulatto.

MM: *Why* [do] *film critics consider your film as a black nationalist project when it is far from that?*
SG: Well, because most film critics aren't too bright. [laughs] They aren't particularly well educated. You know, Roger Ebert comes out of a small town in Illinois, went to the University of Illinois. The only time he's been out of the country is to attend a film festival. He's a nice guy, and I like his reviews because they're totally lacking in pretense as are many of the other reviewers.

MM: *I think they fear your film is really about class conflict in the United States. And for critics to focus on race and claim it a nationalist project is to obscure the fact that laboring whites are also getting their asses kicked by capitalism.*
SG: Definitely. And getting their ass kicked worse than us and they don't even know it.

MM: *And that's the danger of your film! And I don't think that this reality escapes critics. A close reading of the text clearly suggests that black people in*

America have a role to play in social change. At this historical moment, it is to ignite revolution. And that's the message and power of Spook.
SG: You see, the difference is that black people know we're being ripped off and white folks don't. White folks, the Tea Party people, feel angry and don't know why they're angry! "We want our country back." Back from what? [laughs] Who took it? The same people who were in control before control now. And the fact that there's a pigmented president [Barack Obama] doesn't change a damn thing!

MM: *Hasn't changed a thing.*
SG: Yeah! You think he didn't have classmates on Wall Street when he formulated the [Wall Street] bail out? He went to Columbia and Harvard with these cats. He probably knows them by first names. Elite universities are designed to train the offspring of the rich and powerful to rule and their classmates to help them do it. So, he's a trained puppy dog. I never expected anything else. I didn't vote for him.

DW: *Considering such issues, do you think that* Spook *is as relevant today, even though the historical context has changed in some ways?*
SG: Revolution is *always* relevant. I've never been any place where a small group, the rich and powerful—men for the most part—don't rip off everyone else. It's not a question of color. You find it in Africa, in Central and South America. There's always a tight knit group of enormously greedy people who keep most of it for themselves. And whatever else trickles down is stuff they can't keep for themselves. Some has to go to wages; some to buying food. But what you find in the United States, you'll find in Nigeria and other places in West Africa and the world.

MM: Thank you Mr. Greenlee.

NOTES

Interview held March 22, 2011.

1. King Faysal's monarchy was overthrown in a military coup in 1958 by Brigadier Abd al-Karim Qasim and Colonel Abd al-Salam Arif, and Iraq was declared a republic. Five years later (1963), Prime Minister Qasim was ousted in a coup led by the Arab Socialist Baath Party (ASBP), and Arif became president. That same year, the Baathist government was overthrown by Arif and a group of military officers.

2. The Algerian War of Independence began November 1, 1954, with the FLN's (Front de Libération Nationale) attacks against the French military and police and concluded with independence on July 2, 1962.

3. Term used to describe the 1955 pro-Western defense alliance between Iraq, Iran, Pakistan, Turkey, and the UK whose purpose was stated as to maintain stability and peace in the Middle East.

4. Fanon had already published *Black Skin, White Masks* in 1952; he worked in Algeria as the *chef de service* at a psychiatric hospital. In 1959, he published *L'An Cinq de la Révolution Algérienne* [*Year Five of the Algerian Revolution*] (English edition by Monthly Review Press, 1965).

5. April 21, 1967, weeks before scheduled elections, colonels seized Athens, arrested thousands, and took control of state apparatus, means of communication, parliament, and the royal palace. It was alleged that the coup was supported by the US government through the CIA.

6. A high ranking member of the Black Panther Party, Pratt was wrongly convicted and imprisoned for twenty-seven years; eight in solitary confinement. He died in 2011 in Tanzania.

7. Political movement and party active in the Republic of Ireland and Northern Ireland.

8. Whores/prostitutes.

9. First edition was published by Richard W. Baron, March 1969.

10. Of Greek and British ancestry, Lykiard is a novelist, poet, and translator.

11. Founded by Julien Beck and Judith Malina in 1947 and based in New York City, The Living Theatre produced experimental works by Jean Cocteau, Gertrude Stein, and Bertolt Brecht, among others.

12. See Sam Greenlee, *Baghdad Blues* (Bantam Books, 1976; 2007).

13. Dick Gregory with Robert Lipsyte, *Nigger: An Autobiography* (NY: Dutton, 1964).

14. First US edition by Richard W. Baron, 1969.

15. First London edition by Allison & Busby, 1969.

16. By Bantam Books, 1976.

17. Dohrn was among the leadership of the Weather Underground, living underground during the 1970s and on the FBI's Ten Most Wanted List; Bill Ayers was also a key figure in the Weathermen.

18. Frantz Fanon, *The Wretched of the Earth* (Paris: Francois Maspero, 1961; NY: Grove Press, 1963).

19. We believe Greenlee is referring here to Daisy Lee Gatson Bates, who during the Little Rock school desegregation crisis was president of the NAACP in Arkansas; see her memoir, *The Long Shadow of Little Rock* (University of Arkansas Press, 1987), which received a National Book Award in 1988.

20. Greenlee's story calls attention to Spike Lee's most recent film *Chi-Raq* (2015).

21. See Edmund Wilson's meditation on socialist writers and theorists who anticipated the Russian Revolution of 1917, *To the Finland Station* (Anchor, 1940).

22. Acronym for an FBI counterintelligence program during the 1960s that monitored, manipulated, and disrupted social and political movements in the United States, including the Black Panthers, antiwar activists, and the American Indian movement, among others.

23. Actually the Black Panther Party was created in 1966.

24. Fulgencio Batista, two-time leader/dictator in Cuba; 1933–44 and 1952–59.

3. Cinema as Political Activism

CONTEMPORARY MEANINGS IN *THE SPOOK WHO SAT BY THE DOOR*

Marilyn Yaquinto

With the fatal shooting of Trayvon Martin, a seventeen-year-old black male killed by a neighborhood watch captain in February of 2012, members of the African American community in Martin's Florida hometown and supporters across the country took to the streets to demand justice for the slain youth, whose killer was not immediately arrested by police.[1] Mainstream news reports and police authorities framed the outrage as primarily an overreaction by the black community crying racism where there was none.[2] After all, authorities argued, Martin's shooter George Zimmerman is part Latino and, as a fellow minority, could not possibly have racist motivations when he told police he acted in self-defense against an aggressive black youth.[3] As with other communities who have sought justice, demonstrators filmed their protests and witness testimonies, uploaded them to YouTube, and circulated a narrative counter to the one advanced by Florida authorities. That practice of capturing an opposing narrative most conspicuously dates back to 1992, when four Los Angeles police officers were caught on video participating in the beating of unarmed Rodney King. Riots erupted in Los Angeles and around the country after a suburban jury concluded that the four officers had acted appropriately—a verdict that contradicted what people could plainly see on film.[4] The ordeal has led to an explosion of such footage yielding profound outcomes, more recently with events related to the Arab Spring, in which ordinary people exploited visual media to both capture abuses and inspire others to answer the call to action.[5] Such cases speak to the ability of oppressed peoples to use film and video to advance their agendas, with new technologies making it possible for nearly anyone to become a journalist or a political filmmaker. The technologies that make this possible may be ever changing, but the injustices they continue to capture remain familiar to human history.

When Sam Greenlee (1930–2014) cowrote and coproduced the 1973 film *The Spook Who Sat by the Door* (based on his 1969 novel), he took advantage of his era's embrace of emerging options for independent filmmaking, which enabled him to communicate how African Americans, still largely trapped in urban centers, could imagine and execute an insurrection.[6] He included a similar incident in which a black youth is killed in a confrontation between the community and police—the familiarity of the incident as disturbing as the legacies it exposed, which are still in play in contemporary America.

Through the years, theorists and filmmakers, such as Sergei Eisenstein, have left us their experiments, effectively demonstrating the medium's political utility.[7] Cinema's commercial appeal eventually prompted the medium's commodification, increasingly organized into global culture industries that largely serve to disseminate mainstream ideologies that usually affirm rather than challenge the status quo. However, during the intense social and political upheavals of the 1960s, activist filmmakers, including Argentinian filmmakers Fernando Solanas and Octavio Getino, challenged the prevailing hegemony of First Cinema, which they characterized as the industrial, for-profit approach best represented by Hollywood. In their seminal 1968 text, "Towards a Third Cinema," they outlined strategies for challenging that dominance, also describing artists and intellectuals associated with Second Cinema, exemplified by French New Wave directors who tinkered with mainstream conventions but were not necessarily in opposition to the larger sociopolitical order.[8] That terrain belonged to what Solanas and Getino labeled Third Cinema: the "cinema of liberation."[9] Reinvigorating the medium with its progressive potential, Solanas and Getino described an "imperfect" cinema meant to focus less on idealized productions that create spectacle and more on empowering spectators to take action. Or put another way, they conceived of cinema as another revolutionary tool that can facilitate the "decolonization of culture."[10] Whether through documentary or feature film, Third Cinema's aim is to *re*-politicize cinema, which after its commodification tried to mask ideology and exist as "just entertainment."[11]

Solanas and Getino, among other Latin American filmmakers of the late 1960s, pursued cinema that "attempts to intervene,"[12] making political messaging its central focus.

These activist filmmakers were contemporaries of Greenlee, and his 1973 film belongs to this tradition rather than to the blaxploitation genre, with which it is often confused.[13] Despite the film's age and reflection of 1970s-era fashion, music, and street slang, *Spook* remains a relevant political critique as well as a primer on how to plan and execute a revolt, with African Americans comprising the revolutionary vanguard, given their sustained oppression in US history. It embraces Third Cinema's goal to use film as a revolutionary tool, including its embrace of guerilla tactics.

When *Spook* was first released, mainstream political observers and reviewers dismissed it as a dangerous expression of black rage. Fans of blaxploitation complained that it was a poor sample of that genre, especially when compared to mainstream Hollywood products such as *Shaft* (1971).[14] Another audience, though, consisting of political activists, college students, and Left-leaning commentators, recognized *Spook*'s embrace of revolutionary impulses, expressly about black empowerment in America, along with its larger links to class struggles and other human rights movements around the world.

The Organic Intellectual from Chicago's South Side

Spook, both the novel and film, were inspired by Greenlee's experiences growing up on the South Side of Chicago, as well as his years spent abroad as a Foreign Service agent in the late 1950s and early 1960s—a rare career opportunity for a young black male at the time. *Spook* is the story of a black college-educated male who enters CIA training, originally recruited to prove that integration was actively being pursued by the government, as in the circumstances under which Greenlee himself was drawn to the Foreign Service.

However, once inside the CIA, Greenlee's fictional operative intends to return to the ghetto to use his training to lead an armed uprising, mostly of African Americans still living in impoverished urban areas. The title of both the novel and the film play on the double meanings associated with the term *spook,* coupling a pejorative label for black people, rooted in the myth that they are afraid of ghosts, with the nickname given to CIA undercover agents.[15]

Greenlee's project is akin to Gillo Pontecorvo's *La Battaglia di Alger/ The Battle of Algiers* (1966) in its ability to echo the sentiments of Frantz Fanon, who posited that oppressed peoples must resort to violence to reverse the colonial social order, especially through guerilla warfare that engages the lumpenproletariat or urban unemployed as soldiers in such a struggle. *Spook* also was reputed to be screened by groups such as the Black Panthers as a text for organizing an urban guerrilla war. Others charge that the Panthers' ordeal actually inspired *Spook*, although Greenlee points out that his novel had already been rejected by six publishers by the time the Panthers came into existence.[16] Greenlee says he eventually read Fanon and was "amazed at the . . . parallels," but attributes those to having shared with Fanon the same conditions of oppression, despite being continents apart. "The truth is . . . all of us were influenced by our personal experiences within the context of the racist construct. It doesn't matter whether the powers that be speak French or Dutch or German or English. . . . They built their wealth on [the] exploitation of Africa and Asia, built their wealth on enslavement of Africans."[17] Above all, Greenlee contends that he was not looking to capture the story of any particular group, but to tell the truth about his African American community in Chicago, which he believed to be similar to many others across the nation, if not the world. In addition, Greenlee actually critiques radical movements of his era, including the Panthers, charging that most were more about rhetoric than action—and transformed by the media attention, allowing others to interpret their narratives and end goals. Moreover, lacking military experience and the necessary discipline, Greenlee claims they made "targets of themselves," which eventually helped bring about their demise.

Greenlee recalled in an interview, working while in the Foreign Service in both the informational and cultural sectors, both of which produced newsreels in support of foreign leaders, including the Shah of Iran, but which were pitched as locally produced propaganda.[18] Witnessing the fallout of US policies in Africa had a profound effect on Greenlee, who stayed in the service because he was "learning so much"—lessons that would later inform the ideas and actions of his characters. While in Baghdad, he recalls how he saw firsthand how American foreign policy dictated the overthrow of regimes in the region and the installation of puppet governments more favorable to US designs. He also remembers "rubbing shoulders with successful revolutionaries, people who had fought either as armed rebels or as non-violent protestors to rid themselves of the European occupation."[19] During his service, while briefly visiting the United States in 1965, he also witnessed the Watts rebellion, which he came to view as the forerunner of a possible "anticolonial rebellion" at home.[20] He became convinced that such a revolt could take place among African Americans similarly trapped in colonized spaces within American inner cities. Once he returned to his post in Greece, he began drafting the novel version of *Spook*, which was born not only of these experiences, but also of the "grueling realization of the parallel history of African Americans" and the "Third World Country" of the South Side of Chicago.[21]

Greenlee's protagonist Dan Freeman, whose name, fuses together the words *free* and *man*, is similar to Greenlee as a college-educated man loyal to his childhood friends and community.[22] Unlike Greenlee, however, who became radicalized by his government experiences, Freeman enters CIA training with his mission already in mind. Freeman gleans what he can from his rigorous training, and then, after serving a short stint as a "reproduction chief" running a copier in the subbasement of a government office building, he returns to Chicago to launch an urban uprising.

When Greenlee decided to transform his novel into a film, he opted for the action genre as the vehicle, despite its limitations and ability to short-circuit the "psychological impulses" that in a novel allow for the development of meaningful characters.[23] But the format was ideal for depicting the preparation, training, and execution of a military-style operation, along with outlining a "complex political ideology . . . in a way that would be easily understood for the people I wrote for." His community often rejected documentaries as too preachy, so he chose an action film "to get across my message."[24] Although his experiences in part inspired Freeman, portrayed in the film by Lawrence Cook, Greenlee not only had to operate within the conventions of the action genre, but also within the context of black male representations to that point in cinema history. For most of that history, blackness had been used to signify menace, dating back to the now infamous and terrifying would-be rapist Gus in D. W. Griffith's 1915 blockbuster *Birth of a Nation*. As Donald Bogle, among others, has amply noted, this characterization established a baseline with lasting consequences,

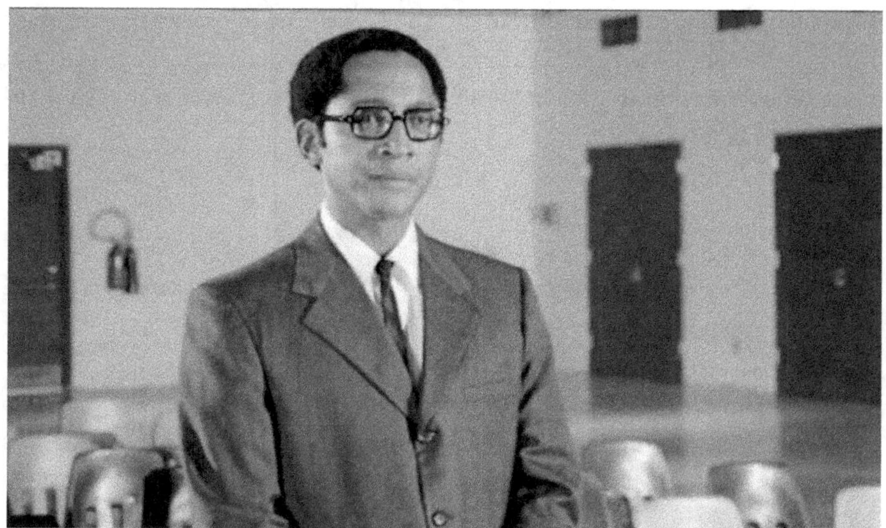

Fig. 3.1 Dan Freeman (Lawrence Cook) in his guise as the quiet, unassuming, and obedient Negro.

one of which was to make the sexualized and violent black "buck" one of the few roles available for black males for decades to come. Other iconic roles included the "coon," who existed for comedy's sake, and the "Uncle Tom," who accommodates the white establishment and avoids making trouble for himself.[25] Freeman co-opts the Uncle Tom stereotype for his story, but does so in a highly strategic manner. Freeman is labeled an Uncle Tom, not only by the CIA but also among his fellow black recruits, who call him a "tom" for refusing to join their plan to keep "the curve down" to avoid having anyone sent home. Meanwhile, Freeman excels in all phases of his training, methodically cataloging advice, including how to make explosives using materials that are readily available in whatever place an operative might find himself. Finally, as the only recruit left in his class, he becomes the target of an instructor who appears determined to break Freeman, challenging him to a showdown that first includes baiting him with racial slurs. Once their martial arts matchup is underway, however, Freeman reveals his talent, leaving his opponent battered and confused, along with exposing Freeman's intensity and seriousness of purpose. Another clever use of the Uncle Tom ruse occurs later in the film, when Freeman and his men seize control of a radio station in order to broadcast their liberation message and to announce "the beginning of our war." Freeman, hiding his identity behind a ski mask, announces he is "the Uncle Tom of your Black Freedom Fighters," which again exploits the customary meanings of the label.

Freeman's Revolutionary Vanguard

Although Greenlee enlisted Ivan Dixon of *Hogan's Heroes* (1965–71) fame to direct the film, most other notable black actors of the era declined to get involved with the project, either in front of or behind the camera. To that time, the only black actor to rise to star status with the arguable clout to take such a risk was Sidney Poitier, whose roles during the 1950s and 1960s had expanded the choices available. Yet, despite his star power, most of his characters continued to be in the service of the white-controlled system, as well as to maintain the taboo against having a sexualized nature. Moreover, by 1973, most black male characters continued to represent blackness as criminal, appearing as the punks who menace the iconic white knights of the mean streets.[26] Two popular films in 1971, *The French Connection* and *Dirty Harry,* had helped to establish the white rogue cop character, who works outside the system to enforce a higher moral and political imperative in order to tame the urban wilderness by any means necessary. It is an American edict first articulated within popular culture in the western, with the "savage" Indian as the target, the nineteenth-century Other standing in the way of the nation's Manifest Destiny.[27] By the late 1960s and early 1970s, contemporary savagery was represented on screen (in feature films and news footage) by ghettoized black males. As Yvonne Tasker notes, "Whilst blackness may be constructed as marginal within Hollywood narratives, it has a *symbolic centrality*" [her emphasis]. This is particularly pronounced in action cinema, a form that is played out over the terrain of criminality, and one that is often directly concerned with the policing of deviance."[28]

At the same time Dirty Harry embodied the white rogue cop as national hero, African American filmmaker Melvin Van Peebles created a groundbreaking alternative in his independently produced *Sweet Sweetback's Baadasssss Song* (1971).[29] It not only ushered in the lucrative style now loosely labeled blaxploitation, but it also introduced the idea of a sexualized black male character as the central focus, with the story told from his perspective as the criminal being hassled and hunted by the cops. Given the box office success of *Sweetback*,[30] Hollywood co-opted the approach but soon replaced innovation with formula and allowed exaggeration to eventually consume the genre—its radical critique all but used up.[31]

It was in this context and environment that Greenlee's Freeman is configured: a sexualized black hero, but one who is also politically informed and can serve as an organic intellectual who offers to lead the struggle for liberation.[32] Greenlee's description of Freeman here alludes to Antonio Gramsci's description of educated elites who recognize their organic links to working-class interests and contribute their insights and labor to counter-hegemonic struggles.[33] As the story advances, Freeman's white shirt and black tie give way to fashionable street clothes in keeping with the times and his community's sensibilities, but unlike the blaxploitation films that *Spook* is often confused with, Freeman does not become a fashion plate, nor does he have a pop soundtrack to validate his currency.[34] In this way, as much as Freeman is situated in a particular time and place, he is also designed to be a figure who can encompass multiple manifestations of blackness and outline a dynamic collective that is better able to confront historically rooted (and globally linked) injustices—an idea that undoubtedly transcends the 1970s.

A few early blaxploitation films produced by black filmmakers other than Van Peebles had demonstrated a measure of oppositionality as well, most notably *Superfly* (1972), in which the superstar drug dealer has the intelligence to envision his doomed fate, curb his greed, and sidestep the gangster's usual downfall. In contrast, Freeman's criminality is not depicted on behalf of personal gain, or to get rich quick as an individual at the expense of his community, but to battle law enforcement on behalf of a liberation movement. It helps explain why some reviewers, expecting another installment of the era's blaxploitation fare, expressed disappointment at Freeman's lack of appetite, ambition, or demonstration of "bling" befitting the era. His gang is also not composed of undisciplined killers who cannot control themselves, but trained revolutionaries who were given something meaningful for which to fight.

Since Freeman's ghetto is largely devoid of a working class to act as a revolutionary vanguard (much like Russia consisted of peasants rather than workers in the manner Marx had envisioned), Freeman recruits from society's outcasts, who are trapped in the decaying neighborhoods of the inner cities and survive by pimping, hustling, and dealing drugs; they will comprise his lumpenproletariat.[35]

Freeman first seeks recruits in a pool hall, where he knows he can find members of the Cobras, the local gang to which he once belonged. At first, they mistake him for the social worker he is pretending to be and challenge him to a fight, which he wins handily despite their numbers, and he earns their respect in the process. He chides them for their crude weapons, pointing out that they will do as much damage to the white establishment as a "mosquito to an elephant's ass."[36] He offers to show them more efficient tools and fighting methods. Once their training is underway, they first balk at his instructions for making homemade explosives, until he reminds them that they will have to "live off the land" and "match technology with spontaneity and improvisation," referencing liberation movements in Algeria and Kenya. He also shows them how city streetlights are laid out on a grid, providing precise measurements for sniper teams to utilize. One of his guerilla fighters later articulates the plan, which is intended to create independent cells that, if discovered, cannot be linked back to the larger organizational structure. These individuals are also trained to replicate themselves. As the movement spreads beyond its initial Chicago operation, these fighters will be forced to go underground, making two moves before reaching a final destination, where they will be given five hundred dollars and new identification papers. Afterward, they will live off the street, where they will recruit new members, establish similar training camps, a chain of command, and an organizational structure that adheres to a policy of tight discipline. Even if arrested, they have been trained to recruit in prison. Later in the film, once the war is launched, his former CIA boss frames the insurrection as the result of "untrained black fanatics," whose leader, once captured, will leave only "ignorant Negroes who won't know what to do without him." Freeman has ensured that his revolutionaries will be able to fight on.

Among Freeman's fighters are men like Shorty (Anthony Ray), an erstwhile drug addict on whom Freeman takes a chance—that is, if Shorty can follow the "no junk" rule.[37] In a poignant scene with Shorty's mother, Freeman delivers a harsh critique of her willingness to look the other way while her son dabbles in petty drug sales because they help her make ends meet. He also tries to urge her to make sure Shorty finishes school, asking, "without an education, what's he gonna do?" Rather than merely preach or

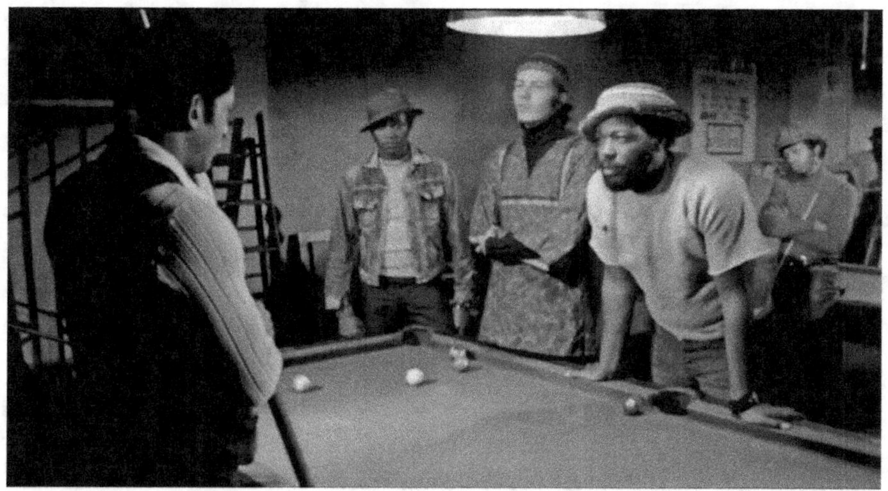

Fig. 3.2 Freeman frequents the pool halls and dive bars of the hood in order to find recruits for his guerilla army.

pass judgment, though, Freeman (and Greenlee) appear to be asking the black community to embrace the discipline necessary to make sustainable change, and to forego the temptations that are designed to derail and distract their discontent. "White folks control your neighborhood—through drugs," Freeman tells Shorty, who he advises to fight back by no longer participating in the trade and, in his own way, disrupt that system. In the end, Shorty fails to measure up and "goes bad," prompting a riot and nearly short-circuiting Freeman's larger plan.

Another important "street" character is the light-skinned Willie (David Lemieux). Few films made by black or white filmmakers up to this time effectively dealt with the complexities of being light-skinned beyond the viewpoint of scorn—à la *Imitation of Life* (1934, 1959)—for the ability to "pass" and reap whatever personal (and largely temporary) rewards might result from deploying such a strategy.[38] In contrast, Greenlee transforms this divisive aspect of black life into another strategic tool. He and Dixon, as director, not only permit Willie a rich moment in which to articulate his anguish about his complicated identity, but they also enable Freeman to deliver a message about inclusivity as a smarter revolutionary approach. Willie explains to Freeman that his motivation for joining the guerilla force is hate for the white man, whom he so closely resembles.[39] But Freeman loses patience with that approach, telling Willie: "This is not about [hating] white folks. It's about loving freedom enough to die or kill for it . . . you're gonna need more than hate to sustain you when this thing begins." Freeman also takes notice of Willie's gift for words, appointing him the Minister of Propaganda to create media products from posters to song lyrics that "talk to the people in the language that they understand." Finally, Freeman urges Willie to value his education, sharing his own story about learning to take reading seriously after realizing his grandmother was learning while helping him. She had advised the young Freeman to get an education because once earned, it is something "the white man can't take away from you."

In another aspect of his fighters' training program, Freeman informs them that they have to learn "how to steal," moving beyond being "experts [at] stealing from your black brothers and sisters . . . [and] learn how to steal from the enemy." Just as Freeman has gone unnoticed in his Uncle Tom disguise, he shows the trainees how their blackness, frequently rendering them invisible in the larger society, can now be used strategically for the cause. He notes that a "black man with a mop, tray, or broom in his hand can go damn near anywhere in this country. And a smiling black man is invisible." In an exercise to prove his point, Freeman sends one of his men dressed as a janitor into the office of an executive of the Chicago Edison power company. The operative manages to steal a pipe right off the executive's desk, the executive too busy and too dismissive of the janitor to note that the theft is taking place. Another way to remain unnoticed, Freeman instructs, is for the men to put track marks on their arms to resemble junkies, which ensures they will be left alone on the streets during the day, leaving their nights available for training.

Freeman also demonstrates how Willie's "lack of pigment"[40] can be deployed as another strategic tool, as he directs Willie and five others to rob a bank to secure a sizable war chest to bankroll their needs. While making their getaway, the men hear a news report confirming that police are looking for six Caucasians, ensuring that their operation remains clandestine, with authorities searching for men who fit different physical descriptions.

Although some critics viewed such scenes as proof that Greenlee was trying to foment a race war, he argues that he was merely identifying race as the site for a revolutionary movement, given the history of race-based injustices in America. By virtue of its underlying philosophy, however, such a revolt could be expanded to include others who suffer oppression in America, including poor whites who are often "just as victimized in the present society," except on the basis of class. In this manner, *Spook* is not necessarily advocating a race war but a wider revolt, with the African American underclass in the vanguard role "given their position now" as American's most persistent underclass.[41] Greenlee ultimately envisioned a union much in the way "John Brown hoped to do."[42] Above all, Greenlee insists his film is about freedom, in this instance, "it just happens in this case it's color-coded." The same concept has been applied around the world, Greenlee explains, citing contemporary conditions in Libya and elsewhere: "They're all the same . . . fed up with being oppressed and dominated."[43]

Blue Trumps Black for Dawson

Police departments were originally developed in part to serve as a domestic army charged with maintaining social order and thwarting insurrections among America's underclass, its Others, whether slaves or unruly immigrant groups that together comprise the "dangerous classes." In *Spook,* that containment agent is portrayed by Freeman's longtime friend turned cop Dawson (J. A. Preston). Dawson also represents a path taken by many Americans from marginalized communities of joining the ranks of the police as a way of climbing into the middle class.[44] Once becoming functioning members of the system, though, in subtle and blunt ways, they absorb the system's codes and concepts of justice, with such internalized biases often directing them to abuse and help contain their own communities.[45]

In the wake of the 1960s US civil rights movement, many urban police departments began actively recruiting black officers, in part to respond to outrage over persistent white control, especially in large cities experiencing a surge of newly empowered black constituencies.[46] Black cops from *Spook*'s era, though, complained about what scholars term "experiential racism," which involves discrimination "motivated by racial stereotyping and racial images that have become so integrated into the woodwork of the society that they are barely noticeable to most white Americans."[47]

Greenlee's black cop character is rooted in these same legacies, which make him doubly conflicted. So few black males have been allowed to portray cop characters, given the meanings attached to the role, and with blackness representing America's most conspicuous Other.[48] Again, Poitier was able to launch a limited challenge, portraying Philadelphia homicide detective Virgil Tibbs in the 1968 film *In the Heat of the Night*. The portrayal was a rare depiction of an intelligent, middle-class black cop. Yet Tibbs is still shown isolated from the larger black community, existing as an anomaly or exemplar of his race rather than to suggest expanding black empowerment as a whole. He also ultimately upholds the system—his "difference" hardly reforming the system or undermining its learned racism.[49] On the other hand, *Spook*'s Dawson is a much richer version, shown interacting with his community and having deep roots within that collective, along with experiencing the "double consciousness," in this case, of having both black and "blue" loyalties. Greenlee explains that he intended Dawson to be a "fully drawn, three-dimensional character," acknowledging that he has cops in his family and understands their conflicting loyalties.[50] In the end, though, Dawson's talent and energies are co-opted by the system to serve as anti-change agents rather than to be utilized on behalf of his race- *and* class-based interests.

Dawson is introduced shortly after Freeman returns to Chicago—Dawson, just in from California, had been demonstrating inner-city riot control as part of his post with the Chicago Police Department. Their relationship is further clarified when Freeman toasts Dawson, calling him the "hoodlum turned cop," referencing both their former memberships in the Cobras. This device of having the two male leads hail from the same neighborhood and now representing opposite sides of the law is another long-standing convention within crime or action films, as is their eventual showdown.[51] In a later scene, Dawson tells Freeman how his estranged wife is going for a master's degree, another reminder of their earned and shared middle-class values, as is talk of Dawson's son excelling in sports, implying that talent will enable him to become eligible for an athletic scholarship to attend college. A scene during Freeman's CIA training revealed that he, too, attended college on an athletic scholarship, prompting his white supervisors to reiterate the stereotype about blacks excelling in sports, and the enduring fetish about the "natural" talents of the black body at the expense of a quality black mind.[52]

In most action films in which male friends occupy opposite sides of the law, blue will eventually trump black or any other identity factor that previously formed the basis of their personal bond. Dawson is no exception. What is unique, though, is that Freeman will attempt to recruit Dawson, not to become a criminal in the traditional sense, but to join an uprising that challenges Dawson to turn his back on the existing political and social order he is sworn to uphold. In this way, Greenlee proposes a powerful possibility, which gets articulated later in the film once the uprising is underway, with reports noting that black bus drivers, garbage men, and other workers have stopped cooperating and essentially shut down the city. As Freeman later explains, the goal is to similarly paralyze the country, not necessarily to overthrow the system, but to fight "whitey to a standstill. . . . There is no way that the United States can police the world and keep us on our ass, too, unless we cooperate. When we revolt, we reduce it to a simple choice."

Even once street violence erupts and both Dawson and Freeman arrive on the scene, Freeman continues the ruse of being a social worker, complying with Dawson's request to calm the crowd and get "the kids to cool it." Freeman has his own reasons to ask the community to resist rioting, explaining the reality of what they have to lose, and the realization that in the end, they will make matters worse for their personal situations and get hurt in confrontations with police. Freeman also does not want them squandering their anger, preferring they channel it into his more carefully planned insurrection, which cannot be so easily curbed by routine street policing and Dawson's riot control methods. Freeman also knows that spontaneous but unorganized riots give the police an excuse to crack down on the community and excuses the political authorities from addressing the underlying grievances behind such rebellions.

While Freeman is frustrated by the riots' ability to rob the community of options, Dawson becomes frustrated by his own lack of control over police response methods, especially when dogs are brought in to work the crowd. Dawson shouts at the cops struggling to maintain control over the snarling dogs: "You know how these people feel about dogs," referring to the use of police dogs against black demonstrators, used most notably during the early years of the civil rights movement. In a revelatory moment in which Dawson is shown at a crossroads in his loyalties, he points a gun at one of the dogs, telling the officer holding the leash that he will shoot the dog if it is not removed from the scene. The officer (who is also black) shouts back that he is only following orders; eventually Dawson lowers his gun and the officer retreats—both men refusing to carry out the command. In this moment, Greenlee and Dixon, if only fleetingly, demonstrate the tension for black cops having to choose among their different identities. After all, black cops were involved in cracking down on demonstrators during altercations with the police during the 1960s, including the "police riot" outside the 1968 Democratic National Convention in Chicago.[53] In *Spook,* after the 82nd Airborne has been called in to help quell the rioting, Freeman remarks that 40 percent of those troops are black, adding, "maybe they'll help us and maybe they won't." Again, this suggests an awareness of the ability of the system to co-opt key members of marginalized communities, making them particularly effective agents of that system, given their access to community leaders, understanding of the cultural codes, and ability to more easily breach the front lines of any resistance.

At the same time Dawson is taking a stand against the dogs, he refers to the black rioters as "these people," still differentiating rather than aligning himself to the community and its collective memory of being subjected to such police tactics. After events further escalate, Dawson chooses sides, shooting off a flare and unleashing all the police resources he has at his disposal to quell the riot. Subsequent scenes depict the violent confrontations between police and demonstrators, with cops brandishing clubs and rioters turning over cars and setting them afire, as well as throwing explosives through windows. It is during these scenes that we learn how the police have killed a child, and rather than be depicted as an isolated tragedy, it is understood as part of a long-standing pattern of collateral damage related to this type of containment method.

Greenlee and Dixon, though, pick a quieter moment for Freeman to finally confront Dawson. It happens during a scene in which they are taking shelter in a car together, expressing their mutual fatigue after three days of rioting. Dawson shares how disgusted he is that the National Guard, brought in to help the overwhelmed police, is composed of "all white" soldiers. In that moment, he acknowledges his black difference, yet, in the next breath, he expresses confusion over having watched people he knows from the neighborhood behave so violently. Freeman takes this moment to press the confused Dawson to see a deeper truth, noting, "Maybe that badge has put distance between you and them." Dawson reacts with anger, saying, "Oh, yeah, I forgot, the pigs over here and the people over there and never the twain shall meet. . . . I grew up down here, too. And I know these people . . . there were some good people out there on the streets the last few nights. Not just hoodlums like they say in the newspapers."[54] When

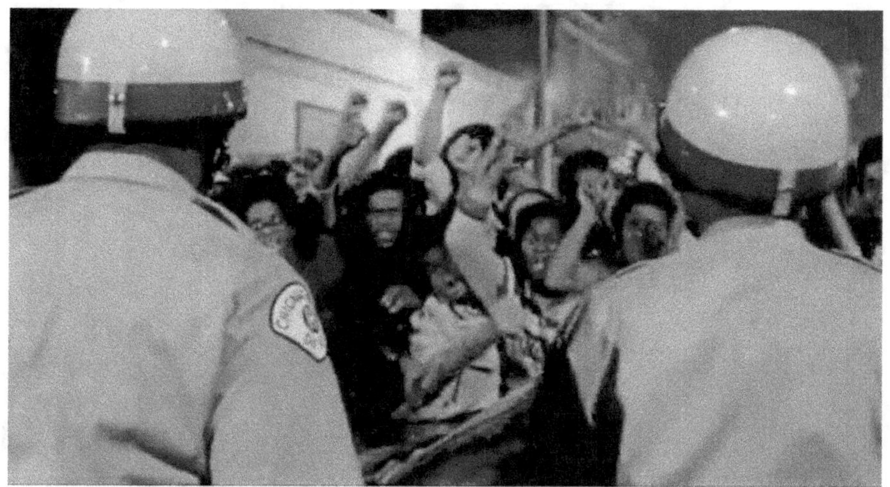

Fig. 3.3 Notwithstanding the best efforts of Freeman and Dawson, the riot quickly escalates.

Freeman pushes further, Dawson again retreats to police blue: "We have to maintain law and order or we might as well be back in the jungle." This is the moment Freeman finally unmasks his thesis, telling Dawson, "The ghetto is a jungle. Always has been. . . . You cannot cage people like animals and not expect them to fight back some day. It has always been an army occupation here, but police badges and uniforms. . . . You and me, cop and social worker. We are keepers of this goddamned zoo." Dawson quickly counters, reminding Freeman that the "streets have to be safe." Freeman then asks, "Safe for who? You are here to protect property, not lives." Dawson then doubles down on his middle-class defense, "Well, that's what it's all about. . . . You worked hard to get what you got . . . you want to keep it just like I do." Freeman responds, "You think because you got a badge and I got a couple of degrees that makes a difference? Do you know what white folks call people like you and me in private? Niggers." Once Dawson seems visibly disturbed by Freeman's words, Freeman quickly retreats, putting his mask back on, in a Fanonian sense, and suggesting the two grab dinner before Freeman must leave to "reassure the white folks."

Eventually, after Joy (their mutual friend and Freeman's longtime girlfriend) reveals her concerns about Freeman, Dawson begins piecing together an accurate picture of what Freeman is doing, which leads to the

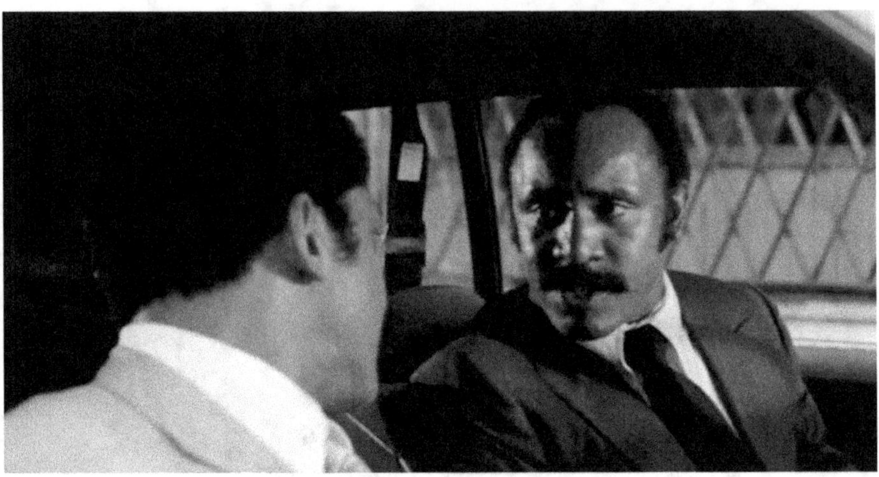

Fig. 3.4 Dawson (J. A. Preston) rejects Freeman's assertion that there is an unbridgeable gulf between the people and the police.

showdown between the two. In their final scenes together, Freeman enters his apartment to find Dawson waiting with a drawn gun. Dawson addresses Freeman by the code name of Uncle Tom and explains how he finally came to recognize the voice on the radio. While Dawson pats Freeman down in the process of arresting him, Freeman maintains his masquerade, asking Dawson to consider why Freeman would risk the trappings of his middle-class life to hatch such a plot. What finally prompts Freeman to drop the facade, though, is when Dawson asks him to deny that he is working with the communists, as he relays reports that assumed no black man could have imagined such a plot without outside help. Dawson explains how the FBI thinks Freeman's plot "is the most sophisticated underground movement in the Western hemisphere. The work of an expert." To that, Freeman asks, "And expertise is a white man's monopoly, right?" It is reminiscent of the era's black gangster Frank Lucas, portrayed by Denzel Washington in the 2007 film *American Gangster*, in which authorities overlooked Lucas's power for so long because they assumed no black hoodlum could possibly outsmart the Mafia.[55]

Dawson finally becomes fully blue, deploying the rhetoric and tools given him as an authority figure when he tells Freeman, "This gun makes me an expert." Freeman, in one last attempt to recruit Dawson, reminds Dawson how that badge and gun only make him a pawn in the system. But Dawson seems particularly outraged that Freeman is recruiting young people to his cause, to which Freeman shouts, "The kids are our only hope . . . . I got to them before they got jailed or killed or turned into Dawsons. And now they'll do anything to be free." Dawson, thinking he finally has Freeman backed into a corner, asks, "Who said you were free?" It is Freeman's response that best iterates Greenlee's thesis, as Freeman notes: "Even on the wrong end of your gun, I'm a lot freer than you are."

As the two men inevitably get into a physical struggle, Dawson is fatally shot—the bullet coming from his own weapon. Such symbolism is most likely intentional on Greenlee's part. It is also echoed in Fanon's writing about violence, especially when perpetrated on the oppressed, who eventually rise up to use violence as a tool of liberation. After Freeman summons his men to the scene to deal with the body, they seem shocked that he has killed his longtime friend, until he reminds them that you "can't hesitate . . . because someone's black," not so long as that black individual is acting on behalf of the system; it was Dawson's job to destroy them, thus, he had to be destroyed.

Class Trumps Gender for *Spook*'s Female Characters

While the Freeman/Dawson matchup is detailed and nuanced, Freeman's relationship with two key female characters is no less vital, though not as fully developed. Even so, they still present far more complex female characterizations than are found in most action films, which tend to feature female characters who represent extremes of a Madonna/whore binary, reduced to their sexual symbolism. In contrast, Greenlee and Dixon give these female characters more to do, especially given the era, including representing the intertwining of class- and race-based conflicts.

Joy (Janet League) is first introduced in the film while Freeman is still undergoing CIA training, revealing a long-standing romantic relationship that links back to the same Chicago community. She now works as a casework supervisor with the Cook Country Department of Welfare, which pays her well enough for her to remark that "since the War on Poverty, all the social workers are making money," to which Freeman adds, sarcastically, "except the poor." As with Dawson's role as a cop, Joy's occupation speaks to ways in which minorities are absorbed into the system to serve its needs rather than the interests of their communities. In this initial scene, despite just having had sex with Freeman, she reveals that she is going to marry a doctor—a move that Freeman admits comes as no surprise. She explains how she is not getting any younger, suggesting that she is no longer willing to wait for Freeman to commit to marriage and children with her.

Once the uprising is underway, and Joy is shown still having a relationship with Freeman despite her marriage, she shares how threatened she is by the Freedom Fighters—not yet privy to his leadership role with them. "All the progress we've made over the last few years will be wiped out," she laments, calling the fighters "niggers" who are threatening "decent people." Hearing Freeman somewhat defend their actions, she asks him, "Whose side are you on?" It is following this meeting that she expresses her concerns about Freeman's emerging sympathies to Dawson, who begins to figure out that Freeman may be the revolutionary leader. While with Dawson, though, Joy sheepishly asks if she is doing the right thing by voicing her concerns, and it is this scene that makes her unlikable and seemingly a traitor to both her lover and her people.

That is one of the major criticisms of the film by Stephanie Dunn, whose 2008 book analyzes the intersection of class, gender, and sexual politics in both *Spook* and *Sweetback*, in particular, and how the two films "configure classed black women as primarily sexualized women motivated by counter revolutionary aims."[56] She ultimately concludes that the female characters' "sexual imagery" situates them as "potential traitors to black liberation who could be used by 'the Man' to maintain white patriarchy unless they willingly yield to black male phallic power, both sexually and politically."[57] Dunn notes that "Joy's ideological distance from the radical, committed Freeman makes it difficult to conceive why the noble Freeman 'can't shake her loose.'"[58] It is clear in the film, though, that Freeman does not need Joy for sex, and freely exercises other options. Nor does he wish to pursue a domestic arrangement with her, clearly having rejected such personal indulgences for himself. One could just as easily make the case that it is Freeman's sense of loyalty that makes him vulnerable to her, which reveals a weakness of sentimentality usually coded as feminine, and which could disturb Dunn's conventional, gendered critique. Instead, Dunn concludes that both the novel and the film "make it clear that her ideological delusion—her commitment to the white status quo—stands as the great flaw that makes her dangerous to the militant black man."[59]

Greenlee says he intended to show that they all came from the "same mean streets," and points to many scenes in the novel that demonstrate Joy and Freeman's shared consciousness. He concedes that Joy lacks depth in the film, but he traces this to a rift between Dixon, the film's director, and the actress who portrayed Joy. The result was scenes that were key to her development were deleted from the film. In one such scene from the novel, Freeman asks Joy if she recalls how it used to be when they were coming up, to which she responds, angrily, "Yes . . . I remember the rats and roaches and the stench of semen and spoiled food and the stairways when the elevator didn't work." Having her recount what it was like to grow up in the projects might have made her a more sympathetic character, Greenlee explains, and might have made clear that she is not just some "bourgie chick who's betrayed Freeman for no reason . . . [but] acting out of fear."[60]

Rather than read Joy as merely representing a diminished female character, or ideologically opposed to Freeman, one could better explain her conflict as a fear of losing her middle-class status and reverting back to the hardships of ghetto life. I would argue that it is Dawson who may be more "ideologically distanced," given his position and more fleshed-out motives, but who proves to be far more dangerous to black solidarity, and to Freeman's project, in particular.

Admittedly, Greenlee explains that his main interest was to "romanticize the lumpen[proletariat]" rather than to be "overly critical of the middle class . . . because you've got warriors in both classes."[61] In Marxist terms, the middle class, or petite bourgeoisie, is positioned between the bourgeoisie and the proletariat, between the owners of capital and the labor they exploit, respectively; the petite bourgeoisie, who can own small-scale businesses but still be classified as workers, have often vacillated in history between being supportive of the exploitive bourgeoisie and siding with the proletarian struggle. Greenlee claims that once members of the black middle class attained a measure of material success, "they abandoned the movement," which allowed the exploitation of more hard-pressed African Americans to continue, since the threat and potency associated with mass-scale solidarity based on race had become diluted.[62]

These conflicts are no doubt woven into the characterizations of both Joy and Dawson. While Dawson represents the physical limits (and counterforce) on the body politic that Freeman is trying to recruit, Joy represents the hearts and minds of the larger black community that do not want to lose what reforms—however measured—it has gained. Rather than exist merely to affirm Freeman's heterosexuality, then, Joy is more representative of a painful rift within the black community, especially regarding strategies for advancement. In her few scenes with Freeman, with their sexual relations rarely the point, she voices objections to his black militancy on behalf of the black middle class, which is perhaps reluctant to risk what "progress" has been earned by individuals to support so militant a revolt, even on behalf of the wider black community. Freeman realizes that it will be much harder to convince people like Joy and Dawson, who have earned a modicum of reward working within the system, mere "crumbs" in Greenlee's view, to risk investing in a more open-ended revolt against forces that will certainly push back hard to retain their privilege and power. Joy also symbolizes the cult of individualism so highly prized in American mythologies, and which has undermined many class- or immigrant-based struggles by overwhelming any sense of collectivity by privileging achievement for the one at the expense of the many. In this light, Joy as a character is less about her gender than about serving as a stand-in for the black middle class, which in Marx's concept of the petite bourgeoisie at the heart of Greenlee's thesis, could go either way once Freeman's revolution is underway.[63] Freeman knows that he must recruit across class boundaries if his revolution is to succeed.

In contrast to Dunn's thesis that Freeman's women are ultimately traitors by essentialized design or sexualized distraction, I see Dawson as the ultimate traitor; he had the potential to be among the guerillas' most effective allies, but he chooses otherwise. Furthermore, if there is evidence of a sexist orientation to Greenlee's story, it is in configuring only males as capable of assuming leadership roles in political movements. But that squares with the gendered politics of the era, when the women's movement was just beginning to make inroads; thus, to isolate any sexism within Greenlee and Dixon's motives is to unfairly apply a presentist lens to a historical text. Greenlee acknowledges that women were active participants in the struggle for black empowerment, although he concedes that it was often limited to supportive roles, in keeping with the gendered politics of the era.[64]

The Dahomey Queen

If we can question Greenlee's use of a diminished female character in Joy, then he should be given credit for transforming the Dahomey Queen character from mere prostitute to ardent revolutionary. Just as Dawson and Joy share a bourgeois orientation, the Dahomey Queen (Paula Kelly) is more akin to Willie, as, despite their gendered differences, they similarly have "nothing to lose but their chains."[65] The Dahomey Queen is a far more complicated character, who also does not exist solely to affirm Freeman's heterosexuality, but to play a more direct role in Freeman's revolutionary vanguard, already comprised of society's other discarded people.

Freeman first meets the Dahomey Queen in a bar during his CIA training and eventually pays her for sex. Rather than focus on scenes that might objectify her to titillate an audience, the emphasis is more on their exchange of ideas, including Freeman telling her how she reminds him of a queen whose portrait he once saw in a book about a great African civilization. At the risk of making her uncomfortable, as few tricks talk to her much after the sex is over, he encourages her to wear her hair in the same natural state worn by the African queen. Later in the film, after she tracks him down to offer to work as a spy, she is wearing an Afro and African garb, which signify her shift in orientation, as well as embracing the era's resurrection of Mother Africa as a source of precolonial strength and Afrocentric pride to be mapped onto her. In a poignant scene earlier in the film, she is seen putting on a wig that enables her to comply with white standards of beauty, which is reminiscent of an earlier scene with Joy, who is shown taking off her wig, with a close-up capturing the wig being put on a faceless, torso-less, white bust. It also intimates a space in which Joy could develop a revolutionary consciousness, if she can grasp how the wig (accommodating white standards of beauty) is as much a socially necessitated mask as Freeman's masquerade as a social worker.

When the Dahomey Queen catches up with Freeman later in the film, she explains how she has graduated from street hustler to having a private "sponsor," who turns out to be the general once in charge of Freeman's training. She had once been interrogated by the general's assistant about Freeman, whom she declared was no "homo," nor had any problems with drugs, gambling, or losing "his cool." But, she warned, "people don't give him no shit either," intimating that Freeman should not be underestimated—words of caution the authorities chose to ignore. At their reunion, the Dahomey Queen reassures Freeman that the general still considers Freeman a harmless Uncle Tom whom he talks about regularly, thereby making her access to the general useful. Out of caution and curiosity, though, Freeman asks why she is sticking her neck out to help him, to which she responds, "I'm black, ain't I?" making clear that she is committed to Freeman's revolutionary project.

In my view, the Dahomey Queen's occupation as a sex worker is less about confirming her sexual utility or Freeman's heterosexuality than about making her the female counterpart to Shorty and the other guerilla fighters—all social outcasts in one way or another. Since the filmmakers omitted even modest depictions of sexual encounters, this character could just as easily have been configured as a cleaning woman. She could have still represented a gendered stereotype and example of a struggling black woman at the bottom of the social order, but one who could also function as a spy, in a manner reminiscent of Freeman's experiment with the "invisible" janitor. Thus, making her a prostitute seems more arbitrary than determinative as a gendered construct, the demands of the action formula notwithstanding. The filmmakers also afford her a small but telling moment, when she boasts of having built up a nest egg from her arrangement with the general. More than empty dialogue, it enables her character to articulate a transformative element not just for her sake, but as a didactic element that is ripe with meaning. As middle class, Joy's labor earns her income and security that rely on a government initiative that was put in place by President Johnson as part of his War on Poverty and his Great Society programs. However, since the 1970s, such programs have faced a sustained effort of dismantling and defunding—a move that would have eventually left Joy vulnerable and perhaps unemployed. In contrast, the Dahomey Queen stashes away money to eventually own her own labor, but, more importantly, invests in an insurrection that holds out the promise of acquiring the power and wealth that will enable her and other African Americans to sustain their gains—even to permanently change the rules that presently put them at a disadvantage.

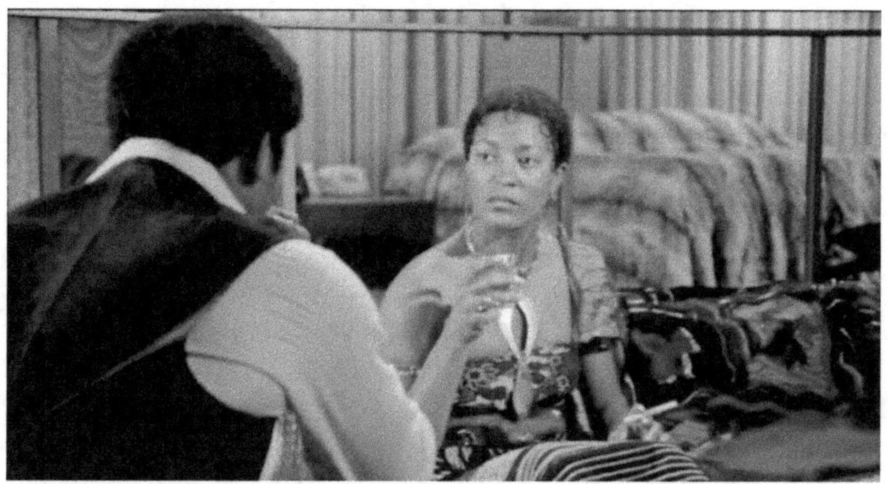

Fig. 3.5 Dahomey Queen (Paula Kelly) commits herself to serving the revolution: "I'm black, ain't I?"

Rather than exist as a sexualized fetish, the Dahomey Queen is contrived to embody both the class *and* race struggles at the heart of Greenlee's story. Moreover, his point is that such people—male or female—have value and, if born under different circumstances, might have been able to pursue more audacious goals and take advantage of what William Julius Wilson would term "life chances." In addition, it is the Dahomey Queen who approaches Freeman, lending her the agency to engineer her own transformation, rather than have the action hero direct her fate. It is also her choice to build on Freeman's suggestion, to educate herself about African history, enough to alter her appearance to reflect her ancestors' rich cultural heritage. Moreover, during the era, to wear African garb was often seen by police as a political gesture meant to convey a separatist mentality.[66] Yet, the Dahomey Queen wears these symbols openly and proudly, another sign that she has strategically aligned herself with Freeman's political project, despite the risks such attire might communicate to authorities. Finally, given the social status of prostitutes (regardless of race), her decision to risk what she had secured for herself by offering to become a spy is profound. In contrast to Joy, who has some advantages should things go wrong (education, occupation, and marriage to a doctor), a prostitute could find herself destitute or worse should her spying be discovered. Law enforcement officials might be reluctant to invest resources to investigate a prostitute's demise, especially when it surfaces that her sponsor was a general. Far from being another of the era's customary depictions of black women as "primarily sexualized beings who are attracted to black phallic power,"[67] it is Dunn who reduces this character's functionality solely to her assumed sexual utility and, in the process, robs her of agency or credit for what she risks to contribute to the revolt. The Dahomey Queen is as much a vital part of the planned insurrection as Pontecorvo's Algerian women, who donned Western costumes to get past Casbah checkpoints in order to place bombs inside the crowded cafes of the more privileged and Westernized sectors of the capital city.

Given the era's gendered roles, the Dahomey Queen is a more feasible attempt at female empowerment, under the circumstances, than arming her with an assault rifle to participate in the street fighting. Such inclusion of armed female warriors in more recent action films attests to the contemporary reality of having women serve in the military and be among the ranks of police; yet, such characters are often no more developed, and even smack of tokenism, given their real existence but persistent absence or lack of seriousness in contemporary cinema. I posit that just as Freeman enables Willie to channel his rage in order to invest in his potential as a revolutionary (rather than self-destruct as a gang member), Greenlee designs a similar crossroads for the Dahomey Queen to exploit in order to become an active participant in the uprising.[68] She and Willie take the leap of faith, whereas Shorty does not, eventually relapsing into life as a drug dealer, with his gender hardly proving to be a determining factor in his failure as a revolutionary.

The Politics of Guerilla Cinema

The notoriety of Greenlee's novel, already a must-read for progressives of the era across racial lines and around the world, enabled the making of the film in the early 1970s to garner its own publicity. On a visit to Hollywood during that time, Greenlee first approached Clarence Williams III about portraying Freeman in the film, given Williams's credentials playing the intense but cool-headed undercover cop on the hit TV show *The Mod Squad* (1968–73). Williams, although declining the role, pointed Greenlee to Dixon, who had recently directed an episode of the show and was looking for the opportunity to direct feature films through his production company, Bokari

Productions. Greenlee and a colleague from his alma mater, the University of Chicago, helped raise the funds independently, drawing most of the money from the black community.[69] After Dixon cut the action footage and shopped it around, United Artists signed on to distribute the film, thinking it was a blaxploitation film.[70] Once studio executives saw the final cut, they were outraged, prompting Greenlee, contract in hand, to force the studio to release the film anyway over the Labor Day weekend of 1973. Many of the riot scenes were shot in Gary, Indiana, after contacting friends on the Gary Police Department who provided squad cars and a police helicopter, not always with express permission. What scenes were filmed in Chicago, "we stole . . . we had to shoot it guerilla style," not having secured permits from the city to do on-location filming. Greenlee explains that the realism of people reacting angrily at the site of police on the streets in riot gear, no matter how staged, also elicited authentic and spontaneous reactions, which made it into the film. United Artists, although initially reluctant to market *Spook*, put Greenlee on a twelve-city tour to promote it after it premiered and "a few venues realized that they had something hot." The film eventually became one of the top box office earners for 1974.[71] However, Greenlee and Dixon contend that the film's run was cut short after FBI agents pressured exhibitors into pulling the film and discouraging any further distribution of prints. Although Greenlee and Dixon regained ownership of *Spook*, with few avenues for distributing it, they finally withdrew it from exhibition.[72]

In the decades that followed, *Spook* became "consigned to cult status and a murky life on bootleg video,"[73] also surfacing in art house theaters or included in special screenings as part of university classrooms or select film festivals. In the early 2000s, Tim Reid—of *WKRP in Cincinnati* (1978–82) and *Frank's Place* (1987–88) fame—met Greenlee, whose film he long considered "one of the most significant Black films ever made . . . [and] ahead of its time."[74] Over the next three years, Reid's production company digitally remastered the film, and eventually released a special thirtieth anniversary edition, appearing first on the black-owned TV One cable channel, where Reid was the senior supervising executive producer.[75]

At the time of the reissue, the United States had just embarked on the war in Iraq, which within a few short years was considered to be an egregious and especially costly mistake for the United States, creating another Vietnam-like quagmire destabilizing domestic and global political realities.

Facing such a similar political environment, the reviews of the newly remastered *Spook* were as divisive as those it garnered back in 1973.[76]

Robert Townsend, who credits Greenlee and *Spook* with inspiring him as a teenager in the 1970s to become a filmmaker, considers Greenlee to be a "true revolutionary . . . [who] continues to speak his mind. He hasn't wavered, his heart, his soul are about change."[77] Townsend also labels *Spook* "guerilla cinema at its best . . . the film made a statement and here we are thirty years later and that statement is still effective."[78] Greenlee, who attended an Indiana University symposium dedicated in part to unpacking his film for its lasting lessons, told students to know history, to exploit opportunities, and to locate allies who can help finance and distribute their messaging, whatever the medium, and ideally across media and platforms. With today's digital technology making it possible to create a film more easily and inexpensively, Greenlee explained that all that stood in their way was the courage of their convictions, and he urged them to avoid being seduced by elites who would advise them to whitewash a black-themed story or to water down a politically provocative film to make it more appealing as entertainment.[79]

In the end, despite being more than forty years old, *Spook* remains politically relevant. Whether regarded as an exemplar of agitprop, black independent cinema, or Third Cinema, it continues to present a thesis that is incredibly complex, and that echoes centuries of complaints about injustice, along with contemporary manifestations of possible remedies. Maybe Greenlee envisioned himself as a modern-day John Brown, but his "imperfect" cinema continues to imagine a fight on behalf of what Greenlee terms the "grassroots people" who grasp that "revolution is always relevant."[80]

NOTES

1. George Zimmerman was subsequently charged with second-degree murder in Martin's death and stood trial a year later. On July 13, 2013, he was found not guilty of all charges.

2. For a sample of conservative news and commentary that claim African Americans, including President Obama, unfairly played the "race card" in the Martin shooting, see Bill O'Reilly, "President Obama and the Race Problem," *The O'Reilly Factor*, July 22, 2013, http://www.foxnews.com/transcript/2013/07/23/bill-oreilly-president-obama-and-race-problem.html.

3. For sample news stories that discuss Zimmerman's ethnic background and its impact on any racist motivations, see Julia Dahl, "Trayvon Martin Case: George Zimmerman's Father Tells a Newspaper His Son Is Not a Racist," *CBS News*, July 12, 2013, http://www.cbsnews

.com/news/trayvon-martin-case-george-zimmermans-father-tells-a-newspaper-his-son-is-not-a-racist/; Chantilly Patiño, "Trayvon Martin Case: Does Race Play a Role, Though Zimmerman's Not White?" *Fox News Latino*, March 21, 2012, http://www.foxnews.com/world/2012/03/21/trayvon-martin-case-does-race-play-role-even-though-zimmermans-not-white.html; both accessed April 23, 2014.

4. After the not-guilty verdict of the four LAPD officers sparked riots in Los Angeles and across the country, President Bush ordered the Department of Justice to retry the officers on violating King's civil rights, which resulted in convictions for two of the four officers. See Douglas O. Linder, "Los Angeles Police Officers' (Rodney King Beating) Trials," *Famous Trials*, http://law2.umkc.edu/faculty/projects/ftrials/lapd/lapd.html, accessed March 28, 2014. I was part of the staff of the *Los Angeles Times* awarded the Pulitzer Prize for Spot Reporting of the riots and subsequent actions.

5. See *Jared Cohen: The Engine of Freedom, FORA.tv*, http://fora.tv/2011/06/22/Jared_Cohen_The_Engine_of_Freedom, accessed April 10, 2014. The video, cosponsored by *Wired* and *The Economist*, features Cohen, adjunct fellow at the Council on Foreign Relations and former advisor to the Secretary of State, discussing the effects of video, web, and social media technologies on political movements.

6. Greenlee's cowriter was Melvin Clay, a friend who was a founding member of The Living Theater. They also collaborated on a stage play, which was scheduled for performance at Chicago's South Side Center for the Performing Arts in 1969. See *Black World/Negro Digest*, April 1969.

7. See David Bordwell, *The Cinema of Eisenstein* (New York: Routledge, 2005); Jonathan Rosenbaum, *Movies as Politics* (Berkeley: University of California Press, 1997); and Jean-Luc Comolli and Jean Narboni, "Cinema/Ideology/Criticism," in *Film Theory and Criticism: Introductory Readings*, ed. Leo Brady and Marshall Cohen (New York: Oxford University Press, 2004).

8. Jean-Luc Godard once noted, "The problem is not to make political films but to make films politically," which he reversed after being radicalized by the violent street demonstrations in Paris and elsewhere during 1968. For more, see Julia Lesage, "Godard and Gorin's left politics, 1967–1972," *Jump Cut* 28 (April 1983), 51–58.

9. Fernando Solanas and Octavio Getino, "Towards a Third Cinema: Notes and Experiences for the Development of a Cinema of Liberation in the Third World," in *New Latin American Cinema—Volume One: Theory, Practices, and Transcontinental Articulations*, ed. Michael T. Martin (Detroit: Wayne State University Press, 1997).

10. Ibid., 37.

11. Paul Smith explains that "any particular film that Hollywood makes will of necessity be bound up in a system of cultural and political formations." In *Clint Eastwood: A Cultural Production* (Minneapolis: University of Minnesota Press, 1993), 89.

12. Solanas and Getino, "Towards a Third Cinema," 47.

13. *Spook* repeatedly shows up on web searches under the genre of blaxploitation; see the blog *Cool Ass Cinema*, where one reviewer noted, "When I began getting into black action films back in the early 1990's, I often lumped them all into the Blaxploitation genre. Since then, it seems even African American authors who have written about the genre, seemingly place any black oriented production into that category. Many consider it an offensive term and I can understand that when important films such as this are saddled with that label. That's why I created this separate category . . . for what I consider movies about African Americans

(*or race relations*) that aren't necessarily about action and violence, but have something serious to say regardless of how offensive, or controversial the subject matter. *Detroit 9000* (1973), *Mandingo* (1975) and *Across 110th Street* (1972) are some films that fit this criteria in my eyes. However, *The Spook Who Sat by the Door* (1973) staunchly represents this category above all others." Venom5, "*The Spook Who Sat by the Door* Review," *Cool Ass Cinema*, July 13, 2010, http://www.coolasscinema.com/2010/07/spook-who-sat-by-door-1973-review.html, accessed July 8, 2014.

14. The film was directed by African American filmmaker Gordon Parks Sr.

15. Michael T. Martin, interview with Sam Greenlee, Indiana University Bloomington, March 22, 2011, 2 (unpublished transcript).

16. Greenlee also claims that his use of the Minister of Information phrase predates the Panthers use. See ibid., 40.

17. Sam Greenlee, panel discussion on *The Spook Who Sat by the Door* as part of the "Cinematic Representations of Racial Conflict in Real Time" symposium, Indiana University Bloomington, March 25, 2010, 23–24 (unpublished transcript).

18. Martin, transcript of interview with Sam Greenlee, 4.

19. Greenlee was in the region about the time the Algerian War of Independence was unfolding and could sense that "a revolution was brewing." See ibid., 1–3.

20. Ibid., 6.

21. Ibid., 5.

22. In the novel, Freeman graduates from Michigan State University; Greenlee attended the University of Wisconsin then the University of Chicago for his master's degree, writing his master's thesis on the Bolshevik Revolution. Greenlee made sure Freeman "dressed the way I dressed, he listened to the same kind of music, ate the same kind of food." Ibid., 41.

23. Ibid., 13.

24. Ibid., 34.

25. See Donald Bogle, *Toms, Coons, Mulattoes, Mammies and Bucks: An Interpretive History of Blacks in American Films* (New York: Continuum, 2002).

26. The description of "knight of the mean streets" is rooted in popular fiction about private detectives, most notably Philip Marlowe, the character created by Raymond Chandler.

27. As Teddy Roosevelt explained, "the American race" needed to vanquish the savage or risk the future of Western civilization. See Gail Bederman, *Manliness and Civilization: A Cultural History of Gender and Race in the United States, 1880–1917* (Chicago: University of Chicago Press, 1995), 5.

28. Yvonne Tasker, *Spectacular Bodies: Gender, Genre and the Action Cinema* (New York: Routledge, 1996), 9.

29. *Sweet Sweetback's Baadasssss Song* tells the story of a black male who earns his living performing in live sex shows in South Central Los Angeles until he is falsely charged with a crime and arrested. After being arrested, he witnesses two white cops brutally beat a black militant, whom he aids before assaulting the cops and then fleeing. He becomes hunted by the LAPD, among others, until he finally makes it across the border to Mexico, vowing to return later to "collect some dues."

30. *Sweetback* grossed more than $10 million during the year of its premier, the most successful independent production on record to that time. The film cost $500,000 to make, including a $50,000 loan from Bill Cosby, according to Jesse Algeron Rhines, *Black Film/White Money* (New Brunswick, NJ: Rutgers University Press, 1996), 43. Also see Gladstone L. Yearwood, *Black Film as a Signifying Practice: Cinema, Narration and the African-American Aesthetic Tradition* (Trenton, NJ: Africa World Press, 2000), 185–216.

31. See Mark A. Reid, *Redefining Black Film* (Berkeley: University of California Press, 1993), 94. Later films such as *The Mack* (1973), *Black Caesar* (1973), and the *Shaft* sequels (1972–3) more resemble the classical Hollywood gangster formula. See Marilyn Yaquinto, *Pump 'Em Full of Lead* (New York: Twayne's Filmmaker Series, 1998).

32. Martin, transcript of interview with Sam Greenlee, 19.

33. Gramsci described such an intellectual as someone who is a "permanent persuader" and "not just a simple orator," a characterization often associated with what he calls "traditional" intellectuals. See Antonio Gramsci, *Selections from the Prison Notebooks* (London: International Publishers, 1971).

34. Greenlee's knowledge and friendship with jazz artists enabled him to secure Herbie Hancock to compose original music for the film.

35. As Greenlee notes, "Bourgeois intellectuals don't make revolutions; they co-opt revolutions. The people who are in the streets . . . are the lumpen." Martin, transcript of interview with Sam Greenlee, 36.

36. *The Spook Who Sat by the Door,* directed by Ivan Dixon (1973: Monarch Home Entertainment, 2004), DVD.

37. A similar prohibition about abusing alcohol and drugs is espoused by the Nation of Islam to infuse a sense of empowerment through self-discipline among its largely African American membership, but in large part based on prohibitions outlined in the Qur'an. See Yusuf Al-Qaradawi, *The Lawful and the Prohibited in Islam (Al-Halal Wal Haram Fil Islam)* (Oak Brook, IL: American Trust Publications, 1999).

38. I am referring mostly to the films of Oscar Micheaux. Also, Greenlee recalls that he has members of his family that "were light enough to pass," which didn't diminish their sense of community, and "it's obvious that among our greatest heroes are people of mixed race or very light in color." Martin, transcript of interview with Sam Greenlee, 43.

39. Ibid., 44.

40. Ibid.

41. Ibid., 16–18.

42. Ibid., 16.

43. Ibid., 16–17.

44. Such minority candidates see police work, a form of civil service work, as a means of acquiring social advancement, benefits, pension funds, and a measure of authority. Also, the term "minority" has been an evolving concept in America; see Noel Ignatiev, *How the Irish Became White* (New York: Routledge, 1995). By 2005 the academy class for the NYPD, the largest (at 37,000) and highest profile police force in the United States, comprised, for the first time , roughly 55 percent nonwhite recruits (specific breakdown: 18.3 percent black, 28.2 percent Latino, and 8 percent Asian American).

45. Tim Wise, one of the leading writers and educators on issues related to race and racism, noted in an appearance on Melissa Harris-Perry's program on MSNBC, March 25, 2012, that not only have most Americans absorbed racist codes, but also that roughly one-third of African Americans have also "internalized biases again their own group." See full interview at http://www.timwise.org/2012/03/tim-wise-on-the-melissa-harris-perry-show-msnbc-32512-discussing-trayvon-martin-case/, accessed April 10, 2014.

46. Geoffrey P. Alpert and Roger G. Dunham, *Policing Urban America* (Prospect Heights, IL: Waveland Press, 1997), 215. In the early 1970s, Baltimore, Newark, Memphis, Miami, and New Orleans had populations with roughly 40 percent minorities but had less than 7 percent minority membership in their police departments.

47. Kenneth Bolton Jr. and Joe R. Feagin, *Black in Blue: African-American Police Officers and Racism* (New York: Routledge, 2004), 27–28.

48. See Toni Morrison, *Playing in the Dark: Whiteness and the Literary Imagination* (New York: Vintage, 1993).

49. The film also seems to suggest that systemic racism is confined to the South, with Tibbs's life in Philadelphia free of racial oppression, which blatantly ignores the racialized history of Philadelphia's police department.

50. Martin, transcript of interview with Sam Greenlee, 20.

51. Cinema history is heavily populated by such matchups, especially in crime films. See Yaquinto, *Pump 'Em Full of Lead.*

52. See John Hoberman's *Darwin's Athletes: How Sport Has Damaged Black America and Preserved the Myth of Race* (New York: Houghton Mifflin Company, 1997).

53. The language of "police riot" was used by the Walker Report, commissioned by President Johnson to investigate reports of police abuse outside the Democratic National Convention in Chicago in 1968.

54. In describing the "us vs. them" mentality, Dawson cites the line of never the "twain shall meet" from Rudyard Kipling's 1889 poem "The Ballad of East and West."

55. See Marilyn Yaquinto, "Denzel Washington: A Study in Black and Blue," *Black Camera* 22, no. 2 (Spring 2008), 3–23.

56. Stephanie Dunn, *"Baad Bitches" and Sassy Supermamas: Black Power Action Films* (Urbana: University of Illinois Press, 2008), 83. In Dunn's study of the female characters in *Spook* and *Sweetback,* she concludes that both films "together demonstrate the exhilarating possibilities of imaging black political and social empowerment on the big screen; at the same time, they anticipate the limitation of that fantasy when filtered through conservative models of gender," 84.

57. Ibid., 75.

58. Ibid., 79.

59. Ibid., 80.

60. Martin, transcript of interview with Sam Greenlee, 24–26.

61. Ibid., 38.

62. Ibid.

63. Ibid., 20.

64. Greenlee acknowledges that "there would have been no civil rights movement if the women hadn't been intrinsically involved. In some cases they worked in the background as organizers, in other cases they were right down in front . . . there's no counterpart [among white women] to Angela Davis—at that time or today." Ibid., 35.

65. Karl Marx and Friedrich Engels, "The Communist Manifesto," in *Karl Marx: Selected Writings,* ed. David McLellan (Oxford: Oxford University Press, 1977), 246.

66. From a 2001 interview with Sylvester A. Lingeman, retired divisional commander for the Detroit Police Department and author of *A Cop's Eyes,* an unpublished memoir (1998).

67. Dunn, *Baad Bitches,* 83.

68. Martin, transcript of interview with Sam Greenlee, 35.

69. Greenlee told a reporter in 1970 that he was looking to raise money from the black community, explaining that his novel, although having been translated into seven other languages to that date, was still being suppressed by a "racist publishing establishment." In "*Spook* Author Says Whites Tried to Spook Book," *Jet Magazine,* August 27, 1970. Greenlee and Dixon estimated the film's costs at $1 million, noting that up to $850,000 came from black investors.

Greenlee also claims that Jesse Jackson was consulted by many of the investors, given his ties to Chicago's black community; but Jackson warned "that [Martin Luther] King would disapprove of a film of this nature and it's against all of his takes on non-violence." As a result of Jackson considering the film to be "dangerous," some investors backed out. Ibid., 28.

70. Ibid.

71. Ibid., 29–30. Greenlee recalls that a number of Chicago area exhibitors told him they had been visited by FBI agents, who urged the film be pulled. The actions and approach of the FBI's now discredited COINTELPRO program, which was finally exposed for abuses and dissolved by Congress in 1971, may help explain the film's disappearance. See *The FBI's War on Black America,* directed by Deb Ellis and Denis Mueller, (1990; CreateSpace, 2009), DVD.

72. Greenlee later enrolled himself in film school and continued writing and publishing, including *Baghdad Blues* (a 1976 novel based on his experiences in 1950s Iraq) and collections of poems: *Blues for an African Princess* (1971), *Ammunition!: Poetry and Other Raps* (1975), and *Be-Bop Man/Be-Bop Woman 1968–1993: Poetry and Other Raps* (1995).

73. Peter M. Nichols, "A Story of Black Insurrection Too Strong for 1973," *New York Times,* January 20, 2004, http://www.nytimes.com/2004/01/20/movies/new-dvd-s-a-story-of-black-insurrection-too-strong-for-1973.html, accessed April 10, 2014.

74. The film is also listed in S. Torriano Berry and Venice Berry's *The 50 Most Influential Black Films: A Celebration of African-American Talent, Determination, and Creativity* (New York: Citadel/Kensington Publishing, 2001).

75. In Lottie L. Joiner, "After 30 Years, a Controversial Film Re-emerges," *The Crisis* (November/December 2003), 41.

76. A high-profile review from 1973 had noted: "The rage it projects is real, even though the means by which that rage is projected are stereotypes. Black as well as white. Mr. Greenlee, who adapted his novel for the screen with Melvin Clay, and co-produced the film with Ivan Dixon, the director, couldn't care less about convincing white audiences of anything except black anger" (Vincent Canby, *New York Times,* September 22, 1973). When rereleased in 2003, the film again was vilified for its divisiveness or lauded for its political boldness. As cited on page three of the unpublished transcript of the "Cinematic Representations of Racial Conflict in Real Time" symposium at Indiana University Bloomington, *TV Guide*'s reviewer noted, "*Spook* is as racially divisive as any film ever made . . . Unabashedly bigoted, stridently hateful; it wants to be incendiary and controversial but only manages thuggish and dull." *All Movie Guide*'s reviewer Sandra Brennan wrote: "This exploitative drama may be too racist for some contemporary viewers." Finally, Jonathan Rosenbaum of *The Chicago Reader* noted: "Possibly the most radical of the black exploitation films of the 70's and that it remains one of the great missing or at least unwritten chapters in black political filmmaking."

77. Robert Townsend, Special Commentary, *The Spook Who Sat by the Door* (Monarch Home Entertainment, 2004), DVD.

78. Ibid.

79. I was part of a panel discussion on Greenlee's film at Indiana University's "Cinematic Representations of Racial Conflict in Real Time" symposium. Other panelists included Terri Francis, Film Studies and African American Studies, Yale University; historian Khalil Muhammad; Karen Bowdre, Communication and Culture, Indiana University; and documentary filmmaker Denis Mueller. Also on hand was Robert M. Young, producer of the 1964 film *Nothing But a Man,* which was the subject of a second panel during the symposium.

80. Martin, transcript of interview with Sam Greenlee, 47.

4. Persistently Displaced

SITUATED KNOWLEDGES AND INTERRELATED HISTORIES IN *THE SPOOK WHO SAT BY THE DOOR*

Samantha N. Sheppard

The 1973 film *The Spook Who Sat by the Door* (Ivan Dixon), an adaptation of Sam Greenlee's novel of the same name, depicts the story of CIA operative-turned-social-worker Dan Freeman (Lawrence Cook).[1] Freeman trains a group of Chicago black youths in counterintelligence and guerilla warfare, molding the undisciplined Cobra gang into the masterful Chicago Black Freedom Fighters. Set during the burgeoning Black Power era, *Spook* is a potent political and social critique of racialized oppression, black middle-class hypocrisy, and the disingenuous racial tokenism of affirmative-action programs. Illustrating the possibilities of a deliberately fomented rebellion, *Spook* dramatizes, as revolutionary, the theme of African American freedom and equality being gained through a political consciousness of armed resistance. With a provocative title, the film's story line plays on the multiple meanings of the term *Spook*. First, the racial slight is based on the premise that black people are frightened by ghosts and, because of their skin tone, look like ghosts in the dark. Second, because they are supposed to be invisible to detection, *Spook* is the nickname given to spies and undercover agents, such as those in the CIA. Third, the term is said to personify the psychological fears of an armed black resistance that haunts white America's consciousness. Embodying all of the above meanings of the term, Freeman is the quintessential spook—a black, ex-CIA agent "who in a Brooks Brothers' suit tried to blow up America."[2] Initially rejected by nearly

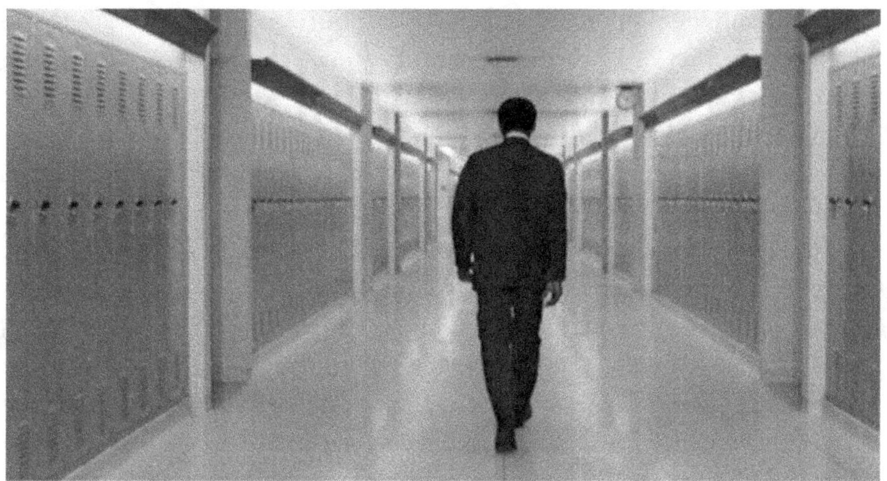

Fig. 4.1 Dan Freeman (Lawrence Cook) walks the basement corridors of the CIA building where he is reproduction chief of the photocopying facility.

forty publishers in America, Greenlee's novel was printed in 1969 by UK publisher Allison & Busby. A Chicago native, Greenlee is a scholar, former first lieutenant in the US Army, poet, and activist. Writing for a black audience, Greenlee believed his work of fiction was "a deliberate departure from traditional black protest novels. Those books were meant to appeal to the moral conscience of white America."[3] Greenlee's novel became an underground sensation, winning the *Sunday Times*'s Book of the Year award for 1969. Because of the book's popularity abroad, Bantam Press approached Allison & Busby to publish the book in the United States. Through word of mouth and a review on WNET's *Soul!* (1968–1973), a syndicated black public-affairs television show in New York, the novel's relative, yet potent, success in America made Greenlee the subject of FBI surveillance and, in conjunction with the film, is said to have been the catalyst for the government's sabotage of his career.[4]

For Greenlee, "the book is about white faces and black masks . . . and is a warning that African masks have historically and traditionally served the dual function of entertaining and threatening the enemy."[5] In the book, Freeman's self-constructed persona as both Uncle Tom and black militant figure is the guise in which the hypocrisies of the black middle class and white America are revealed, showing how the powers of both groups are unequal in relation to each other but equally destructive to the black community. An outsider within, Freeman chooses not to integrate into the burning buildings of institutionalized racism but rather to convert a gang of black youths into revolutionaries and to train them in the use of explosives to figuratively and literally set ablaze the pillars of injustice themselves.[6]

The novel, which has attained a certain cult status, was adapted for the screen by Greenlee and Melvin Clay. Following the release of the film, directed by the legendary actor, television director, and producer Ivan Dixon, in 1973, *Los Angeles Times* staff writer Kevin Thomas called *Spook* "one of the most terrifying movies ever made."[7] Thomas notes that the terror lies not only in the violence the film depicts but also in the fact that it "was filmed in Gary, Indiana, with the cooperation of its black mayor, its police department, and at least a sizable portion of its citizenry."[8] With black people of varying levels of power, skill, and ability "acting" together to tell the story of how, in fact, the master's tools (which in this case include cameras, film stock, and key grips) can be used to dismantle the master's house, the film's run was, somewhat predictably, short-lived. *Spook* was removed from theaters shortly after its release amid rumors of interference and intimidation by the FBI's Counter Intelligence Program.

As *USA Today* columnist DeWayne Wickham notes, to understand *Spook* we have to take into account the fact that the film comes out of a period of hard-fought gains in black America, including the Civil Rights Act of 1964, the Voting Rights Act of 1965, and the Fair Housing Act of 1968. In addition, *Spook* is situated during the political and social transition from the civil rights movement, with leaders such as Martin Luther King Jr. and Fannie Lou Hamer, to the Black Power era, with figures such as Stokely Carmichael (Kwame Ture) and Angela Davis. Using violence as a metaphor for active black opposition and an aggressive control of one's own destiny, Wickham explains that the "movie had a message that in the early 1970s scared the hell out of some white folks. It was a message that said to Black folks: you can resist, you can respond."[9] Moreover, "if accepted as the message movie it was meant to be, the protest film it was intended to be," *Spook,* then and now, Wickham contends, has the potential to raise the level of sociopolitical and historical consciousness in viewers, particularly those in racially subjugated communities.[10]

In this article, I continue this process of historically analyzing *Spook* and the level of consciousness that the film's production history and diegetic narrative raises. Aided, in part, by Christine Acham and Clifford Ward's 2011 documentary *Infiltrating Hollywood: The Rise and Fall of "The Spook Who Sat by the Door,"* which focuses on *Spook*'s production and mysterious disappearance, my historical analysis looks at the ways in which *Spook* is both a product of social, cultural, and political forces and a producer of historical meaning when those forces are analyzed alongside and against the film's narrative.[11] *Spook* can, thus, be constructively analyzed and historicized within the related contexts of its own production and exhibition history; black film production in Los Angeles in the 1970s; documentary television coverage of blacks in the late 1960s; and the history of black gangs—particularly Chicago's Blackstone Rangers—and social violence. The specific historical facts and themes of *Spook* are used to read interrelated histories and narratives of black experiences of film and social change, and I argue that, while these particular histories of *Spook* do not give a complete view of the film's historical significance (which could never be done, since as time passes, films accrue and disperse meanings), these histories do reveal much about the film's sociopolitical and cultural value. We are thus able to catch a glimpse of how a film that has been persistently displaced throughout history makes visible connections—textually and socially—to both local and distant moments, contexts, films, images, and communities. By providing contextualized "situated knowledges" of *Spook*, then, this article favors partial but revealing perspectives on the film as a text of and significance to black history and cultural production.[12]

Producing Radicalness: The Enduring Relevance of *Spook's* Controversial Release(s)

Spook's production and exhibition histories are important industrial sources of insight into the film's sociopolitical and cultural significance. Through analyzing its industrial history, we can see how *Spook* has made connections to and produced meanings in different historical periods. For example, in "Theorizing Historicity or the Many Meanings of *Blacula*" Leerom Medovoi explores the way in which *Blacula* (William Crain, 1972) not only represents multiple histories but also gains meaning through its negotiated readings in different historical moments.[13] Focusing on how a film text performs "what it *means* in the sense of what it *does*," Medovoi explains that a historical analysis of a film's performativity "demands attention not only to its representational codes and conventions, but also to the actual sites of its production and consumption."[14] A film steeped in controversy and exhibited sporadically over the course of its existence, *Spook*'s radical themes also mirror its production and reception histories. As a "radical" text, *Spook* rebels against a fixed historical placement and a rigid social significance to one time period over another. In fact, *Spook*'s enduring ethos of radicalness—conjured by the narrative and its controversial release history—is what helps to produce connective and connected meanings to histories and narratives situated in different spatiotemporal moments. Therefore, to understand what *Spook* means historically in the sense of what it does to and throughout history, the film's production and exhibition history must first be summarized.

After shopping the film to studios and being rejected, Greenlee and Dixon, who also served as producers, struggled to finance the film independently. According to Greenlee, some potential investors were discouraged from contributing to the film by unknown sources, thought to be members of the FBI.[15] In the end, Greenlee and Dixon raised nearly a million dollars, mainly from black investors, and the film was produced by black-owned Bokari Ltd.[16] As previously noted, while *Spook* is set in Chicago, the film was shot primarily in Gary, Indiana. Chicago's Mayor Richard J. Daley refused to allow any filming in the city, but Dixon's cast and crew were welcomed by Gary's first African American mayor, Richard Hatcher. Mayor Hatcher offered full support to the production, even providing local police and a helicopter for a shot of the main riot scene.[17] While filming primarily in Gary, Dixon did shoot (steal) a few scenes in Chicago. Taking a cue from the film's narrative, in which Freeman teaches the Cobras to "match technology with spontaneity and improvisation," the one scene filmed in Chicago—in which Freeman teaches the gang how to use the city streets as tools for warfare—was shot guerilla style. "To get this memorable shot the actors and a crewmember took a handheld camera onto the [L] platform. They filmed the scene, got on the [L], took some images in the moving train and got off at the following stop before they could be questioned."[18]

Distributed by United Artists (UA), which also kicked in completion funds, *Spook*'s limited exhibition history is rife with controversy based on its radical vision of insurrection. Released in October 1973, the film was quickly pulled from theaters across the country. According to a March 20, 1975, letter from Bokari Ltd. to investor Harry Schrogg, the film is said to have grossed $884,996.62 through February 1975, but UA, which by that time had recovered its investment, pulled the film from circulation.[19] Although Bokari Ltd. was able to recover the rights to the film, the nearly fifty prints of *Spook* disappeared.[20] The surviving negative copy, saved by Dixon, was stored in a vault under a different name for nearly thirty years. *Spook* was basically extinct, save for VHS copies of the film that were stolen and circulated in the 1980s and 1990s. In 2004, African American producer and actor Tim Reid and his company, Obsidian Home Entertainment, premiered the film at the Los Angeles Film Festival, and a digitally remastered version of *Spook* was released on DVD through Monarch Home Video.[21] Offering a somewhat skewed view of black film history, particularly black independent film, Reid said that "this movie is the only true black radical movie ever made" and that "there is nothing that comes close to this movie in terms of black radicalism."[22]

Reasons given for the film's removal from theaters vary; however, the influence of the FBI's Counter Intelligence Program is a common denominator in the discourse surrounding the film's disappearance.[23] Greenlee attests that "exhibitors from across the country reported that men who identified themselves as members of the FBI 'requested' that the owners remove the film from the theaters."[24] Given its dramatization of armed stealth, *Spook*'s disappearance becomes "pure political paranoia, or one of those strange-but-true episodes that could only have happened during the political turmoil of the 1960s and early 1970s," and Dixon believed that a "robbery of an armory in Compton, which mirrored an episode in the film, was so disturbing to UA that the company quickly dropped 'Spook.'"[25] Paranoia, politics, and the police state of the actual time underpinned the radical nature of the film, and its stunted and intermittent run defines the way in which *Spook* performed at the time of its release and subsequent rereleases and also the way the film is remembered today.

Viewers have used *Spook*'s curtailed exhibition and the controversy over the film's subject and suppression to connect and negotiate thematically interrelated moments throughout history. For example, in a 1976 article in the *Tri-State Defender* on Memphis's black-owned Towne Cinema Theatre's first-anniversary celebration of the film's disappearance, the author notes that "in the wake of Watergate and recent disclosures about the country's intelligence system, 'The Spook Who Sat by the Door' is back—more relevant than ever."[26] The author aptly notes *Spook*'s profound relevance to 1976's moment of political controversy, cover-up, surveillance, and FBI terrorism of people of color.

A displaced (and thought to be erased) film that has exhibited itself in one way or another in every decade since its release, *Spook* is a powerfully significant and signifying text.[27] As Tim Reid correctly observes, "Even in today's context" of black film production, *Spook* is "a radical movie." Set against black film history, *Spook* still articulates a freedom not yet realized and a dream not yet fulfilled within Hollywood's depictions of African Americans. For example, in the film Freeman and the Cobras discuss black representation in Hollywood narratives. Freeman asks the Cobras about the plantation movies seen on television, decrying irreverent story lines of "no chains, no whips, just a bunch of happy darkies waiting on Master Charlie and digging it." In this scene, the Cobras begin to act out these narratives, typical of such racist films as *Gone with the Wind* (Victor Fleming, 1939). The film's sarcastic and comical tone reminds us, as Clyde Taylor says of Ralph Ellison's *Invisible Man,* that "funny things happen when black people show up at masquerades of their spook image."[28] Halting the revelry in the film's scene, Freeman's contextualization that the Cobras "have just played out the American dream" functions in contrast to the nightmare he intends to enact; he states, "What we have now is a colony, what we want to create is a new nation." In imagining a liberated black future, *Spook* still seems radical in relation to Hollywood's black representations. The criticism of middle-class sensibility in *Spook* challenges assimilationist films of the 1980s, such as *Beverly Hills Cop* (Martin Brest, 1984). The liberation-minded black youth in *Spook* also challenge the nihilism of the hood films of the 1990s, such as *Menace II Society* (Albert Hughes and Allen Hughes, 1993). Finally, the sociopolitical awareness in *Spook* challenges the neo-minstrelsy and revisionist cinema of the 2000s, such as *Soul Plane* (Jesse Terrero, 2004) and *The Help* (Tate Taylor, 2011).

As a product and producer of historically contingent meaning, *Spook* goes beyond providing significance to and critiquing black representation in the dominant culture of film production. The title itself is often referenced to point to the marginalized status of African Americans in society.[29]

In an enduring age of inequality, *Spook*'s form of social diagnosis and critique is rather telling. For example, in his article "Obama's Candidacy Recalls Cult Film," Kevin Weston argues that *Spook* puts the racial politics of the 2008 presidential race—following the Reverend Jeremiah Wright controversy and Obama's subsequent speech on race—into clear focus.[30] Weston believes that "[l]ike the Spook in the movie, Obama has made a living [in Chicago] winning white votes by playing the role of the non-threatening black man America can trust."[31] However, functioning as the black militant side of Obama's "Freemanization," Wright taught Obama "the skill of speaking to the choir and gathering a flock, with flair and audacity, while shouting truth to power and the people."[32] To Weston, "[f]ear of an '08 Spook is what [Hillary] Clinton—and if Obama is the nominee, the Republicans—will use to try bring Chi-town's finest down."[33] No longer at the door, Obama's in the House. While espousing nowhere near the leftist politics of *Spook*'s protagonist, the racial and political fears—questions of citizenship and socialism—that still circulate around President Obama are reminiscent of *Spook*'s integrationist critique. As Freeman (and fellow Chicago native Kanye West) explains, in a society built on and sustained through white racial tyranny and capitalism, even a successful, well-bred, and well-read black man can be reduced to a derogatory stereotype.[34]

Moreover, in the wake of the Occupy Wall Street protests, one cannot help but think of *Spook*'s narrative. Meyer Canton's 1973 *New York Times* review of *Spook* states, "Should we fail to meet the legitimate demands of the millions of poor, ill housed, hungry, sick, and degraded Americans, we may, someday soon, find ourselves faced with a very real spook who sat by the door."[35] With the film's rerelease in 2004 during the height of the Bush era, *Spook* moves throughout a history of conservative intransigence. As Canton warns, today there are multicultural spooks sitting by doors, colleges, financial institutions, and government agencies demanding radical reform. In this sense, the film can be and is remembered as a text that can inspire change just as much as a text that reveals stasis. In a conversation with a group of black youths, an elderly Sam Greenlee encourages students not to "stand in line for a white man to sign you a check to make a movie."[36] Encouraging them to be active agents in the way they are imaged and imagined, Greenlee uses the history and legacy of *Spook* as a tool for education and the support of black-created and black-controlled arts. Similarly,

Dixon has stated that *Spook* "enabled him to say to anybody who questioned [him] about race [to] look at the film."[37] A performative text and product of particular historical forces that engendered a legacy of radicalness, *Spook*'s subject matter and exhibition history reproduce radical reflections on black experiences throughout history.

Producing a Hybrid Film: *Spook's* Dual Appeal to Black Cultures of Production in the 1970s

To flesh out a historical analysis of *Spook*, we must also consider the film's displacement in two categories of Black film production in the 1970s: blaxploitation and independent black film production, specifically the period of the LA Rebellion at UCLA. By analyzing the ways in which *Spook*'s production, narrative, and exhibition appeal to both these cultures of production, I argue that *Spook* highlights the way in which both blaxploitation films can be and LA Rebellion films are "visions of a liberated [Black] future."[38]

Independently financed, *Spook* secured distribution by "selling" the film to UA as a type of "generically" violent blaxploitation film. According to Greenlee, only the film's action scenes were shown to UA, "which agreed to distribute the film thinking it would be the usual Blaxploitation fare."[39] Greenlee recalls that when UA "saw the final cut, they went up the wall."[40] "'A deathly silence descended over the room. . . . So I told them: look we got a contract and in the first paragraph you ask for six copies of the script. Don't blame me if you don't have anybody over here who can read. You got a contract; put the damn thing out there.'"[41] Stealthily portraying the film as both "the usual" and "not the usual" blaxploitation fare, Greenlee and Dixon employed the codes and conventions of blaxploitation to secure distribution for a film that they actually believed to be "too political to be called a blaxploitation film."[42]

The context of *Spook*'s production during the blaxploitation cycle reveals much about the way we think (and don't think) about blaxploitation and the politics of representation within the genre. In regard to its political engagement and social relevance, *blaxploitation* is a term and category (coined by Junius Griffin) that is fraught with contention—and the overuse of scare quotes.[43] Whether considered a genre, style, or production period, blaxploitation has come to define "the film industry's targeting [of] the black audience with a specific product line of cheaply made, Black-cast films shaped with the 'exploitation' strategies Hollywood routinely uses to make the majority of its films."[44] To Cedric Robinson, "blaxploitation was a degraded cinema": "It degraded the industry which prostituted itself to political and market exigencies and constructed the genre of an urban jungle; it degraded the Black actors, writers, and directors who proved more affectionate to money than to the Black lower classes they caricatured; it degraded its audiences who were subjected to a mockery of the aspirations of Black liberationists."[45] Notwithstanding their own exploitation of the Hollywood system in selling *Spook,* Dixon and Greenlee are quick to displace the film from its temporal context. According to Dixon, "Pretty much all those blaxploitation films were junk" because "there were too many pimps and drug dealers. Those pictures were dealing with the crud of society, instead of dealing with ordinary people."[46] While films such as *Superfly* (Gordon Parks Jr., 1972), to an extent, glorify a deleterious lifestyle, blaxploitation films, *Superfly* in particular, have a much more important relationship to black agency, political relevance, and social significance to black film, aesthetics, and cultural industries than has been acknowledged by both scholars and *Spook*'s creators.[47] As Peter Stanfield explains, "Although [Cedric] Robinson is justified . . . there is enough evidence to suggest that, however speculatively, blaxploitation films *do* express 'political' concerns."[48] For Stanfield, revealing these concerns "requires a more oblique approach to the ways in which the historical specificity of Black social experience registers in these films."[49] Thus, beyond its temporal location, *Spook*'s historically situated depictions of Black social discontent—perpetrated through violence—make the film's political concerns akin to those of many blaxploitation films.

With films such as *Shaft* (Gordon Parks, 1971), *Foxy Brown* (Jack Hill, 1974), and *Blacula,* black film production in the 1970s is marked not only by Hollywood's financial crisis but also by African Americans' emergence as lead actors, directors, and crew members in the Hollywood industry. These films engaged both abstractly and concretely with the contemporaneous social experiences of the black community, particularly the "rejection of nonviolent protest" in the 1970s.[50] Blaxploitation films, or black action films, are thought to be "popularized versions of this discontent."[51] As a result, the blaxploitation film cycle in Hollywood is predicated on a distilled recuperation and production of black content into a commoditized form that can be sold to the discontented. Therefore, let us go back to the way in which, using scenes of violence, *Spook* was sold to UA as "the usual" blaxploitation fare. Although images of violence are central to blaxploitation films, the violence in these films "referenced black sociality, or transcoded, however fancifully, black political struggles and aspirations of the times."[52] Raising sociocultural consciousness through fighting, guns, and the hipness of being one ba-a-a-a-d mother, "the genre's reliance on narratives of destruction and hypermasculine empowerment both countered and was complicit in the growing discourse of urban African American criminality, whose foundational roots were in the urban unrest of the 1960s inner city."[53] Like many blaxploitation films, *Spook*'s scenes of violence reference aggressive black sociality, particularly that of urban rebellions and violent struggles for equality.

For instance, several of *Spook*'s scenes of violence depict police brutality, such as the mass race-riot scenes that mirrored the ones that took place across the country in the late 1960s. Using a shaky, handheld camera, Dixon highlights the *liveness* of the riot scene. Actor Paul Butler (who plays Do-Daddy Dean) remembers that the scene felt real and that it turned into a real riot that forced many in the cast and crew to retreat to their motor homes.[54] Here, *Spook* shows how in both production and representation of revolt, the film contains a documentary impulse of real black resistance. This impulse is consumed by the film's black participants and black viewers "as a part of a widely shared and widely recognizable reality."[55] With overturned and burned police cars, anger in the faces of rioters, and a cacophony of visual and aural chaos, the scene is an uproarious expression of past and present black anger and angst. Blending their own experiences within the fictional narrative, the rioters in the scene are active black agents, literally and figuratively acting out a history of racial uprisings. *Spook* depicts its assault by and on "the Man"—perhaps the most recognizable character in the blaxploitation period—as both fantastical and factual. As Freeman explains, "The ghetto is a jungle. Always has been. You cannot cage people like animals and not expect them to fight back someday." The film overtly alludes to the historically violent aggression by whites against blacks struggling for equality: invoking the history of the South's reaction to black civil disobedience, police officer Dawson (J. A. Preston) rails against the police's use of dogs to control the angry Chicago residents, saying, "You know how these people feel about dogs." In this regard, like *Spook*, many blaxploitation films—from *The Legend of Nigger Charley* (Martin Goldman, 1972) to *Mandingo* (Richard Fleisher, 1975)—use histories of white violence and racialized oppression to narrativize circumscribed tales of black liberation.

Therefore, to consider *Spook*'s appeal as a part of the blaxploitation period's engagement with black sociality, attention must also be paid to the role of the black audience as consumer of these films containing violent expressions of social discontent. As a cycle marked by the viewership of a youthful, urban black audience, "these films were made possible by the rising political and social consciousness of black people (taking the form of a broadly expressed black nationalist impulse at the end of the civil rights movement), which translated into a large black audience thirsting to see their full humanity depicted on the commercial cinema screen."[56] *Spook*, in this context of blaxploitation, can be situated as a cultural product of the period that inspired desires and fictionalized the discontent of its audience.

While *Spook* should be understood in relation to the blaxploitation film cycle, the film's independent production and subject matter is also related to other black independent films of the time period. Dixon's film can be productively read against independent black art films, especially those created by the black filmmakers at UCLA in the late 1960s through the 1980s. While often considered the antithesis to blaxploitation, *Spook*'s appeal to the LA Rebellion's representational codes and conventions reveals many textual connections. Moreover, because of its diegetic narrative and Greenlee and Dixon's discursive displacement of the film outside of blaxploitation, *Spook* can and does engage with the film work of the LA Rebellion.

Alternatively called the "Los Angeles School of Black Filmmakers," the LA Rebellion, a term coined by Clyde Taylor, describes the group of political, creative black film artists who worked to produce antiracist, alternative films that could serve the black community and narrate more authentic representations of black life.[57] In 1986, Taylor argued, "By the turn of the next century, film historians will recognize that a decisive turning point in the development of black cinema took place at UCLA in the early 1970s. By then, persuasive definitions of black cinema will revolve around images encoded not by Hollywood, but within the self-understanding of the African American population."[58] A film using the codes of Hollywood but not coded by it, *Spook*'s historical and social significance revolves around the images encoded by the LA Rebellion. Like *Spook,* LA Rebellion films grappled with black social discontent. For example, *Spook's* narrative of resistance and black consciousness can be read in relationship to Haile Gerima's *Child of Resistance* (1972), Bernard Nicolas's *Daydream Therapy* (1977), the films of Jamaa Fanaka, and Larry Clark's *As Above, So Below* (1973). Gerima's *Child of Resistance,* based on a dream Gerima had after Angela Davis was imprisoned, relates themes of a political awakening to black youth. In the case of *Spook,* the Cobra gang members are the children of resistance and function as an oppositional force for black liberation. Nicolas's *Daydream Therapy* narrativizes the lyrics of Nina Simone's rendition of "Pirate Jenny" and links an armed resistance to pan-African consciousness and global black-liberation struggles. Using a scene of fantastical violence against a white oppressor, *Daydream Therapy* is the "revolutionary dream" that *Spook* turns into a reality.[59] Pointedly, Jamaa Fanaka's entire oeuvre—including *Welcome Home, Brother Charles* (1975), *Emma Mae* (1976), and *Penitentiary* (1979), which all received theatrical distribution during his time at UCLA—also co-opted and recoded the conventions of "the usual" blaxploitation fare. In his production style, Fanaka, like Dixon and Greenlee, uses the aesthetic conventions of blaxploitation to produce alternative narratives of black male agency and social opposition.

Although *Spook* was not made within the UCLA Film School's production culture, the film was screened at UCLA. In 1974, connecting *Spook* and the LA Rebellion, Dixon's film and Clark's *As Above, So Below* were screened together at UCLA's First International black Filmmakers Festival.[60] The story of Jita-Hadi (Nathanial Taylor), a Chicago native with military training, recruited to help fight to overthrow the US government by an underground black militant group, *As Above, So Below's* plot is strikingly similar to *Spook's* own. According to Allyson Nadia Field, "Like *The Spook Who Sat by the Door* and *Gordon's War, As Above, So Below* imagines a post-Watts rebellion state of siege and an organized black underground plotting revolution. With sound excerpts from the 1968 [House Committee on Un-American Activities] report 'Guerilla Warfare Advocates in the United States,' *As Above, So Below* is one of the more politically radical films of the L.A. Rebellion."[61] Contextualizing *As Above, So Below's* narrative of armed resistance, Field suggests how *Spook* conjures up memories of and connects to other relevant and related texts on sociopolitical armed resistance also released in 1973.

It would appear that *Spook* is a part of both dominant cinema and counter-cinema.

A hybrid of sorts, *Spook* reminds us that, while often viewed as antagonistic, blaxploitation and the LA Rebellion are not mutually exclusive categories. Invoking the metaphor of call-and-response, Guerrero argues that both blaxploitation and the LA Rebellion "arose out of same revolutionary circumstances at the time" but "just took different paths."[62] As a text that embodies both paths in its narrative and production, *Spook*'s history provides a way to reciprocally consider the production, politics, and cultural products of two Los Angeles-based black production cultures in the 1970s.

Producing (Re)visions of Rebellion: *Spook's* Televisual Images and Imaginings

In her discussion of the films of the 1970s, Paula Massood explains that particular attention must be paid to the role that television imagery had in shaping associations of black experiences.[63] According to Sasha Torres, television and images of African Americans have "collided at crucial moments in television history with industrial self-interest, cynicism, and even, on occasion, the desire to do the right thing, to produce not only the content of television's programs, but their form and reception as well."[64] Torres explains how the civil rights movement used television's coded identification to "[ask] its viewers, black and white, to identify *with* nonviolent black protest and *against* the violent representatives of the southern state."[65] However, in the wake of the Watts revolt in 1965, many nationally broadcast white television programs began to depict blacks in very circumscribed and stereotyped ways. As Mark Reid notes, "Destruction and the destructive seemed to define the black community. The combination of televised news coverage of the urban uprisings and the militant rhetoric of black armed resistance intensified white middle-class America's opinion of blacks as a violent people."[66] Displacing dominant narratives of urban rebellion, *Spook*'s representation of black insurrection challenges television's vision of the black social experience in America.

In this regard, *Spook*'s critique of dominant televisual images is similar to that of the popular 1970s black television-news programs on public television. Following the published report by the National Advisory Commission on Civil Disorders in 1967, these programs were commissioned after the racial crisis of the late 1960s, and they documented urban rebellions, interviewed black artists and political figures, and showed black cultural life during this turbulent time period.[67] Devorah Heitner explains: "These shows marked a turning point in the portrayal of African Americans in the media. For the first time, Black producers, editors, writers, and on-air talent took control of the way Blacks were portrayed on TV."[68] These programs included PBS's *Black Journal/Tony Brown's Journal* (1968–2008); WNET New York's *Soul!*; WGBH Boston's *Say Brother/Basic Black* (1968–); Detroit's WTVS *Colored People's Time/American Black Journal* (1968–); and New York's WNEW *Inside Bedford-Stuyvesant* (1968–1970). For example, the program *Say Brother* "took on controversial issues like Black Power, school integration, youth uprising, and police brutality."[69] Similar to these programs, *Spook*'s uses of television and its representation of revolt function to reveal the truth behind the unrest of urban rebellion and to project on the screen the maligned racial truths of African American experiences in the 1960s and 1970s.

Spook engages with the American mass media's representation of blacks by subverting the dominant narration of these representations through props of mediation, most noticeably television screens. By focusing on television, a medium that purposefully "installed" itself within the domestic space of the home and the domestic gender and racial politics of the United States, the medium's relationship to the politics of representation of black popular-culture images during this time period is connected to *Spook*'s narrative.[70] As "blacks drew from popular [television] culture a distorted image of themselves," *Spook*'s engagement with preconceptions of black agency produced a fictive and rebellious intervention into the historical performance of its visible black-liberationist politics.[71]

In *Spook*, the role of television as a tool of surveillance, misinformation, and mediation is dramatized. For example, when Freeman and other potential black candidates meet for CIA training, the television is used as a tool of surveillance. The candidates are unknowingly being watched and listened to by two white CIA officials. The shot reveals a large television screen, and the audience becomes a voyeur like the officials. Viewing the black candidates talking freely about tokenism and integration, the white officials stare knowingly at the screen. The shot cuts back to the television to reveal four additional screens monitoring the group and the building. Here, television is a function of the state, a Janus figure watching the comings and goings of the black recruits. Additionally, television news functions as a medium of misinformation. For example, in the scene in which the National Guard general (Byron Morrow) holds a press conference, the news cameras mediate the event. At the press conference, the general claims that there has been no police brutality in the city, a lie that Freeman and the Chicago Black Freedom Fighters (the name of the newly trained Cobra gang) dispel via their radio broadcasts. Radio, a medium that carries voices and not images, is helpful for maintaining the anonymity of the underground revolutionaries, but it is clear that television is the place to hear and see "legitimated" discourse about blacks, as manipulated by whites.

Television is not only a middle-class aesthetic prop in Freeman's domestic double life (it is located in his apartment and in the room he uses while employed by the CIA) but also a medium of social transmission. For example, in the film's final scenes, images of the violent insurrection of the Chicago Black Freedom Fighters are cut back and forth as a voice-over of a broadcast reporter states: "The newest outbreak in the black section of Oakland brings to a total of eight the number of uprisings by black guerillas in cities across the nation. The president has declared a state of national emergency." The shot slowly fades into Freeman's apartment. Freeman is standing near a window and in front of the television. Both the vastness of the window and the structural placement of the television serve as looking glasses. The disembodied voice of the broadcaster filters through this referent via a lap dissolve. For a brief moment, the viewer can see both images of Freeman's apartment and images of the insurrection, layered on top of each other. While the voice-over offers one version of the events, the content look on Freeman's face as he looks out of the window and the camera's cut to the African masks in his apartment subvert the dominant narrative of the newscaster with the alternative truth of the images of black revolt.

With this representation of televised rebellion, *Spook* produces an oppositional stance on white-authored, authoritative televised news of urban revolts. In doing so, *Spook*'s subversive representation of revolt informs and challenges images of urban rebellion. Focusing specifically on the Watts rebellion, which has become both a local and a metaphorical representation of social unrest in the 1960s, *Spook* is clearly in dialogue with dominant televised images of Watts.[72] According to Greenlee, "I was also inspired by the Watts rebellion. Because of my experience in revolutionary and post-revolutionary situations in the Middle East, I knew not only because of the outbreak, but because of the rage I found everywhere among Blacks, that it would be only the first in a series of rebellions that might lead to organized armed struggle."[73] Therefore, it is productive to read the film's images of revolt against documentary images of Watts that circulated in the news. With its focus on media and mediation, *Spook* produces a revision of Watts history and imagery of black rebellion in, for example, programs such as "Watts: Riots or Revolt?" and KTLA's *Hell in the City of Angels*.

In the *CBS Reports* (1959–1999) episode "Watts: Riots or Revolt?" that aired four months after the Watts rebellion, Watts is positioned as a wasteland. The televised documentary seeks to answer a series of questions about Watts: "Was it a local riot or the beginning of a national revolt? What started it? Will it happen again?" The dominant (white) narrative of the program focuses disproportionately on white agency in explaining the meaning, both historically and contemporaneously, of the event. White authorial voices—including the broadcasters, Los Angeles Police Department chief William Parker, the McCone Commission, and Daniel P. Moynihan—narrate the images of the rebellion, which is constructed notably as a riot and not a rebellion. While there are interviews with Watts's residents and African American leaders, these moments of agency are edited to discredit black voices of dissent. For example, after a group of black leaders' attempts to point to the reasons for the revolt—blaming it on police brutality, bad schools, poor conditions, and so on—the statements are eschewed by the news reporters. The story shifts to saying not only that the mobs hated authority but also that they generally hated white people. This misses the point that, as Freeman decries, "it's not about 'hate white folks'; it's about loving freedom enough to die for it." In language that codes the victim as the one at fault and constructs a tone of us versus them, the documentary situates its African American subjects as ignorant, stupid, and less civilized than their white counterparts.

"Watts: Riots or Revolt?" depicts the black city as a land of destruction and places the blame on its black residents. The broadcaster states that Watts is "a ghetto but not a slum." Over images of the "ghetto," a disembodied voice states, "[Most] of the residents are newcomers who joined the modern gold rush to California of the last twenty-five years; many are newcomers from the most backwards parts of the deep south, poor and ignorant negroes who have no skills to offer a big city employer, no desire for classroom learning, not even the knowledge of how to live in urban surroundings, not even the knowledge of how to use plumbing." African Americans are called "back-country refugees" in a "land of golden promise." The documentary relays televised images of blacks as lawless residents of beautiful Southern California. In many respects, the documentary functions like a Hollywood film, weaving a based-on-true-events story about the drama that was the Watts revolt. Its Hollywood narrative is structured with a dark villain (black people), a white hero (the state), and a happy ending in which the white hero successfully saves (contains) the city from its dark predators. Just as Hollywood loves to remake and recycle previous tales, the "sequel" to this narrative would come out in 1992 after another "alleged" moment of police racial injustice and brutality.

Overall, the documentary assigns no blame or fault to the conduct of the officers in the arrest that served as the catalyst of the Watts rebellion. White agency to quell the rebellion and, more important, to explain its significance is privileged. The latter point here is quite important. Not only does the documentary not really attempt to understand the principal events and causes of the nightmare of Watts, but it does so for the historical benefit and pacification of its non-black viewers. In the end, the documentary answers its questions about whether Watts was a riot or revolt, stating, "Revolt, yes, as it was a formless striking out." By discrediting the rebellion as a failure, the historical meaning of the televised images of black uprising is not only depoliticized but also pathologized.

Similar to "Watts: Riot or Revolt?" the KTLA program *Hell in the City of Angels* is a documentary about the events of August 11. A "special program" that aired at the end of the riots, *Hell in the City of Angels* paints an even bleaker picture of Watts. Filled with wide-angle shots of Los Angeles taken from a helicopter, the documentary, like the aforementioned one, operates as a Hollywoodesque narrative. As the helicopter shot of Los Angeles surveys the city, the camera zooms in on footage of the city, displaying burned and charred buildings. The voice-over states, "Then with the suddenness of a lightning bolt and fury of an internal holocaust . . . there was hell in the City of Angels!" The title of the program takes over the screen, and a loud, pulsating horror film soundscape demarcates the images of a city ablaze as hell on earth. Many of the images in the documentary, which attempts to give an informative chronology of the events, are detached (shot from a camera in a helicopter), showing Watts's burned buildings and cars. With images of black bodies narrated over by white voices, most of the documentary centers on whites pontificating on the "why" question of the rebellion without much self-reflection.

These images of Los Angeles are narrated over by a broadcaster expounding on the beauty of the environment, describing the area as "not an abject slum" like New York City or Detroit. This rhetorical maneuver, also used in the other documentary, is calculated. In creating a narrative against the black residents, the documentary reassures its non-black viewers that, though a ghetto, Watts is a community that isn't all that bad. In other words, if Watts is a ghetto, then it is a place that just happens to be poor, a notion that enables the documentary to avoid discussing the systematic disinvestment by major industries, the government, banks, and shops, as well as the housing policies and racial discrimination that would make it a "slum." Thus, the documentary's potent images of black insurrection are coded as the nonsensical antics of blacks destroying their own slice of the city. The images produced by *Hell in the City of Angels* add to the national imagery of lawless African American resistance, constructing blacks as violent reactors to a misunderstanding of the Los Angeles Police Department's law-abiding actions. With Watts positioned as a hell on earth, blacks are depicted as suitable inhabitants because of their unrepentant sins, breaking the first commandment of social existence by being black and poor in white America.

What does it mean to consider *Spook*'s televised images of rebellion in relationship to news documentaries such as "Watts: Riot or Revolt?" and *Hell in the City of Angels*? In *Revolution Televised*, Christine Acham also analyzes "Watts: Riot or Revolt?" explaining that documentaries such as this "could not quite contain the emotions and politics of a rising vocal black population."[74] In the same way, *Spook*'s aforementioned lap dissolve from the scene of insurrection to Freeman's apartment operates as a form of discursive and social documentary excess.[75] In this scene of the film, the reality of the uprising, Freeman's training of the urban youth, does not comply with the narrative reality of the broadcaster. What one sees and hears on television about the warfare is not the truth, and the cinematic dissolve destabilizes the boundary of the television's images of insurrection with the imaginings—the American nightmare—that Freeman has orchestrated. This scene in

Spook operates as an intervention between its referent (rebellion and televised programming on black insurrection) and its own discourse (revolution), liberating the "containment designed to account for historical reality" to expose the "excess remains" of black agency, history, and political truths.[76]

Dixon's film recodes the "nightmare" of Watts as the first step in black liberation. Breaking the containment of the history of Watts and the documented historical accounts on television, *Spook*'s revolutionary warfare produces a narrative that sees the rhetoric and reality of explosion—like those so vividly manipulated in *Hell in the City of Angels*—as the precursor to liberation. As a reviewer in the *Sacramento Observer* wrote in 1973, the film may address itself "to the question posed by the late Black bard Langston Hughes: What happens to a dream deferred? . . . [D]oes it explode?"[77] The film's literal explosions and black urban warfare not only have historical meaning in relation to America's televised representations of urban rebellions but also illustrate how black agency functions to recode urban unrest as necessary to freedom.

Producing Utopia under Destruction: *Spook's* Gang-Related Potential

In historicizing the production history and narrative of *Spook*, interrelated histories of black gangs and social violence can also be analyzed. In the film, Freeman's "big time[,] bad-ass Cobras" are the foot soldiers for the movement for social change. Unlike the black gangs at the time and today, the Cobras are depicted as black heroes of freedom. Suspected of everything wrong in the ghetto but not suspected of having a liberationist outlook or ability, the Cobras are a paradoxically visible and invisible force to be reckoned with. *Spook*'s representation of the Cobras, who are trained in military tactics and counterintelligence, is significant to the history on black youth potential in gangs in America. In this context, the narrative presence of the Cobras indirectly speaks to the history of Chicago's Blackstone Rangers (the Stones) and directly to the misused discontent of black male youth in gangs across America.

Rebellious and defiant black youths are the future in *Spook*. In reading the film in relation to the Stones, who "have been painted as victims of circumstances, as champions of social change, and as brainwashed dupes ready to bomb federal buildings," *Spook*'s youthful freedom fighters narrate a fantastical vision of displaced hope for black liberation.[78] Indeed, in

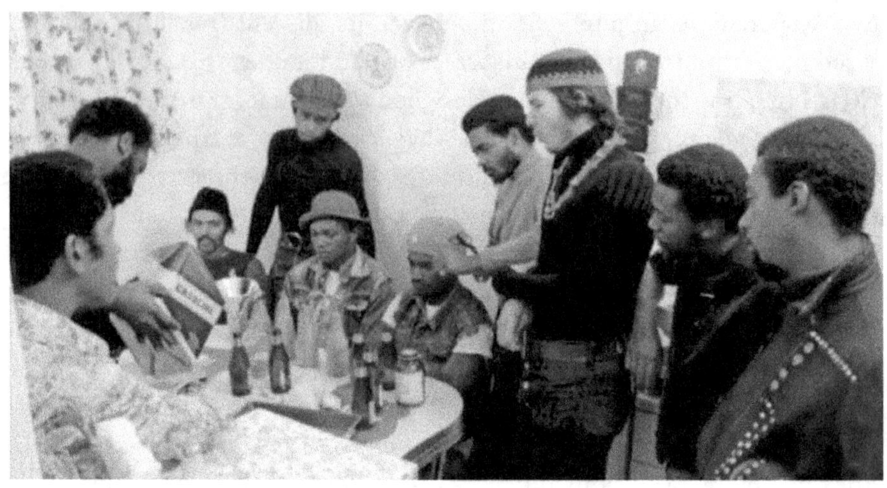

Fig. 4.2 Freeman discusses revolutionary strategy with the members of the Cobra street gang.

considering the violence and self-destruction of the Stones, *Spook*'s use of the Cobras as a potential force of and for black liberation and resistance offers discursive space for the representational meaning of black gangs as dispossessed warriors of a promising black utopia that is under social destruction. *Spook* produces an alternative-generational social experience for many black male and female youths who were and currently are members of the most violent gangs in America.

In the film, as mentioned, the Cobras are a street gang in Chicago that Freeman trains in guerilla warfare. Taking them to task for their ineffective and uneducated assault on the police during the prior summer's riot, Freeman condemns irrational gang violence. Moreover, other forms of illogical gang violence are alluded to in the film. For instance, when Dawson is introduced in the film, Freeman learns that Dawson was at a seminar on riots and gang violence in Los Angeles. Los Angeles is the home and birthplace of the most deadly black gang in America, the Crips, which was founded in 1971 by Stanley "Tookie" Williams and Raymond Washington in South Central Los Angeles. In his memoir *Blue Rage, Black Redemption*, Williams recalls that the gang "fought and often died for a causeless cause."[79]

Alternatively, the Cobras are shown as the perfect group for Freeman to indoctrinate because, as the Cobra Pretty Willie explains, the group is filled with a bunch of wasted talent starving for purpose. Teaching them how to "mess with whitey," Freeman operates as a paternal mentor figure, giving them that purpose, teaching them discipline, and providing political and cultural knowledge to the Cobra gang.

While *Spook* is not directly the story of the Stones, the similar social history of the gang is rather illuminating in relation to the film, particularly since Sam Greenlee grew up in the birthplace of the Stones, which was founded by Eugene "Bull" Hairston and Jeff Fort in the early 1960s on Blackstone Avenue in the Woodlawn neighborhood of Chicago. Natalie Y. Moore and Lance Williams explain that the organization "has a long and controversial legacy of criminal charges ranging from defrauding the federal government to drug trafficking to conspiracy to commit domestic terrorism."[80] There were many social and cultural influences on the Stones, including the Black Power and Black Nationalist movements. Under the direction of Presbyterian Reverend John Fry and the Woodlawn Organization, "the Stones and rival gang, the Disciples, received nearly a million dollars in federal funding. But at the time the two groups were in constant combat killing each other and ruining the peace in the neighborhood."[81] Nonetheless, over the course of their history (which continues to this day), the Stones have been engaged and disengaged with the Black Power and Black Nationalist politics and political figures. Although internal strife, greed, drugs, crime, and systematic government interference mark these moments of political awareness, the Stones did have opportunities to become involved in radical movements. In fact, the FBI became concerned with the politicization of the gang, worrying about the Stones' "real and imaginary relationships with the Black Panthers, the Nation of Islam, and the New Afrika."[82] The FBI used surveillance and a campaign of misinformation to create friction among the Stones and rival gangs in order to suppress an "'interlocking directorate' with other youth gangs to carry out revolutionary acts against the government."[83] Although the Stones never latched on fully to any specific political oppositional force such as the Black Panthers, founder Eugene "Bull" Hairston "encouraged all Stones to wear Afros to reflect a sense of pride in being black. Although most Stones . . . weren't as pro-black as Bull, they all, to a certain degree, considered themselves Black Nationalists."[84]

Similar to the Stones, the Cobras in *Spook* are not tied to any black-liberation movement in particular but to an ideology of Black Nationalism. While there are posters of Malcolm X and a graffiti proclamation of "Black

Power" in the bar the Cobras frequent in *Spook*, the politics of Malcolm X and the Black Panthers are not directly suggested, outside of the film's clear implication that change must come by any means necessary. Despite the iconography of resistance surrounding them prior to meeting Freeman, the Cobras initially function, like the Stones, as a pedestrian, undisciplined, and unorganized street gang that do drugs and steal from and hurt the black community. The film shows that under the tutelage of Freeman, the Cobras' potential power for change is realized; they become the Freedom Fighters as Freeman teaches them that it is necessary to use their assets (e.g., environment, skills, race) in calculated and liberating ways.

The ideological message of resistance in *Spook* is contained in the related histories of the potential encoded in black youths and gangs across the nation, including but not limited to the Stones and the aforementioned Crips. Greenlee stated that his choice to use a gang for Freeman's strategy was deliberate because "they cannot be infiltrated, unlike the Black Panthers. The Panthers told anybody who showed up with a good rap to come on and join. . . . You have to grow up into the street gang. You can't just show up one day and say you want to join."[85] Even Freeman had to earn the trust of the Cobras; it is both their closed ranks and their youthful ignorance that make them the best agents of armed resistance. This sentiment is expressed, for example, in the scene in which Dawson holds Freeman at gunpoint. Dawson is disgusted that Freeman is using kids in guerilla warfare. Freeman replies: "Who else am I going to involve? People like you and me? The kids are our only hope, and I got to them before they got jailed or killed or turned into Dawsons [a former gang member turned police officer]. And now they'd do anything to be free." Thus, the Cobras are positioned as being in the perfect interval space for black collective resistance.

Indeed, the Cobras' underground operation and youthful rage made them perfect for Freeman's indoctrination. With Freeman's help, the Cobras (turned Chicago Black Freedom Fighters) spread vision, mission, and training to black gangs across the nation. This story line produces a way to read the significance of the history of actual gang formations during this time. Writing about the day of the founding of his gang, Crips cofounder Stanley "Tookie" Williams says:

> It would have been a police photographer's Kodak moment to have captured all of us on film that day. Standing and sitting around on the bleachers was

> the largest body of black pariahs ever assembled. I'm convinced that had the Black Panther party still been recruiting . . . Huey Newton and Bobby Seale would have salivated over the untapped youthful potential we represented. Throughout this state and country, we embodied only a small division within a multitude of reckless, energetic, fearless, and explosive young black warriors. Though we were often seen as social dynamite, I believe we were the perfect entity to be indoctrinated in cultural awareness and trained as disciplined soldiers for the black struggle. Nevertheless, this opportunity to mold us as a valuable resource was never seen in its true potential by society, schools, churches, community programs, civil rights movements, or other black organizations.[86]

By contrast, *Spook* dramatizes the potential of the "reckless, energetic, fearless, and explosive young black warriors" as fully realized. Lacking discipline and guidance, the Crips, the Stones, and the hundreds of other black gangs across America are labeled as a "lost generation[,] . . . forgotten prodigies who disappeared, children buried alive in a sandlot" who went from potential revolutionaries to "dope dealing capitalists."[87] Unlike the Cobras, whom Freeman commanded not to take drugs, black gangs in America (while not alone) aided and continue to aid in the spread of drugs in the black community. Not letting the institutional factors that feed on and perpetuate gang violence and illegal activities off the hook, the sad fact is that the nascent black youth Williams describes (and others like them) rose to become one of the most deadly forces against—and not for—the black community.

By reading *Spook* against this history of the Stones, the Crips, and the potential of all black gangs in the 1960s and 1970s, we can see how the film represents an alternative society of gangs, which, if they had taken a different, more radical, direction could have continued the fight for black liberation after the rise of the Black Panther Party. In this sense, gang violence would be a welcome tool for black liberation, as illustrated provocatively in the scene in *Spook* after Freeman kills Dawson. Surprised he killed his own best friend, Freeman tells the Cobra's Do-Daddy Dean: "Don't tell me who I killed and what it cost me to do it." *Spook* implies a certain kind of "freedom dues" paid in killing one's own black brother that are unfortunate, but necessary, for the larger cause of black liberation. Freeman states that there are a lot of "Dawsons" out there and that the Cobras can't hesitate to kill them because they are black or they will be the ones killed. However, the perversion of these freedom dues by black gangs, marked by the enormous

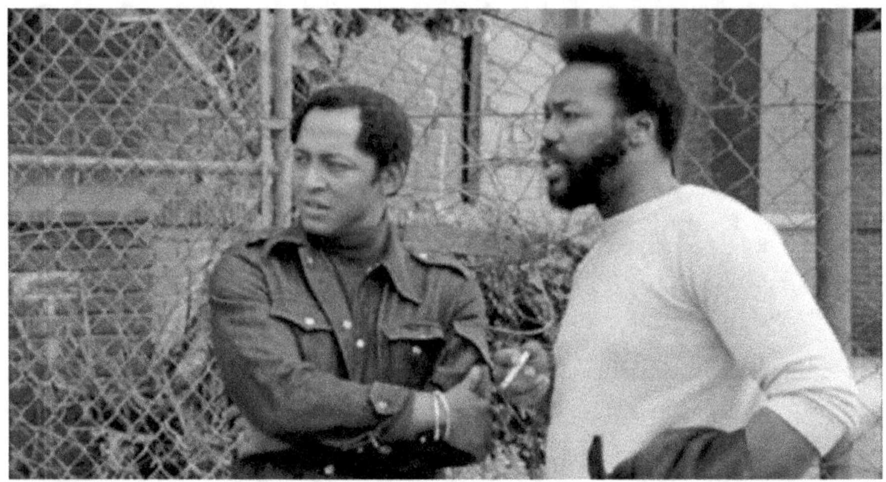

Fig. 4.3 Freeman and Do-Daddy (Paul Butler) discuss the readiness of Cobra members to go underground in preparation for armed rebellion.

collateral damage of young and old black lives, is a tragic reality of the growing violence of black-on-black crime. Consequently, black gangs spoiled (and continue to spoil) their potential for being positive personifications of angry and dangerous black youths. Embracing and exploiting the negative, they went from being angry at oppression to being anger that oppresses others. They went from being dangerous to dominant forces of inequality to being a dominant force of danger in the black community.[88] *Spook* presents a harrowing alternative social reality of a radical dramatization of American gang warfare, in which the Cobras' insurgency not only facilitates but also begins a revolution for black freedom.

In analyzing and historicizing *Spook* in the context of its production and exhibition, 1970s black cultural production in Los Angeles, black televisual images, and the history of Chicago's Blackstone Rangers and the legacy of gang violence in America, the sociopolitical and cultural discourses around the film's politics of production and representation can be situated within and suggestive of knowledge about and around the film. *Spook,* a film that has been persistently displaced, is both timely and timeless, moving throughout the bends and arcs of history while shedding light on its various and varying textual and discursive meanings. *Spook*'s complex relationship to the past, present, and future can be and should be contextualized within the rebellious and radical narrative of the film itself.

NOTES

1. Sam Greenlee, *The Spook Who Sat by the Door* (London: Allison & Busby, 1969).

2. Martin Arnold, "Police and Panthers: Urban Conflict in Mutual Fear," *New York Times*, October 26, 1970.

3. Christine Acham, "Subverting the System: The Politics and Production of *The Spook Who Sat by the Door*," *Screening Noir* 1, no. 1 (Fall–Winter 2005): 118.

4. Greenlee, quoted in Corey Hall, "Bookin! Racism and Revolution Discussed by Novelist Sam Greenlee," *Hyde Park Citizen*, July 31, 2003.

5. "Author of 'Spook' Speaks at Merritt," *Oakland Post*, May 11, 1972.

6. See Patricia Hill Collins, *Black Feminist Thought: Knowledge, Consciousness, and the Politics of Empowerment* (New York: Routledge, 2000), 5. Harry Belafonte recalled that in a conversation with Dr. Martin Luther King Jr., King feared he was integrating black people into a burning house. When Belafonte asked what they should do, King replied that they should become firefighters. Harry Belafonte, "The Journey: The Long Road to Freedom" (keynote address, Dartmouth College, Hanover, NH, January 15, 2007).

7. Kevin Thomas, "Melodrama with Powerful Message," *Los Angeles Times*, December 19, 1973.

8. Ibid.

9. DeWayne Wickham, introduction to *The Spook Who Sat by the Door* (Ivan Dixon, 1973; Monarch Home Video, 2004), DVD.

10. Ibid.

11. Christine Acham is one of the leading scholars on *Spook*. The opening five minutes of *Infiltrating Hollywood: The Rise and Fall of "The Spook Who Sat by the Door"* (Christine Acham and Clifford Ward, 2011) succinctly historicize the production and politics of the film. Using archival footage, photos, and primary-source documents, the opening montage shifts from images and moments of African Americans at the turn of the twentieth century to the civil rights movement up to the Black Power era.

12. See Donna Haraway, "Situated Knowledges: The Science Question in Feminism and the Privilege of Partial Perspective," *Feminist Studies* 14, no. 3 (1988): 575–599.

13. Leerom Medovoi, "Theorizing Historicity, or the Many Meanings of *Blacula*," *Screen* 39, no. 1 (Spring 1998): 1–28.

14. Ibid., 13.

15. Acham and Ward, *Infiltrating Hollywood*.

16. See Lottie Joiner, "After 30 Years, a Controversial Film Re-emerges," *Crisis*, (November-December 2003): 41.

17. Acham and Ward, *Infiltrating Hollywood*.

18. Acham, "Subverting the System," 121.

19. RENAISANCEtv, "TGE Presents Sam Greenlee Film Discussion 'The Spook Who Sat by the Door,'" April 12, 2011, http://www.youtube.com/watch?v=RM5VnVDAz1E.

20. Acham and Ward, *Infiltrating Hollywood*.

21. Lewis Beale, "'Spook' Unearths a Radical Time Capsule of a Movie," *Los Angeles Times*, February 28, 2004.

22. Ibid.

23. Earl Calloway, "Sam Can't Be Spooked," *Chicago Defender*, August 24, 1974; "Controversial Black Film Comes to Memphis," *Tri-State Defender* (Memphis, TN), June 19, 1976; Lottie Joiner, "After 30 Years, a Controversial Film Re-emerges"; Beale, "'Spook' Unearths a Radical Time Capsule of a Movie"; Peter Nichols, "A Story of Black Insurrection Too

Strong for 1973," *New York Times*, January 20, 2004; Acham, "Subverting the System," 113; Acham and Ward, *Infiltrating Hollywood*; "TGE Presents Sam Greenlee Film Discussion 'The Spook Who Sat by the Door."

24. Greenlee, quoted in Acham, "Subverting the System," 124.

25. Beale, "'Spook' Unearths a Radical Time Capsule of a Movie."

26. "Controversial Black Film Comes to Memphis."

27. Screened intermittently up until 1975 in theaters across the nation, the film has had special screenings in every decade. For example, in 1982, the film was screened at St. John's Episcopal Church in Los Angeles. See "Film on Black Rebellion Set," *Los Angeles Times*, January 22, 1982; Beale, "'Spook' Unearths a Radical Time Capsule of a Movie." In "TGE Presents Sam Greenlee Film Discussion 'The Spook Who Sat by the Door,'" Greenlee notes that the film was bootlegged and that hundreds of copies circulated underground in the "hood," stating, "I made a film about guerilla warfare that became a guerilla film."

28. Clyde Taylor, "LA Rebellion: Creating a New Black Cinema" (keynote address, UCLA Film & Television Archive, Hammer Museum's Billy Wilder Theater, Los Angeles, CA, November 11, 2011).

29. For example, see Jacqueline Stewart, "The Scholars Who Sat by the Door," *Cinema Journal* 49, no. 1 (Fall 2009): 146–153.

30. Kevin Weston, "Obama's Candidacy Recalls Cult Film," *Athens News*, March 31, 2008.

31. Ibid.

32. Ibid.

33. Ibid.

34. In the film, Freeman tells black police detective Dawson: "Listen, you think because you got a badge and I got a couple of degrees that makes a difference? Do you know what white people call people like me and you in private? Niggers, Daws! Niggers." West's song "All Falls Down" echoes this sentiment. He raps: "For that paper / look how low you'll stoop / even if you in a Benz / you still a nigga in coupe." Kanye West, featuring Syleena Johnson, "All Falls Down," *College Dropout* (Sony Music Studios, February 24, 2004), CD.

35. Meyer Canton, "This 'Spook' Has No Respect for Human Life," *New York Times*, November 11, 1973.

36. "TGE Presents Sam Greenlee Film Discussion 'The Spook Who Sat by the Door.'"

37. Reelblack, "IVAN DIXON—Legendary Actor & Filmmaker (Interview)," March 30, 2008, http://www.youtube.com /watch?v=SzAggNOozMo&feature=related.

38. Ed Guerrero, "LA Rebellion: Then and Now" (roundtable discussion, UCLA Film & Television Archive, Hammer Museum's Billy Wilder Theater, Los Angeles, CA, November 11, 2011).

39. Greenlee, quoted in Nichols, "A Story of Black Insurrection Too Strong for 1973."

40. Ibid.

41. Greenlee, quoted in Acham, "Subverting the System," 123.

42. Greenlee, quoted in Beale, "'Spook' Unearths a Radical Time Capsule of a Movie."

43. Junius Griffin, quoted in "NAACP Takes Militant Stand on Black Exploitation Films," *Hollywood Reporter*, August 10, 1972.

44. Ed Guerrero, *Framing Blackness: The African American Image in Film* (Philadelphia: Temple University Press, 1993), 69.

45. Cedric J. Robinson, "Blaxploitation and the Misrepresentation of Liberation," *Race and Class* 40, no. 1 (July-September 1998): 1.

46. Ivan Dixon, quoted in Beale, "'Spook' Unearths a Radical Time Capsule of a Movie."

47. See Eithne Quinn, "'Tryin' to Get Over': *Super Fly*, Black Politics, and Post-Civil Rights Film Enterprise," *Cinema Journal* 49, no. 2 (Winter 2010): 86–105.

48. Peter Stanfield, "Walking the Streets: Black Gangsters and the 'Abandoned City' in the 1970s Blaxploitation Cycle," in *Mob Culture: Hidden Histories of the American Gangster Film*, ed. Lee Grieveson, Esther Sonnet, and Peter Stanfield (New Brunswick, NJ: Rutgers University Press, 2005), 286–287.

49. Ibid.

50. Mark A. Reid, *Redefining Black Film* (Los Angeles: University of California Press, 1993), 70.

51. Ibid.

52. Ed Guerrero, "Black Violence as Cinema: From Cheap Thrills to Historical Agonies," in *Violence and American Cinema*, ed. J. David Slocum (New York: Routledge, 2001), 214.

53. Amy Abugo Ongiri, *Spectacular Blackness: The Cultural Politics of the Black Power Movement and the Search for a Black Aesthetic* (Charlottesville: University of Virginia Press, 2010).

54. Acham and Ward, *Infiltrating Hollywood*.

55. Valerie Smith, "The Documentary Impulse in Contemporary African-American Film," in *Black Popular Culture*, ed. Gina Dent (Seattle: Bay Press, 1992), 57.

56. Guerrero, *Framing Blackness*, 69.

57. See Ntongela Masilela, "The Los Angeles School of Black Filmmakers," in *Black American Cinema*, ed. Manthia Diawara (New York: Routledge, 1993): 107–117. These filmmakers include Charles Burnett, Larry Clark, Julie Dash, Haile Gerima, Ben Caldwell, Bernard Nicolas, Billy Woodberry, Alile Sharon Larkin, Jamaa Fanaka, Zeinabu irene Davis, and Barbara McCullough. See Clyde Taylor, ed., *The LA Rebellion: A Turning Point in Black Cinema: Whitney Museum of American Art 26*, exhibition catalog (New York: Whitney Museum of Art, 1986).

58. Ibid.

59. See Nikki Giovanni, "Revolutionary Dreams," in *The Collected Poetry of Nikki Giovanni: 1968–1998* (New York: Harper Perennial Modern Classics, 2007).

60. "Black Film-Makers Fest to Open Sunday," *Los Angeles Times*, April 26, 1974.

61. Allyson Nadia Field, ed., *"As Above, So Below": L.A. Rebellion Creating a New Black Cinema*, exhibition catalog (Los Angeles: University of California, 2011).

62. Guerrero, "LA Rebellion."

63. Paula J. Massood, *Black City Cinema: African American Urban Experiences in Film* (Philadelphia: Temple University Press, 2003), 86.

64. Sasha Torres, *Black, White, and in Color: Television and Black Civil Rights* (Princeton, NJ: Princeton University Press, 2003), 4.

65. Ibid., 11.

66. Reid, *Redefining Black Film*, 74.

67. Devorah Heitner, "A History and Overview of Black-Identity Public Affairs TV," *Broadcasting While Black*, February 28, 2009, http://www.thirteen.org/broadcastingwhileblack/uncategorized/broadcasting-while-blacka-history-and-overview/.

68. Ibid.

69. Ibid.

70. See Lynn Spigel, *Make Room for TV: Television and the Family Ideal in Postwar America* (Chicago: University of Chicago Press, 1992).

71. J. Fred MacDonald, *Blacks and White TV: Afro-Americans in Television since 1948* (Chicago: Nelson-Hall Publishers, 1983), xv. This period is also important for the representation

of Blacks on prime-time television. Television programs from 1972 to 1983 depicted African Americans in new and exciting and, simultaneously, old and denigrating ways. On the one hand, this era had programming that ridiculed Black subjectivity. On the other hand, the programs of the era gave Blacks more screen time and finally dealt with relevant social issues for Blacks. These issues included the racial, political, economic, and social problems that were plaguing American society. Examples of programs during this time are *The Jeffersons* (CBS, 1975–1985), *Get Christie Love!* (ABC, 1974–1975), *Good Times* (CBS, 1974–1979), *That's My Mama* (ABC, 1974–1979), *What's Happening!!* (ABC, 1976–1979), and *Sanford and Son* (NBC, 1972–1977). Even with such programming, there was a lack of diverse character portrayals of both Black men and Black women on the television screen. See Herman Gray, *Watching Race: Television and the Struggle for "Blackness"* (Minneapolis: University of Minnesota Press, 1995); Robin R. Means Coleman, *African American Viewers and the Black Situation Comedy: Situating Racial Humor* (New York: Garland Publishing, 2000).

72. The Watts rebellion began on August 11, 1965, after the Los Angeles Police Department stopped and arrested Marquette Frye. The event was the tipping point in a struggle against racial injustice in Watts, lasting until August 15, 1965. Sixteen thousand members of the National Guard were brought in to stop the rebellion; thirty-four people died (all but five were Black), four thousand were arrested, and there was more than $200 million in property damage. See Gerald Horne, *Fire This Time: The Watts Uprising and the 1960s* (Charlottesville: University of Virginia Press, 1995), 3.

73. Greenlee, quoted in Acham, "Subverting the System," 117.

74. Christine Acham, *Revolution Televised: Prime Time and the Struggle for Black Power* (Minneapolis: University of Minnesota Press, 2004), 40.

75. Bill Nichols, *Representing Reality* (Bloomington: Indiana University Press, 1991), 143.

76. Ibid.

77. Review of *The Spook Who Sat by the Door, Sacramento Observer*, November 14, 1973.

78. Natalie Y. Moore and Lance Williams, *The Almighty Black P. Stone Nation: The Rise, Fall, and Resurgence of an American Gang* (Chicago: Lawrence Hill Books, 2011), 1.

79. Stanley "Tookie" Williams, *Blue Rage, Black Redemption: A Memoir* (New York: Simon and Schuster, 2004), xviii.

80. Moore and Williams, *The Almighty Black P. Stone Nation*, 1.

81. Ibid., 3.

82. Ibid., 71.

83. Ibid.

84. Ibid., 38.

85. Greenlee, quoted in Hall, "Bookin!"

86. Williams, *Blue Rage, Black Redemption*, 89.

87. Ibid., 85; Greenlee, quoted in "TGE Presents Sam Greenlee Film Discussion 'The Spook Who Sat by the Door.'"

88. Amir Sulaiman's poem "Danger," the positive personification of this shifting identity of "anger-angry" and "dangerous-danger," relates the transition to educated, active, and resistant collective freedom and liberation. See Amir Sulaiman, perf, "Danger," in *Russell Simmons Presents Def Poetry Jam*, season 4, episode 5, produced by Russell Simmons and Mos Def, aired August 15, 2004 (New York: HBO Video, 2005), DVD.

5. Subverting the System

THE POLITICS AND PRODUCTION OF *THE SPOOK WHO SAT BY THE DOOR*

Christine Acham

To discuss African American filmmaking or black representation in the 1970s, one cannot ignore the blaxploitation phenomenon. Born of converging economic, social, and political factors, the films of the era remain a vivid reminder of this moment in film history. The African American community had entered a new phase in the black freedom movement. America was witnessing a political shift from African Americans' engagement primarily in nonviolent civil rights tactics toward their participation in more vociferous Black Power actions. African Americans were also concerned with representational issues and expressed frustration over the continuing servile roles played by blacks in Hollywood films and network television. As film historian Ed Guerrero discusses in his book *Framing Blackness: The African American Image in Film,* at this time, many in the African American community were frustrated by the mainstream images produced by Hollywood. By 1967 Sidney Poitier had become the number-one box office star in the United States. His success was based on mainstream US acceptance of the roles that he played, which were typically sidekick characters who supported white counterparts in obtaining their dreams. For example, Poitier won an Academy Award for his role in *Lilies of the Field* (1963), a film in which he helps a group of nuns construct their church. Hollywood placed the majority of their black filmmaking efforts into his vehicles. Considered a positive image by many, Poitier was seen as an integrationist hero, but films such as the 1967 Academy-Award-winning film *Guess Who's Coming to Dinner,* in which he was actually allowed to have a love interest, were considered sadly behind the times.[1]

It is generally accepted that the blaxploitation film era was kicked off with the production of the 1971 Melvin Van Peebles film *Sweet Sweetback's Baadasssss Song.*[2] The film was independently made for $150,000. Although it was rated X and did not have a full mainstream release, the film grossed over 10 million dollars in its first year.[3] Hollywood studios were experiencing financial difficulties due to their production of extravagant yet underperforming films. The success of *Shaft* (1971) and *Superfly* (1972) made Hollywood more aware of the viability of black film audiences. Movie studios soon relied on a slew of cheaply made black-themed films to reestablish their economic viability. The term blaxploitation was coined as a derogatory term for African American–cast films that relied on exploitative tactics—sex, drugs, and violence. As time went on, blaxploitation films were often written or directed by white people and indeed the production economy, surrounding these films reflected that of the Race Films of the silent era: white-financed films starring black actors.[4]

Considering the root of the word and the pressure placed on Hollywood to halt the production of these films, one can easily understand the negative connotations the word blaxploitation elicits. However, what is important to note is the way in which the criticism of these films is class based. This situation can be compared to the arguments that raged around the television program *Amos 'n' Andy.* While *Amos 'n' Andy* was criticized by political organizations such as the NAACP, the show was enjoyed by a cross section of the African American public, who recognized the roots of the comedy in the performances of local black clubs—or the "Chitlin' Circuit."[5] A similar situation is apparent with the films of the blaxploitation era. Oral histories report that many African Americans (while acknowledging the overblown characteristics of many of the films' protagonists) still found the films enjoyable (*Baadasssss* 2002). At a time when African Americans' battle with oppression heightened, and worsening inner-city problems were evident, films that celebrated overcoming *The Man,* in whatever form, were empowering and enjoyable. However, with the political push for integration and an attempt to uplift the African American population, these images were seen as reveling in highly functionalized and very negative aspects of African

American society. With political pressure on Hollywood to end the production of these films, the financial recuperation of the industry, the eventual loss of profits from these films, and the studios' ability to find crossover films that appealed to both black and white audiences, the production of blaxploitation films slowly petered out.[6]

The impact of the blaxploitation film movement did not end in the 1970s, and the re-embrace of blaxploitation in 1990s and contemporary hip-hop music, fashion, and culture solidified the film movement's relevance within the history of black popular culture. The historical dismissal of one of the most prolific periods of black representation by groups within the film and black communities creates three central problems. First, this type of critique ignores issues of spectatorship and pleasure. Second, it overlooks the fact that during this era black people did gain opportunities to participate in the production of some of these films. Their involvement resulted in the creation of a body of films representative of a complex time in black social and political history. Directors, writers, producers, and actors of this era still have an influence on contemporary African American films and filmmaking. Finally, the tendency to consolidate all black-themed films created during this period under the rejected rubric of blaxploitation means that many significant films have been ignored or forgotten.

While discussing the significance of blaxploitation films, this article specifically focuses on the film *The Spook Who Sat by the Door* (1973). While many 1970s black-themed films were using limited black talent, *The Spook* not only boasted a black cast but also had black director Ivan Dixon and black writer Sam Greenlee. Although United Artists provided $200,000 in finishing costs and distribution, the film was produced with $850,000 raised from black financial organizations.[7] Released in 1973, the film's politically controversial subject matter led to its suppression by local and federal policing organizations. The film disappeared from many theaters across the country within a week of its release. What made this film so dangerous to the US government that they pulled it from theaters? In order to read the politics of the film, it is important to address the personal and political views of Sam Greenlee, author of the novel and screenplay *The Spook Who Sat by the Door.* Further research sheds light onto the roots of his thinking, the creation of the text, the film's connection to global issues of colonization and repression, and why the government feared the potential impact of the film.

Iraq, *Baghdad Blues*, and the Creation of the Original Spook

In the 1950s Sam Greenlee, upon completion of his undergraduate degree, became an Army ROTC commissioned lieutenant assigned to the 31st Infantry Dixie Division National Guard out of Mississippi. Greenlee was already well aware of the ways in which race worked in American society; however, this was his first encounter with what he describes as "deep southern bigotry." As he arrived at the entrance of the camp, he saw a huge billboard decorated with the Confederate Flag. The billboard read "Welcome to Dixie and the 31st Infantry Division." He was initially placed within division headquarters, and his uniform included a stars and bars insignia. From the beginning, Greenlee refused to wear the stars and bars, and when confronted he explained that he saw it as a symbol of the slavery of his ancestors. He was almost court-martialed due to his political stance, but he threatened to bring in the NAACP to fight his case. Greenlee understood that the NAACP was highly invested in the integration of the military and would not want to become involved; however, those in command were not aware of this fact and granted him a transfer out of division headquarters, so he would not have to wear this racist symbol.

Greenlee then worked under the command of a superior officer whom he described as fair and was even promised a company at age twenty-four; however, when he finished his tour, he chose to leave the military and was honorably discharged. He enrolled in graduate school at the University of Chicago to study international relations. At that time a representative of the United States Information Agency (USIA) visited the University of Chicago and spoke to students about the cultural and informational side of the agency, the divisions that dealt with public relations, music concerts, newspapers and radio. Greenlee took the qualifying examination and thought he would get a clerical job when he was finishing his thesis. The recruiter, however, put his application into the pool for the Junior Officer Training program, and he was eventually offered the position.

In 1957 he received his first post as a member of the Foreign Service in Baghdad. During this time Iraq was still under the rule of a British- and US-supported monarchy and in the midst of a period of instability. The country was a hotbed of anti-European and anti-American sensibilities. When Greenlee arrived in Iraq, he knew nothing about the situation in the country.

However, because he was socially ostracized as a black man within the Foreign Service and viewed as suspect by his fellow officers, Greenlee spent his time in the city getting to know local Iraqis. From these contacts he began to understand the negative feelings of many Iraqis toward the monarchy and knew that a revolution was imminent. Although Greenlee reported this information to the officers in command, they rejected his theories. Greenlee realized that although members of his organization claimed to be Foreign Service agents, they had little to do with the actual Iraqi people. Instead they spent time with other white officers and government officials in Baghdad. By July 14, 1958, King Faysal II of Iraq and the Iraqi monarchy were overthrown. Faysal II, his chief minister Nuri as-Said, and several members of the royal family were assassinated. The country was then taken over by Abd al-Karim Qasim, an Iraqi general and politician.[8]

As a black man, Greenlee had a different experience in Iraq. As he reports, Iraqis made a distinction between the white officers and himself. They saw him as a brother who also lived under a repressive state government. When the revolution broke out, he was able to drive freely around Baghdad in an embassy vehicle. According to Greenlee most Iraqis understood that African Americans were part of a global struggle against white chauvinism. It was at this time that Greenlee truly began to understand the global connections between African Americans and other oppressed colonial bodies around the world; he knew that he needed to inject these ideas into his writing in order to bring this information to a wider black American public.

Greenlee began writing the book *Baghdad Blues* while still in the Foreign Service. Although fictional, it has autobiographical aspects. The story follows an African American man, Dave Burrell, who joins the Foreign Service and is assigned to the United States Information Bureau in Iraq. Burrell soon realizes that he is a glorified office boy whose opinions are dismissed and feared. He is expected to discuss the importance of US policy in Iraq, "we were acting as a propaganda office for the Iraqi government . . . to make the king, the crown prince, prime minister, and their development plans for the country attractive . . . if we could work it in we said a few nice things about the United States."[9] Burrell gets an alternate impression of what is going on in Iraq. He befriends Ali and Jamil, two Iraqis from different backgrounds, who introduce him to the ideas of working-class Iraqis and the young intellectuals. Burrell "realized that a black skin was an asset in Iraq, and after living in the States all my life, that sure as hell was new."[10] The Iraqis accept Burrell as they see the connections between their oppression in Iraq and his struggle as a black man in the United States. Burrell understands that the only way that Iraq should be run is by a government of popular choice, not one imposed on them and supported by foreign governments.

While *Baghdad Blues* was published after *The Spook,* these life experiences in Iraq clearly led to the formulation of the plot and characters within *The Spook.* Greenlee witnessed the dismissive attitudes and repressive actions that whites and those in power displayed toward Arabs and Asians while he was in the Foreign Service. He recognized this treatment as the same experienced by blacks in America. Greenlee understood that African Americans were also living under a repressive government not of their choosing. He also read the books, articles, and speeches of authors and activists such as Franz Fanon and Malcolm X, and he realized how similar these were to his own thoughts and conclusions about the situation of blacks in the United States.

As Greenlee remembers, "I was also inspired by the Watts Rebellion. Because of my experience in revolutionary and post revolutionary situations in the Middle East, I knew not only because of the outbreak, but because of the rage I found everywhere among blacks, that it would be only the first in a series of rebellions that might lead to organized armed struggle." When Greenlee returned to the United States, he saw the level of anger in the faces of black Americans in his hometown of Chicago. He knew that they expressed similar beliefs to those of the oppressed in prerevolutionary Iraq. He further explains, "I decided to write [*The Spook*] so that the people who would do it, would do it right. *The Spook Who Sat by the Door* . . . is a handbook on urban guerrilla warfare, organization, supply and propaganda. All of it's in there and that's what made it so threatening."[11]

Black Power, *The Spook,* and the Chicago Connection

When Greenlee returned to Chicago in the mid-sixties, the political climate reflected that of urban centers across black America, societies influenced by the rise in Black Nationalism and Black Power ideology. Even with the passing of the Civil Rights Act (1964) and the Voting Rights Act (1965), African Americans still faced racial intolerance and discrimination. Growing frustrated with the slow progress of the civil rights movement, many black political organizations became inspired by the Third World freedom movements. These groups were influenced by the writings of social and political theorists and reflected a new Black Power ideology. The FBI increased its surveillance of these black activists while COINTELPRO, an FBI counterintelligence program, specifically attacked the ranks of the Black Panther Party, which FBI head J. Edgar Hoover described as "the greatest threat to the internal security of the country."[12]

By setting the novel in Chicago, Greenlee wrote about a city with which he was intimately familiar and situated the characters within a specific local racial history. Chicago came to national attention as a focal point of Martin Luther King and the Southern Christian Leadership Conference's (SCLC) attempt to deal with racism and poverty in northern cities. King negotiated with Chicago Mayor Richard J. Daley to improve the living and working conditions of the city's poor black population. While Daley initially stonewalled, he signed an agreement in 1967. However, it was a lame duck policy that left Chicago residents with little to show for King's efforts.[13]

Greenlee completed the novel *The Spook Who Sat by the Door* in 1966 and wanted to publish it immediately, but he was unable to find a US publisher willing to accept the book. The novel was eventually published in March 1969 by London publishing house Allison and Busby. Greenlee states that he wrote the book as "a deliberate departure from traditional black protest novels. Those books were meant to appeal to the moral conscience of white America. I don't do that. My book is for black people."[14] The book and the film, *The Spook Who Sat by the Door,* tell the story of Dan Freeman, the first black man to integrate the all-white Central Intelligence Agency (CIA). The story begins as the fictional Senator Gilbert Hennington, who is running for reelection, realizes that he will lose if he is not able to regain the black vote. Looking for a hot button campaign issue, he decides to accuse the CIA of discriminatory hiring practices. Under public pressure, but with no intention of integrating the organization, the CIA accepts its first class of black recruits.

The CIA hopes to get rid of the black candidates one at a time, as they assume that the men will fail either the physical or academic challenges. However in Greenlee's narrative, the one black man who survives the training appears to be the typical "Uncle Tom" to all of his classmates. Dan

Freeman stays under the radar and becomes the first black member of the CIA. Freeman, whose job title is "reproduction section chief," is actually a glorified copy boy who works out of a basement office. He is eventually moved upstairs, and as Greenlee describes in his novel, "[h]e was given a glass enclosed office in the director's suite. His job was to be black and conspicuous as the integrated Negro of the Central Intelligence Agency of the United States of America. As long as he was there, one of an officer corps of thousands, no one could accuse the CIA of not being integrated."[15] Freeman spends several years with the CIA and plays the "good Negro": unassuming, undemanding, and clearly not a radical. Due to his conservative attitude during his tenure with the CIA, Freeman draws little attention. When he informs his superiors that he has decided to move back to his hometown of Chicago to work with local gangs and to improve his community, he is not seen as any kind of threat. Freeman is considered a "safe Negro" and, after some basic security checks, raises no suspicions.

However, Greenlee plays on the double meaning of the word spook, a derogatory term for African Americans but also a synonym for the word spy. Freeman is literally the spook who sat at the door of the CIA and learned everything he could. When he moves back to Chicago, he turns his social work job into an opportunity to train local gang members to take over Chicago and eventually the United States. In duplicate scenes the audience witnesses Freeman training the Cobras in the tactics that he learned in the CIA. The group encourages armed resistance throughout Chicago and disrupts the political structure, leaving the city unable to function. Freeman also sends members of the Cobras to major cities across America to train at local sites. Freeman teaches a foolproof plan in which even the assassination of key members of the organization will not stop the black revolution. As the film closes, it is indicated that Freeman, although possibly fatally injured, has instigated the black revolution, and a news reporter is heard discussing the uprising of black rebel forces in major cities across America.

Greenlee based Dan Freeman after himself, someone who was able to glean information from the military and return to the community to teach individuals what they needed to do for armed revolution. Through his novel, Greenlee saw himself as a propagandist, showing African Americans that they too could participate in a similar revolution—one that would overthrow what he conceived of as the colonization of African Americans within US borders. Greenlee believed that the novel could have been an additional impetus to revolution and could have also saved lives, because according to Greenlee, success comes with proper preparation and "on the ground training is disastrous for a revolutionary."[16] He believed that his knowledge would have been helpful to black activists. Greenlee's beliefs are further validated when one considers what happened as the Black Panthers rose to prominence in the city of Chicago.

Under the leadership of then twenty-one-year-old Fred Hampton, the Panthers focused on the poor social and economic circumstances of the black community. As was traditional in other cities, the organization produced a newspaper, held community meetings, offered free job and educational training, and had breakfast programs. Hampton raised the ire of the FBI and the Chicago police who tried to eliminate the organization's social programs and encourage gang violence between the Panthers and the local gang, the Blackstone Rangers. By infiltrating the organization, the police and FBI planned an illegal raid on Hampton's apartment that led to the assassination of the Chicago Panther leader on December 4, 1969, while he slept.[17] Greenlee believes that books such as *The Spook* could have prevented such tragedy and benefited the Panthers and Hampton, who were learning "on the ground" to be revolutionaries.

However, Bantam Press did not publish the book in the United States until 1973 and it was turned into a film later that year. Greenlee regrets the timing of the US release of the book and film, as "it wasn't until the movement was almost over that the armed militants understood that they needed to be on the ground. The Panthers learned that too late. The nonviolent movement was above ground and the armed revolutionaries were underground. They finally understood that they needed to reach the community . . . but [by] then they were infiltrated."[18]

Repression and Oppression: Keeping the Spook behind the Door

The continued panic over the state of black politics in Chicago specifically and in the nation overall led to the reaction over the production and release of the film *The Spook Who Sat by the Door*. The outcome of *The Spook* represented the greatest fears of the US government as to the potential of groups such as the Black Panther Party; this was evident from the moment of production to that of distribution.

Upon completion of the screenplay, Greenlee went to Los Angeles to ask Clarence Williams III to play Dan Freeman. While this did not work out, Greenlee did meet Ivan Dixon who was directing an episode of *The Mod Squad*. They had dinner, and Dixon told Greenlee how much he wanted to direct the film. When Greenlee told him he had a script, Dixon was excited but told him that he did not have the money to buy the rights. Greenlee responded, "Let's form a partnership and we will both own fifty percent of nothing." Dixon shopped it among the majors, but they all turned him down. He went abroad to countries such as Algeria and Nigeria but was unable to secure funds. Greenlee went back to Chicago and wrote a proposal to raise the money. Dixon's brother, an attorney, became the major fundraiser. Greenlee reports that some investors were discouraged from putting their money into the film by various governmental agencies.

The IRS in one case influenced a prominent doctor by threatening to audit him from the present day back to his years in medical school. Dixon began shooting with $45,000 in the account and continued to raise money along the way.

Both Dixon and Greenlee wanted to shoot the film in Chicago to maintain the verisimilitude of the production. However, the film office in Chicago refused to grant their company film permits and offered no explanation. According to Greenlee, all outdoor images of Chicago were "stolen guerilla filmmaking style."[19] In one scene Dan Freeman discusses the logistics of street assassination with one of the gang members while standing on the Chicago L platform at Sixty-Third and College Grove. To get this memorable shot, the actors and a crewmember took a handheld camera onto the platform. They filmed the scene, got on the L, took some images on the moving train, and got off at the following stop before they could be questioned. The film production moved to Gary, Indiana, where African American Mayor Richard Hatcher opened the doors of the city to the film crew. He offered Dixon all of the support that he needed to complete production of the film. For one scene in particular, Greenlee recalls that Hatcher offered Dixon the help of the local police force to participate in a riot sequence. Thus the film showed actual residents of Gary taking out all of their actual and fictional aggression toward the police force within the scene. Dixon's use of a handheld camera, which is literally shoved around by the rioting bodies, adds an intimate understanding of the emotions present. The Gary chief of police also offered Dixon the use of a helicopter for a postriot scene. As Greenlee described, "the shot would have cost over $100,000."[20] Instead a cameraman got the sweeping overhead shot with a handheld camera.

Operating under a very tight budget, the filmmakers encouraged a group of Washington, DC investors to provide finishing funds. However, the group first contacted Jesse Jackson to ask his opinion. Jackson, concerned about issues of integration, invoked the memory of Martin Luther King and strongly suggested that they not invest.

According to Greenlee, filmmakers then used alternate tactics to finish *The Spook*:

> We cut the action footage and shopped it around and United Artists picked it up, and they thought they had a blaxploitation film. When they saw the final cut, a deathly silence descended over the room. They did not bother to look at the dailies. White folks trust dumb niggers and loyal niggers and that's the only kind they had been in contact with out there in Hollywood, because most of the blacks in the film industry tap-dance and do anything to get into a movie or make a movie. Along comes this radical little dude like me who doesn't give a damn about Hollywood or white folks. They did not know who they were dealing with. So I told them, look we got a contract and in the first paragraph you ask for six copies of the script. Don't blame me if you don't have anybody over here who can read. You got a contract, put the damn thing out there.[21]

What happened to the film upon its release is something that has become part of black film history lore. The film disappeared. As Greenlee discussed, in the first week, the film grossed a half-million dollars. Encouraged by the numbers, United Artists arranged a twenty-one city tour for Greenlee. Soon thereafter, reports started coming in that the film was opening on Friday and closing on Sunday even when theaters had paid for a three-week contract. African Americans across major American cities recall seeing the film when it opened and then upon return to the theater it was gone. Others remember hearing about the film and being unable to locate it.

Upon noticing the disappearance of the film from Chicago theaters, Greenlee began his own investigation. Some of the more progressive black distributors and theater owners let him know what happened. Representatives of the mayor's office visited one particular exhibitor, who owned three theaters and two drive-ins. They informed him that if he did not pull the film from all of his theaters, he would face city inspection in the near future. They suggested that the theaters would have difficulty in passing that inspection. The threat was not all that veiled. Other exhibitors from across the country reported that men who identified themselves as members of the FBI "requested" that the owners remove the film from the theaters.

Finally, Greenlee reports, "a contingent of the FBI sat down with the executives of UA and they agreed to take the film off the market."[22] Once the forty to fifty film prints were taken out of distribution, they disappeared, and the author presumes that they were destroyed. Indeed the film could only be found on bootleg copies passed from individual to individual or available at offbeat internet sites. Dixon and Greenlee, upon realizing the fate of the film, hid a copy of the negative in a film vault, registering it under a false name. It was this copy that was used to prepare the film for DVD release and to restore it for its premiere at the Los Angeles Film Festival in June 2004. While it is significant that the film has finally found an audience, the author contemplates the film's potential impact had it escaped suppression in the 1970s.

The Spook reads like a handbook for revolution, the details and plans garnered from the training of the US government. There are clear connections between the politics of the film and the fears of a white nation surrounding the Black Power movement. The revolts in major cities across America proved that many in the black population were outraged by the lack of progress and incessant racism. Federal and local governments considered it too dangerous to screen *The Spook* for volatile black audiences. The film relayed a powerful message of self-reliance and black power. Considering the appeal of such sentiments to a frustrated black audience, it is clear why the government believed that it could not afford to have *The Spook* in circulation.

NOTES

1. Ed Guerrero, *Framing Blackness: The African American Image in Film* (Philadelphia: Temple University Press, 1993).

2. Donald Bogle, *Toms, Coons, Mulattoes, Mammies, and Bucks* (New York: Bantam Books, 1973).

3. Guerrero, *Framing Blackness*, 86.

4. Thomas Cripps, *Slow Fade to Black* (London: Oxford University Press, 1993).

5. Thomas Cripps, "Amos 'n' Andy and the debate over racial integration," in *American History/American Television*, ed. John E. O'Connor (New York: Unger Books, 1987), 33–54.

6. Guerrero, *Framing Blackness*.

7. Christine Acham, interview with Sam Greenlee, San Diego, CA, April 2004.

8. Tariq Ali, *Bush in Babylon: The Recolonisation of Iraq* (New York: Verso, 2004).

9. Sam Greenlee, *Baghdad Blues* (New York: Bantam Books, 1976), 34.

10. Ibid., 82.

11. Acham, interview with Sam Greenlee, San Diego.

12. Clayborne Carson, David J. Garrow, Gerald Gill, Vincent Harding, and Darlene Clark Hine, eds., *The Eyes on the Prize: A Civil Rights Reader* (New York: Penguin Books, 1991), 529.

13. Ibid.

14. Christine Acham, telephone conversation with Sam Greenlee, March 2004.

15. Sam Greenlee, *The Spook Who Sat by the Door* (Chicago: Lushena Books, 2002). Originally published 1969.

16. Christine Acham, interview with Sam Greenlee. Los Angeles, CA, June 2004.

17. *Eyes on the Prize II: A Nation of Law (1968–1971)*. PBS. Television series episode, 1990.

18. Acham, interview with Sam Greenlee, Los Angeles

19. Acham, interview with Sam Greenlee, San Diego.

20. Ibid.

21. Ibid.

22. Ibid.

6. *The Spook Who Sat by the Door*, Screenplay

Sam Greenlee and Melvin Clay

INT. FREEMAN'S APARTMENT

Film opens with a close-up on two African statues while music plays in the background. "A Bokari Ltd. Production" appears on screen.

INT. SENATOR HENNINGTON'S OFFICE

Senator Hennington sits at his desk. Mrs. Hennington and Willa—a young black woman—sit opposite him.

SEN. HENNINGTON — All right, this is the gun map for the reelection. So give it to me straight.

MRS. HENNINGTON — Well, there are no major defectors for campaign contributions, dear. The war chest is in excellent shape.

SEN. HENNINGTON — Good. Very good. What is our image?

Senator Hennington walks around to the front of desk. Willa consults the papers and files in her lap.

WILLA — We've programmed the latest polls, Senator. Louis Harris gave us a random pattern sampling with peer group anchorage; Gallup, a saturization vertical syndrome study with horizontal personality back stopping; and N. O. R. C. ran an ethnic study with racial and religious breakdown, status group compensation, and socioeconomic balancing.

SEN. HENNINGTON Yes, good. But am I winning or losing?

WILLA Losing, Senator.

SEN. HENNINGTON Losing? But why? The computers had me ahead last December!

WILLA It checks out on both computers, plus the one we have at the safety valve, back-stopped and cross checked. If the elections were held today, you would lose by 1.846 percentile.

SEN. HENNINGTON 1.846 percentile. Oh, yes. The computers don't lie.

MRS. HENNINGTON Isn't there a possible breakthrough with any of the peer groups? How are we doing on the Jewish vote?

WILLA The Senator is solid with the Jews, Mrs. Hennington. The Negroes are the trouble spot.

SEN. HENNINGTON The Negroes! (*sighs*) I'm the best friend those people have in Washington!

WILLA The computers indicate a sharp decline immediately after your Law and Order speech last winter.

Senator Hennington turns around and looks at his wife. She glances at him and looks away.

SEN. HENNINGTON All right, all right. Now let's see if we can come up with some ideas here. First, how do we retrieve the lost Neg . . . Black vote?

MRS. HENNINGTON Gil, why don't we accuse the CIA? Their racially discriminatory hiring policy? They have no Negroes, except on a menial level you know.

SEN. HENNINGTON Are you certain? I mean that may be it.

MRS. HENNINGTON — I'm positive. But I'll check it out with our man over at personnel.

SEN. HENNINGTON — Good.

WILLA — Whoever they select will be the best-known spy since 007.

INT. CIA HEADQUARTERS
A group of black recruits are being sworn in en masse.

Beginning Credits

CARSTAIRS — You may now stand. Raise your right hand and repeat after me: "I do hereby swear to uphold the laws of the United States of America and those laws governing the Central Intelligence Agency."

The group of recruits repeats the oath.

Opening credits of film. Multiple shots move in and out of recruits being examined and processed through the CIA's induction procedure.

INT. CIA MEDICAL EXAMINATION ROOM
Recruits proceed through multiple lines for physicals.

INT. CIA CLASSROOM
The recruits sit for a written exam.

INT. CIA INTERVIEW ROOM
A doctor is administering a psychological examination of a recruit.

CIA OFFICIAL — What do you see in this ink-blot?

RECRUIT — I see a man.

Screen zooms out to show more one-on-one interviewing and questioning.

INT. CIA CLASSROOM
A now depleted group of recruits sit at desks completing another exam.

INT. CIA CLASSROOM

A single recruit stands before a panel of CIA officials for an oral examination.

RECRUIT — If I were undercover as a political or economic officer at an embassy and I was questioned about racism in the United States, I'd point out that they also have racial and religious troubles, a thing like that isn't resolved overnight, and that our country is firmly behind racial progress and great strides are being made here.

CARSTAIRS — Thank you.

INT. CIA CONFERENCE ROOM

A group of ten recruits are gathered together. Carstairs and Calhoun are also present.

CARSTAIRS — And so on behalf of the director of our agency, I'd like to offer congratulations on completing our tough preliminary training course. After weeks of physical and psychological testing, you ten men have survived the more than forty already sworn in who, in turn, were selected from the careful screening and security check of hundreds. You men, therefore, represent the best of your race. The survivors of our regular training course, to begin tomorrow, will be the first of your race to join the finest intelligence and espionage fraternity in the history of mankind. I must emphasize, however, that you are by no means agents as yet. Now the selecting out process continues right up until graduation day. So, uh, keep on your toes, keep your noses clean, and I hope to congratulate you on joining the team at the end of the training course. Thank you.

Carstairs leaves room with Calhoun. One of the recruits follows them to the door, peers out, and turns around back to group.

RECRUIT 1 Well, ain't it groovy to be a spy?

RECRUIT 2 Right on.

RECRUIT 3 We are the first spooks to be spooks for the CIA.

RECRUIT 4 Hey man, you know how much this Scotch cost in the commissary? Three dollars. Shiv-*ass* Regal!

RECRUIT 5 Yeah, and it's cheaper overseas.

RECRUIT 6 Yeah, and rent-free housing overseas, too.

RECRUIT 7 Hey, you went to Fisk didn't you? I'm from Howard. Say, you a frat man?

RECRUIT 8 Yeah, man. Alpha.

RECRUIT 7 No kidding, baby, so am I!

Multiple conversations take place simultaneously as the recruits chat together.

RECRUIT 1 We got it made now.

RECRUIT 6 Yeah, but don't forget what Carstairs said. They can still flunk us out.

RECRUIT 4 Yeah, I don't think Carstairs would be uptight if we all flunked out.

RECRUIT 5 You know that PT Instructor Calhoun hates us.

RECRUIT 2 Hey, man, it doesn't matter how they feel. The word is integration. From the top. Now some of us have gotta make it, and we're it. You just have to understand the theory of tokenism. Look they grade on a curve, none of us get too eager, gentleman's C for everybody, right?

ALL RECRUITS Right.

Recruits clink glasses and continue chatting.

Screen zooms out to show that the recruits are being recorded and watched by the General and another CIA official.

INT. CIA TRAINING FACILITY—FACTORY INTERIOR

Recruit runs through factory and places an explosive on a large machine.

INSTRUCTOR Four more seconds.

There is an explosion at which point the lights turn on and the exercise ends.

INSTRUCTOR As you can see, gentlemen, there is one quick way to fail this course.

EXT. CIA TRAINING GROUNDS

RECRUIT Then we take the two wires, place them here, and we crimp them together, making the connection positive. Take the switch there, and throw it.

EXT. CIA TRAINING GROUNDS

Instructor and recruits walk in a single file line away from a car.

INSTRUCTOR All right, we'll operate the ignition by remote control.

Vehicle explodes.

EXT. CIA TRAINING GROUNDS

Instructor works and speaks with one of the recruits next to a post where they have planted an explosive.

INSTRUCTOR Always use those materials which are easily accessible to any citizen of the country in which you are operating. Okay.

They walk away. Explosive goes off.

EXT. CIA TRAINING GROUNDS

Man parachutes to the ground and lands.

INT. CIA GUN RANGE

Recruits practice target shooting.

INT. CIA SWIMMING POOL

Recruits dive into pool wearing full wetsuits and oxygen tanks.

INT. CIA ROOM OVERLOOKING THE SWIMMING POOL

The General and Carstairs talk as they observe the recruits through a large glass window.

GENERAL	How long before this experiment in integration ends?
CARSTAIRS	There are only six left in the group, General.
GENERAL	And?
CARSTAIRS	The top-ranking man academically will fail the physical requirements. He's no athlete. Another figures to flunk this week's exam. But one might make it.
GENERAL	You assured me two weeks ago that no one would survive.
CARSTAIRS	Somehow I forgot that Freeman even existed. He has a way of fading into the background. But he's been among the top three in academics and first in athletic training.
GENERAL	Yes, they do make good athletes. Which one is he?
CARSTAIRS (*POINTING*)	That one.

INT. CIA, FREEMAN'S ROOM

Dan Freeman is sitting at his desk working at a typewriter. There is a knock on the door.

FREEMAN	Come in.

A group of his fellow recruits enter the room.

RECRUIT 1	Hey, Freeman.
FREEMAN	Hey, come on in.
RECRUIT 1	Listen, we're going into Washington. Do you want to come along with us?

FREEMAN — No. Got some studying to do.

RECRUIT 2 — They've been letting us in town for a month now man and you ain't been out of here yet. You're going nuts in here.

FREEMAN — Well, maybe next time.

RECRUIT 3 — Maybe you ought to cool it.

FREEMAN — Cool it?

RECRUIT 3 — Cool it. If you weren't so eager to please the white man and send the grading curve up, there'd be three times as many of us here now. What kind of Tom are you anyway?

FREEMAN — Same as you I guess. Except that I don't try to have it both ways. And you better watch what you say about white folks behind their back. This place could be bugged.

RECRUIT 3 — Are you are calling me a Tom, man?

FREEMAN — Well, none of us were picked for our militancy now, were we? Now why don't you go away and let me alone.

RECRUIT 3 — Why don't you join the team, man?

FREEMAN — Team? Man, I'm not playing any games.

RECRUIT 3 — Man, you just don't belong. I think you'd be happier with a mop in your hands.

FREEMAN — Like your mamma?

RECRUIT 3 — Let's step outside now.

FREEMAN — No. No. You don't want to step outside with me. Because, baby, I would kick your ass.

Recruit 3 moves aggressively toward Freeman.

RECRUIT 1 AND 2 — Come on now, man.

Recruits 1 and 2 pull Recruit 3 away to the door.

RECRUIT 3 No. This fool is crazy.

Recruits 1, 2, and 3 all leave and shut the door. Freeman takes a moment, grabs his jacket, and walks out the door.

INT. BAR IN WASHINGTON—NIGHT

Freeman enters a barroom. He looks around and then sits down at the bar counter.

FREEMAN A glass of Courvoisier. And, uh, would you give the young lady down the end of the bar whatever she's drinking?

We see Dahomey Queen sitting at the opposite end of the bar counter to where Freeman is sitting.

BARTENDER Yes.

The bartender pours a glass for Freeman and then one for Dahomey Queen.

BARTENDER This is from the fella at the end of the bar.

Dahomey Queen gets up and walks over to Freeman.

DAHOMEY QUEEN Thank you.

FREEMAN My pleasure.

DAHOMEY QUEEN You're looking for some action?

FREEMAN Yeah. How much?

DAHOMEY QUEEN Fifteen and five. Five for the hotel.

FREEMAN Yeah. And all night?

DAHOMEY QUEEN Not on Saturday, baby.

FREEMAN Okay.

Freeman and Dahomey Queen get up to leave.

INT. HOTEL—LATER THAT NIGHT

Freeman pours a drink and hands it to Dahomey Queen sitting at dressing table.

FREEMAN	You know, you remind me of someone.
DAHOMEY QUEEN	Oh, really? Who?
FREEMAN	A queen.
DAHOMEY QUEEN	Look, baby, all you got to do is give me my bread. You don't have to talk no trash.
FREEMAN	No, really.
DAHOMEY QUEEN	What kind of queen?
FREEMAN	A queen from Dahomey.
DAHOMEY QUEEN	Dah-who? What the hell is Dahomey?
FREEMAN	Dahomey was a great nation in Africa.
DAHOMEY QUEEN	Africa?
FREEMAN	No, really. I got a book with a picture, and you look just like her. I'll give you the book.
DAHOMEY QUEEN	Sure.
FREEMAN	No. You two could be twins except that she, um, uh, wore her hair different.
DAHOMEY QUEEN	How?
FREEMAN	Oh, it's kind of like natural, you know, the way it grew.
DAHOMEY QUEEN	I do.
FREEMAN	You look good like that.
DAHOMEY QUEEN	Look, honey, if you a hairdresser, maybe I can get you a boy?
FREEMAN	No, no, no. You'll do.

DAHOMEY QUEEN Good. Why don't you just be a trick and stop talking all that shit about queens and kinky hair?

FREEMAN Okay, okay. Listen, can I get you another drink?

DAHOMEY QUEEN Mmm-hmm.

Freeman pours Dahomey Queen a glass. He then moves away and sits on the end of the bed. Dahomey Queen walks across the room and stands in front of Freeman.

DAHOMEY QUEEN You really got a book with a picture in it that looked like me?

FREEMAN I'll bring you the book.

DAHOMEY QUEEN When?

FREEMAN The next time I see you.

INT. CIA HEADQUARTERS—GYMNASIUM

Mr. Soo, the judo instructor, finishes a session with one of the recruits. He says a few words in Japanese, turns to rest of the group, kneels, and bows. The recruits bow to Mr. Soo in turn, stand up, and turn to each other and bow. They turn back to Mr. Soo and bow. They begin to file out of the gymnasium.

CALHOUN Mr. Freeman, you will stay for additional instruction.

Freeman and Calhoun stand on the judo mat, facing each other.

CALHOUN Mr. Freeman, I don't think you people belong in our outfit. I don't have anything against the rest of the group. They . . . they just don't measure up. But you, I don't like.

FREEMAN I . . . I don't understand, sir.

CALHOUN Well I don't like your phony humility, and I don't like your style. Now this is a team for men. Not misplaced cotton pickers.

FREEMAN Yes, sir.

CALHOUN — Stow the "yassah boss." It doesn't work on me. I'll give you a chance. Just go up to the office and resign. Otherwise we fight. Now your black belt matches my own, so you won't be able to whine brutality. Equal opportunity you people claim you want? Mr. Soo, shinpan.

Calhoun and Freeman bow to each and begin fighting. Freeman goes down three times.

CALHOUN — Rest?

FREEMAN — No. There ain't no rest for the weary.

Freeman and Calhoun fight again. Freeman takes down Calhoun four times. Calhoun concedes defeat.

MR. SOO — Calhoun-san, are you all right?

INT. HOTEL—NIGHT

JOY — Hey, baby, don't look so sad. I'll be back in a month.

FREEMAN — Well, at least you won't have to stay in a hotel. They let us start commuting in two weeks, and I'm gonna get us a pad.

JOY — You know I don't mind this place too much. Kind of reminds me of that hotel off campus, remember?

FREEMAN — Listen, what would happen to the Cook County Department of Welfare if the starved caseworker missed work tomorrow?

JOY — Casework Supervisor!

FREEMAN — Okay, okay, Miss Victim! What would happen?

JOY — You wanna play hooky?

FREEMAN — Yeah. I found a beautiful restaurant last week.

JOY — Oh, do they have shark's fin soup?

FREEMAN — No, it's a West Indian restaurant.

JOY	Oh, shark's fin soup with beans and rice, right?
FREEMAN	Yes.
JOY	Hmm, hope they stay open late.

INT. GENERAL'S OFFICE

General is practicing his putting across the office carpet. Carstairs sits in a large straight-backed armchair.

CARSTAIRS	They've all been eliminated except Freeman, sir.
GENERAL	Will he make it?
CARSTAIRS	I think so. He has written and oral finals this week.
GENERAL	Security?
CARSTAIRS	Checks out so far. Routine security checks in the training barracks. And checks on his activities in Washington. Of course he's only been allowed out of the training area for the last two months.
GENERAL	Anything suspicious?
CARSTAIRS	No, sir. He checked into a colored hotel, spent his weekends in the ghetto. Mostly on U Street.
GENERAL	That's pretty tough territory.
CARSTAIRS	Yes, sir, but he seems at home there. He grew up in a neighborhood much like it in Chicago.
GENERAL	How'd he get through college?
CARSTAIRS	Athletic scholarship.
GENERAL	That figures. Also explains the Calhoun incident.
CARSTAIRS	Sir, in fairness to Calhoun, Freeman has been studying judo privately for years.
GENERAL	Politics?
CARSTAIRS	Apolitical. He was involved in civil rights activity as a student but nothing pink or radical.

GENERAL — Men or women?

CARSTAIRS — Women. No hint of homosexuality. Developed a liaison with a prostitute on U Street. Also has a girlfriend in Chicago. Apparently, he's known her since they were college students.

GENERAL — Why don't you run a final six-nine security check?

CARSTAIRS — It's already in progress. It should be finished in a few days.

GENERAL — Run up a dossier on this whore and give it to me. Leave Freeman's file. Secure of the security he's in?

CARSTAIRS — Yes, sir.

GENERAL — Figured out something for him to do?

CARSTAIRS — Yes, sir.

GENERAL — Well, like it or not, it looks as if we're integrated.

INT. BAR—NIGHT

Dahomey Queen is sitting in a booth drinking with a CIA agent.

CIA AGENT — Do you know if he takes any dope? Heroin, LSD, marijuana, pills?

DAHOMEY QUEEN — No. He don't even smoke. He ain't no junkie, baby.

CIA AGENT — Does he have a tendency to boast? Brag about himself.

DAHOMEY QUEEN — He don't talk about himself at all. Most regular tricks want to tell you the story of their whole lives.

CIA AGENT — Does he gamble?

DAHOMEY QUEEN — If he do, I don't know about it. Took him to a joint one night . . . craps, poker. If he get in, I get a cut. He just stand around and look.

CIA AGENT — Would you say he's violent? Uncontrollable temper?

DAHOMEY QUEEN — Temper? Nah. He'll never lose his cool. But people don't give him no shit.

CIA AGENT — How do you mean?

DAHOMEY QUEEN — He's one of them quiet kind of cats that people just don't mess with it. Like that time I was telling you about. The cat that owned it owed me some bread. He started to get off the wall about it. Then he check out Freeman. Just standing there quiet, digging the action. And the cat—baaad, make two of Freeman!—check out Freeman, look at me. Give me my bread. Thought about that that night. He ain't my man and nothing like that, but I know that if I got in trouble, he'd be in it. I think he'd be real bad once he get going, too.

CIA AGENT — What about his sexual habits?

DAHOMEY QUEEN — Hm?

CIA AGENT — You think he might be homosexual?

DAHOMEY QUEEN — No. You're wasting your time there.

INT. CIA CLASSROOM

Carstairs is giving Freeman an oral examination.

CARSTAIRS — What is the guiding principle of an underground guerilla army?

FREEMAN — To live off the country. To rely on nothing in the way of logistics or supplies, which cannot be obtained easily and simply, whether legally or illegally.

CARSTAIRS — What happens in an underground organization when the first- or second-in-command are killed or captured?

FREEMAN Each man is trained to handle positions three steps ahead of him in grade. The operations officer takes over, and the others move up two grades.

CARSTAIRS Fine. That concludes our oral examination, and let me congratulate you on being the first Negro officer in the Central Intelligence Agency. We've programmed your aptitude into our computer personnel system. You're to be our new Top-secret Reproduction Center Section Chief.

INT. CIA STORAGE/COPY ROOM

Freeman stands next to a copy machine collecting printouts. Doris walks in and pats him on the shoulder.

DORIS Hey.

FREEMAN Oh, hi, Doris. What brings you all the way down here to the third subbasement?

DORIS The General needs someone to give a guided tour for a bunch of senators. You think you can handle it?

FREEMAN Yeah. I think I can handle it.

DORIS Good. The senators are in the General's office now.

FREEMAN Okay.

INT. CIA HALLWAY

As they walk along the hallway together, Doris begins to talk.

DORIS Freeman, you don't like me do you?

FREEMAN What makes you say that?

DORIS You never seem very friendly when you bring top-secret documents to the office. Sometimes it seems like you don't even know I'm around.

FREEMAN Oh, it's just that I'm preoccupied with my duties. I just wanna make good here, that's all.

DORIS You're very ambitious aren't you?

FREEMAN Yeah. I wanna be the best Reproduction Section Chief they've ever had.

DORIS But you are. Everyone says you're doing much better than expected.

FREEMAN Well, I certainly hope so.

INT. GENERAL'S OFFICE

General, Carstairs, and three senators stand as Freeman enters the office.

GENERAL Gentlemen, our Mr. Freeman. He'll conduct your tour. Senator Barton, Senator Chambers, Senator Wilson.

FREEMAN Right this way, gentleman.

As Freeman and the senators leave the office, Senator Barton stays behind briefly and speaks quietly to the General.

SENATOR BARTON General, I'm delighted. A member of your personal staff already. Now that's integration in action.

Senator Barton follows the other Senators and Freeman out of the office.

GENERAL You know, that's not a bad idea. Put him on my personal staff. If he doesn't bungle this tour, we'll keep him up here.

CARSTAIRS Yes, sir. We can put him out in reception. All our visitors could see we're integrated.

INT. HOTEL ROOM IN WASHINGTON

Freeman sits on a bed. Joy's voice can be heard in the background.

JOY I'm not coming back to Washington anymore, dear. I'm getting married.

FREEMAN — A doctor or a lawyer?

JOY — A doctor.

FREEMAN — He seems like a nice cat.

JOY — I'm sorry, but I'm not getting any younger.

FREEMAN — And I'm not in your bag, right? I always knew it had to happen someday. It's all right, baby. Baby. Joy, let's say goodbye right.

Joy removes her wig and places it on a mannequin bust and walks toward Freeman.

INT. CIA LIBRARY

Freeman is sitting at a table, which is covered with books and journals. He is making careful notes as he reads.

INT. CIA HALLWAY

Freeman walks down the hallway and enters the copy room.

INT. CIA FREEMAN'S ROOM

Freeman sits on his bed reading.

INT. GENERAL'S OFFICE

A black waiter clears a meal away from General and Freeman seated at a table. The waiter then serves them both coffee.

GENERAL — Dan, I'm certainly pleased with the way you've fitted into the agency. How long have you been with us now?

FREEMAN — A bit more than five years, sir.

GENERAL — And you've done well. You're a credit to your race.

FREEMAN — Thank you, sir.

GENERAL — Hard work, Dan, no shortcuts. Other minorities have pulled themselves up by their bootstraps.

FREEMAN	Yes, sir.
GENERAL	You're a perfect example, Dan. Fine natural athlete—no denying your people are great in sports.
FREEMAN	Well, thank you, sir, but, uh, we still have a long way to go.
GENERAL	Right. There's still the cultural gap to be closed. It's a question of evolution. Of course it will take generations. In the meantime, you people must earn respect by serving the country. Freeman, you people must serve.

General takes a cigar and Freeman lights it for him beating the waiter to it.

INT. CIA HEADQUARTERS—HALLWAY
General and Freeman are walking the long hallway.

FREEMAN	General, I want to serve.
GENERAL	I don't understand.
FREEMAN	Your comments last Friday afternoon convinced me that I can make a real contribution. So I'm going back to Chicago and work with my people and, uh, show them the way.
GENERAL	Now don't be hasty, Freeman. Perhaps you should think this thing over. After all you do set an example for your people to follow.
FREEMAN	Well I realize that General, and I have thought about it. But I've decided to take this position with the Social Service Foundation and help my people help themselves. Use what I learned here.
GENERAL	Well, I'll be sorry to see you go, Dan. Take all the time you need to phase out here. Be sure to let us know how things are going in Chicago.

The General shakes Freeman's hand and walks off.

FREEMAN — All right, sir. I will.

Freeman walks off in the opposite direction along the hallway.

INT. GENERAL'S OFFICE—CONTINUOUS
The General picks up the telephone.

GENERAL — Carstairs, bring in Freeman's file.

Carstairs enters the office and hands the file to the General.

GENERAL — Freeman's leaving us for a do-gooder outfit in Chicago.

CARSTAIRS — More money?

GENERAL — What else? Check out this foundation he's to work for—saturation in-depth security check.

CARSTAIRS — And Freeman?

GENERAL — He's safe enough. A routine surveillance of the foundation's clean. Phone tap, random and regular checks on his activities and associates.

CARSTAIRS — I'll telex the Chicago office today.

EXT. AIRPORT—DAY
Plane landing at the airport.

EXT. FREEWAY
Freeman is being driven from the airport into the city.

DRIVER — Dan, we really got our work cut out for us. Some of the baddest young dudes in Chicago, if not the country, are operating right here in our territory—the King Cobras.

FREEMAN — I used to be a Cobra.

The driver and Freeman laugh.

DRIVER	You?
FREEMAN	Yeah, they used to call me Turk. That gang goes back over thirty years. Listen, do they still hang out down at that, what is it, Pete's?
DRIVER	Yeah, you can find them there any night. Except now they own the place.

INT. RESTAURANT—DAY

Mrs. Duncan is sitting at a table eating. Freeman walks in and addresses her.

FREEMAN	Hello, Mrs. Duncan.
MRS. DUNCAN	Oh, Mr. Freeman, hi. Why don't you join me?
FREEMAN	Good. Listen, that looks good.
MRS. DUNCAN	It is delicious. You ought to try some.
FREEMAN	Mrs. Duncan, how is your son Shorty doing?
MRS. DUNCAN	Oh, Shorty is doing just fine. He got a job now making good money. In fact, he just bought me a color television set.
FREEMAN	What I hear is that he's not only running numbers and pushing drugs, that he's hooked.
MRS. DUNCAN	No, he ain't no real junkie. Sure he shoots up now and then. But I don't think he got no more than about a twenty or thirty dollar a week habit. And that ain't no habit.
FREEMAN	Well, did you ever think that he could end up in jail?
MRS. DUNCAN	Not unless somebody turned the heat on in the precinct. And then I can't hardly see why they'd be after Shorty cuz he ain't into it that much.
FREEMAN	Shorty ever think about finishing at least high school?

MRS. DUNCAN No, he don't want no part of the school. You know how them teachers are.

FREEMAN Well, without an education, what's he going to do?

MRS. DUNCAN Mr. Freeman, you know there ain't nothin' out there for us. Right out there on those streets where Shorty is.

EXT. STREET—A FEW MINUTES LATER

Shorty Duncan is standing in a doorway where he completes a drug deal. Dan Freeman walks down the street to speak with him.

FREEMAN How you doing, Shorty?

SHORTY Hey, Turk.

FREEMAN I just saw your mother inside the restaurant.

SHORTY Yeah, I was just on my way down there to lay some bread on her.

FREEMAN Shorty, the word is on the vine that you're not making your payoffs to the cops.

SHORTY That's just a rumor, Turk.

FREEMAN You mind if I give you a little advice?

SHORTY No, go ahead.

FREEMAN Why don't you just quit dealing altogether?

SHORTY Ah, man, you know I can't do that, Turk. It's survival.

FREEMAN Did you ever stop to think what would happen on these streets if we cut off the flow of drugs altogether? White folks control your neighborhood, do drugs, and you deal them?

SHORTY So what you gonna do now? Give me a sermon?

FREEMAN No, no sermon, Shorty. I just thought I'd ask.

Freeman walks off down the street. Shorty heads in the opposite direction.

INT. POOL HALL—NIGHT
Freeman is in Pete's Pool Hall playing a game of pool alone. Three Cobras—Do-Daddy, Pretty Willie, and Stud—walk into the pool hall and head straight to Freeman's table.

DO-DADDY	This our table.
FREEMAN	I only want to talk to you.
DO-DADDY	No talk, social worker. You better split.
FREEMAN	You know who I am?
STUD	Yeah, flunky. We know who you are.
FREEMAN	(*sighs*) Let's go out in the alley. This won't take long.
PRETTY WILLIE	You don't want to go out there, man. That's the way you want to go. Right now.

Freeman puts down his pool stick and walks out the back door to the alley. The three men look at each other and then follow him.

EXT. ALLEY BEHIND THE POOL HALL—CONTINUOUS—A FEW MOMENTS LATER
Freeman waits by the door and attacks Pretty Willie and Stud. When Do-Daddy walks out, Freeman pulls out a gun and points it at him.

DO-DADDY	Next time, social worker, we have us a piece, too.
FREEMAN	Shuddup! Then listen, big time bad-ass Cobras. Pop and wave to pigs from the rooftops during the riots last summer? Oh yeah. I know what you're into. Them .22 rifles and pistols did about as much damage as a mosquito to an elephant's ass. What did you expect to hit from that range with those weapons at night? You might as well have thrown the damn pieces at the pigs. You really want to mess with whitey? I can show you how. I can show you how.

INT. GYMNASIUM
In an echo of the first scenes at the CIA training camp, Freeman is now teaching martial arts to the Cobras.

EXT. REMOTE FIELD—DAY
The Cobras gather around a table to examine and activate an explosive device.

FREEMAN — You twist the wires to make contact. And throw the switch.

EXT. REMOTE FIELD—DAY
Two Cobras run a cable from the primed explosive toward Freeman and other members of the group, who are all standing some distance away.

FREEMAN — Come on bring it on here. Easy. Easy now. Take your time. Touch it off.

The explosive goes off and the group disperses.

EXT. REMOTE FIELD—DAY
Cobras and Freeman walk away from a car.

FREEMAN — All right. I'll operate the ignition by remote control.

The car explodes.

EXT. REMOTE FIELD—DAY
Freeman is instructing the Cobras in generalized combat training.

EXT. REMOTE FIELD—DAY
Freeman instructing the Cobras in combat with firearms.

EXT. REMOTE FIELD—DAY
Freeman teaches the Cobras target shooting.

EXT. REMOTE FIELD—DAY
Simulated war zone with explosives and grenades.

INT. KITCHEN IN APARTMENT

Freeman and a small group of Cobras are making gasoline bombs at a kitchen table.

FREEMAN	What's wrong, Willie?
PRETTY WILLIE	What we doing messing around like a high school chemistry class? Man, anybody can make explosives like this.
FREEMAN	Okay, Willie. You go order us some plastic and detonators from Marshall Fields.

Group laughs.

FREEMAN	Everything on this table can be obtained easily from a drug store or hardware store or medical supplies. If we can get sophisticated equipment, we'll use it, but we don't rely on it. We live off the land. We match technology with spontaneity and improvisation. Men against machines; brains against computers. Now if you don't think it can work, you check out Algeria, Kenya, Korea, and in Nam. Can you dig it?
PRETTY WILLIE	I understand now. It's cool.

EXT. TRAIN TRACK PLATFORM—DAY

FREEMAN	You find out in a country how difficult a range estimation is, but in the city the problem is simplified. A city block is twenty to fifty yards north to south. One hundred and fifty yards east to west. The lampposts are a standard thirty yards.
DO-DADDY	So we got reference points all over?
FREEMAN	Right. And since the buildings act as a funnel for the wind, you can fire on zero windage. Now run it down to the sniper teams, and I'll be in my pad all night if you need me.

DO-DADDY Cool, Turk.

FREEMAN Okay.

Freeman walks away.

EXT. SHOT OF THE CITY—NIGHT

JOY (V.O.) How's the new job coming?

FREEMAN (V.O.) It's, uh, all right.

INT. FREEMAN'S APARTMENT—SAME SCENE

JOY All right? The word's out on the grapevine how much money you making.

FREEMAN Well, nothing's changed about the gig except the bread.

JOY But I used to know you when you thought making money was obscene. Making a contribution was your thing.

FREEMAN Well, there's no reason why I can't do both.

JOY That's what I used to try to tell you, but you wouldn't listen. Since the War on Poverty all the social workers are making money.

FREEMAN Everyone except the poor.

JOY Now that's the old, Dan. But you have changed.

Joy gets up from the couch and kisses Freeman.

JOY Maybe I should have waited.

FREEMAN Well, too late to talk about that now. You already have a husband.

JOY Yeah, after a fashion. He goes his way and I go mine. By the way, Dawson's back from California.

FREEMAN Daws?

INT. CLUB—NIGHT

Scene opens with a band playing and a belly dancer performing. Freeman walks in with two women and recognizes Dawson sitting with a woman next to the entrance. Freeman walks by Dawson and brushes and taps Dawson's face awkwardly and annoyingly to get his attention.

DAWSON Excuse me. Look, excuse me.

Dawson gets up and recognizes Freeman.

DAWSON Aw, hey!

FREEMAN How you doing?

DAWSON Okay.

Freeman introduces his female companions.

FREEMAN This is Peter Dawson. Alenna. Sylvia.

DAWSON How are you?

FREEMAN I came down to see you. I came down to see you. And we're going over to have a drink. Can you get over with us, some day? Well, if you can, okay? Come on girls.

DAWSON Hey, Turk, how come you always offer to pay me back the fifty you owe me when we're about to be stuck up?

FREEMAN Because I'm good to you. Trust me.

Freeman walks toward the women and sits down with them.

DAWSON Hey, baby . . .

Dawson sits down next to his date and whispers something in her ear. He then crosses the bar to join Freeman's table.

DAWSON Okay.

FREEMAN What are you having?

DAWSON Uh, cognac.

FREEMAN So how you been, dummy?

DAWSON (*laughing*) Okay.

FREEMAN Joy tells me that you were in California.

DAWSON Yeah, I conducted a fifteen-week seminar on inner-city riot control.

FREEMAN What's that?

DAWSON Well, it has to do with the Chicago Police Department's approach to street gangs.

FREEMAN And they sent you?

DAWSON Who better? Five year warlord with the Apaches.

FREEMAN Oh yeah. (*addressing the women*) I'll tell you, this is an ex-hoodlum turned cop.

A waitress brings a tray of drinks to the table. Freeman raises his glass to Dawson.

FREEMAN Here's to old friends rediscovered.

DAWSON And to new ones.

FREEMAN Tell me about this new job.

INT. GYM HALL TRAINING

FREEMAN Next stage of your training program is to learn how to steal.

Cobras all laugh.

FREEMAN Yes, sir. I know you are all experts in stealing from your black brothers and sisters. Now you will learn how to steal from the enemy.

INT. OFFICE BUILDING RECEPTION AREA—DAY

Stud dressed in janitorial clothing and carrying a mop and a bucket walks down a hallway into an office space past reception. He enters through a door off to the side.

FREEMAN (V.O) Remember, a black man with a mop, tray, or broom in his hand can go damn near anywhere in this country. And a smiling black man is invisible.

INT. OFFICE—CONTINUOUS

Stud enters the Chicago Edison president's office with a mop and bucket and starts straightening curtains while the president sits at his desk on the phone.

FREEMAN (V.O)	The president for the Chicago Edison's a collector of pipes. Stud, you will rip off the president's pipes while he is in his office.

Stud starts to clean windows then starts collecting items unnoticed from the president's desk while the president sits at his desk. Stud starts to leave, the president looks at him and turns away. Stud collects the last pipe from the office.

INT. PRETTY WILLIE'S APARTMENT—NIGHT

Freeman sits in the living room of Willie's apartment toying with a large decorative knife.

FREEMAN	I wanna talk to you, Willie. The brothers tell me you write.
PRETTY WILLIE	Yeah.
FREEMAN	Good. We need a propagandist. So you are the Minister of Information. I want you to set up a group and use whoever you want.
PRETTY WILLIE	What you want? Like some posters, music, poetry?
FREEMAN	Anything. Just so long as you talk to the people in a language that they understand.
PRETTY WILLIE	I know about six of the cats that I can use. You know there's a lot of wasted talent in the Cobras.
FREEMAN	Good, let's use it. And give me an outline in two weeks.
PRETTY WILLIE	Mmm, one week, man. It ain't no problem.
FREEMAN	Beautiful. I understand that you're still registered at the university.
PRETTY WILLIE	You know I got to take a few courses each semester, man. Keep that bread coming from home.

FREEMAN — You ever intend to get a degree?

PRETTY WILLIE — Now what do I need with a status symbol?

FREEMAN — That's all it is to you?

PRETTY WILLIE — For a black man in this country? What else is there?

FREEMAN — You know how my grandmother learned to read?

PRETTY WILLIE — No, huh?

FREEMAN — Along with me. Remember those reading primers?

PRETTY WILLIE — Dick and Jane? Yeah.

FREEMAN — When I first got into those books, my grandmother used to wait for me to come home from school, so she could help me with my reading. And she would follow the whole thing line for line. One day, I don't know why, I just read the line wrong, and I realized she couldn't read. I went into the bathroom and locked the door. And I cried. And every day after that, I ran home so that my grandmother could help me read. And man, the first time I saw her really read . . . "Get your education, boy" she used to say. Because that's the only thing the white man can't take away from you. And she was right.

PRETTY WILLIE — You know, I can't figure you, man.

FREEMAN — What's to figure?

PRETTY WILLIE — I mean, what are you in this for? You want power, you want revenge, you know? What is it?

FREEMAN — It's simple Willie. I just wanna be free. How about you?

PRETTY WILLIE — So do I. And I hate white folks.

FREEMAN	Hate white folks? This is not about "hate white folks." It's about loving freedom enough to die or kill for it, if necessary. Now you gonna need more than hate to sustain you when this thing begins. Now if you feel that way, you're no good to us, and you're no good to yourself. Have you ever killed a man, Willie?
PRETTY WILLIE	No.
FREEMAN	I have. In Korea. And when you spill a man's guts in the gutter, you see how fast hate disappears. Unless you like killing, and I don't think you will. Now some of the Cobras will. Stud will.
PRETTY WILLIE	Why Stud?
FREEMAN	Because he's a killer. He doesn't know it yet, but he is.

Freeman stands up and puts the knife back on the wall.

FREEMAN	I have another job for you, Willie.
PRETTY WILLIE	What's that?
FREEMAN	We need money. So I have a bank job case. The only thing about it is that I can't have the job connected with the Cobras.
PRETTY WILLIE	How you gonna do that?
FREEMAN	We'll use Red Beans, Benny Rooster, Paul Monty, JT, Johnny, and Tom. And you lead the team.
PRETTY WILLIE	All the yellow niggers, right? Look man, I am tired of that. I am not passing. I am black. Do you hear me, man? Do you understand? I am black! I am a nigger! Do you understand me? I was born black, I live black, and I'm gonna die probably because I'm black. Because some cracker that knows I'm black better than you, nigger, is probably gonna put a bullet in the back of my head.

INT. BANK—DAY

The bank robbery is in place. Pretty Willie holds a shotgun to the face of a bank teller.

PRETTY WILLIE — Stick up. Put your hands up. Move. Get on the wall. Get on the wall. Now. Move. Put your hands up. Hands up.

As the gang run out of the rear of the bank carrying sacks of stolen cash, Willie fires the shotgun twice.

EXT. ALLEY BEHIND THE BANK—CONTINUOUS

The gang leap into a getaway van and drive off. As they pull out into traffic, we see Dan Freeman watching them from a corner across the street.

INT. INSIDE VAN—CONTINUOUS

Taking off the wigs and clothes used during the robbery, Willie and the others put their own clothes back on.

EXT. PARKING LOT—CONTINUOUS

The van stops in a parking lot. They all jump out and into a sedan car parked nearby and drive away. They are listening to the news on the car radio.

RADIO ANNOUNCER — Chicago police are seeking six heavily armed men after a daring daylight robbery today of a southwest Chicago bank. Bank authorities estimate the theft to be in excess of three hundred thousand dollars. The men have been described by eyewitnesses as six Caucasian males between the age of twenty to thirty. Police warn that these men are armed and dangerous.

EXT. BASKETBALL COURT—DAY

The Cobras are playing a game of basketball on an outdoor court. Freeman and Do-Daddy stand watching.

FREEMAN — Recruitment and training group ready?

DO-DADDY — They had their final exams last week.

FREEMAN — Transportation set?

DO-DADDY	They make two moves before they reach their final destination. Check for tails along the way. Pick up instructions as they go along.
FREEMAN	Logistics?
DO-DADDY	There'll be five hundred dollars and new identification papers waiting for them when they reach the other end. After that, they live off the street.
FREEMAN	And when they get there?
DO-DADDY	Locate and identify a gang like the Cobras, set up training, a chain of command, organization, and a very tight discipline.
FREEMAN	And?
DO-DADDY	No junk.
FREEMAN	Good. I want the men assigned to Boston, New York, Philadelphia, Detroit, New Orleans, and Los Angeles to move out within ten days.
DO-DADDY	Man, they got some bad brothers in New Orleans.
FREEMAN	You got that right. And stagger the rest of them over the next month. There'll be monthly reports until we make contact and weekly reports after that. Now if they get busted in the street hassle, they recruit in prison, and we replace them. Any questions?

Do-Daddy shakes his head.

INT. FREEMAN'S APARTMENT

FREEMAN	Hey.
DAWSON	Hey, man, I just got off duty, and so I'd thought I'd stop by.
FREEMAN	Beautiful, beautiful.

DAWSON Hey, Joy!

JOY Hi Pete. How are you? How's the family?

DAWSON Oh, just fine. Just fine. Hey, Freeby, I think my oldest boy is gonna be an athlete.

FREEMAN Come on.

DAWSON Oh yeah, man. You remember that move I used to make coming off the baseline?

FREEMAN Yeah.

DAWSON Well, he's got it, man. He's got the head and shoulder thing and everything. I didn't teach him that move. You know I went to the game the other day, and there it was. It reminded me of myself twenty years ago.

FREEMAN I like to see that. The next time you go to a game, take me along.

DAWSON That's a bet.

FREEMAN Okay.

JOY How's Eileen?

DAWSON Ah, just fine. She's back at school at nights, and she got a master's last year. Now she's going for a PhD.

JOY Any chance of you two getting back together again?

DAWSON I don't think so. I mean it's not easy being the wife of a cop.

FREEMAN Say, I hear Jugg's in town. How about us catching a set?

DAWSON The three of us? Like old times?

JOY Hey, I'm sorry but I have really got to go home.

DAWSON — Ah, boo!

JOY — Listen, we'll make it over next week. Okay?

Joy leaves the room to fetch her coat.

DAWSON — Okay. (*turning to Dawson*) Can't cut her loose can you?

FREEMAN — No. And she knows me too well.

Joy reenters the room.

JOY — Okay. Have a good time.

DAWSON — Mmm-hmm.

JOY — For me?

DAWSON — Yeah. Bye-bye.

JOY — Bye-bye. Talk to you later?

FREEMAN — Yeah.

Joy and Freeman kiss goodbye, and Joy exits.

FREEMAN — Listen.

DAWSON — Yeah.

FREEMAN — Listen, let me get this coat on. We go down there, and we catch two sets.

DAWSON — Okay. Then we have a nightcap and a late dinner at The Avenue.

FREEMAN — Mmm-hmm.

DAWSON — Then we cut out all this fooling around and go see these two chicks that I came over to tell you about before I found out that Joy was here.

FREEMAN — Oh, yes. Splendid.

EXT. TRAIN TRACKS—DAY

Camera shows the view from a moving train. We pass extensive buildings, lots, and telegraph wires. The train arrives at a platform, and Freeman, Do-Daddy, Stud, and Pretty Willie exit the train, walking down the station steps to the city street below.

INT. GYM HALL TRAINING

FREEMAN What happens in an underground organization when the first and second in command are either killed or captured? Daddy?

DO-DADDY Each man is trained to handle positions three steps ahead of him in grade. The operations officer moves up and takes command. And everyone else moves up two grades.

FREEMAN Good. Now, we're almost ready.

INT. FREEMAN'S APARTMENT—NIGHT

We see an open box full of syringes.

PRETTY WILLIE We ain't no junkies.

FREEMAN From now on everyone gonna think you are. You put needle marks in your arms, and you keep them fresh. And no pig is gonna bust you for the things that we'll be doing as long as you got those tracks.

DO-DADDY AND STUD Yeah, man!

PRETTY WILLIE During the daytime we'll be nodding. Nighttime we get out there and do it.

FREEMAN We are gonna get our own. Stop begging for crumbs.

STUD How?

FREEMAN What we got now is a colony. What we want to create is a new nation. In order to do that, we gotta pay a different kind of dues. Freedom dues.

DO-DADDY — Right on.

FREEMAN — Now according to Mr. Charlie, we have never paid any dues. You dig those plantation movies on television?

STUD — Yeah.

DO-DADDY — Yeah.

FREEMAN — No chains, no whips. Bunch of happy darkies just waitin' on Massa Charlie and his family and digging it.

The group all laughs at this portrayal. Do-Daddy and Pretty Willie begin to act out a parody of a plantation movie.

DO-DADDY — Lordy, lordy, lordy. It's Colonel Beauregard come home from de war.

PRETTY WILLIE — My faithful retainer, George! The war is over and we lost. You're not a slave anymore, George. You're free.

DO-DADDY — Free massa? Is that bad massa? I gonna die?

PRETTY WILLIE — You're free, George. You can leave the plantation.

DO-DADDY — I wan' stay wiff you.

PRETTY WILLIE — But I can't pay you, George. The Carpetbaggers mortgaged the plantation.

DO-DADDY — Oh, don't let that worry you none. Why I wouldn't know what to do with no money. And don't let that mortuary thing worry you either. Everything's gonna be all right.

PRETTY WILLIE — Bless you, George.

Freeman and Stud play imaginary guitars and hum "I Wish I Was in Dixie."

PRETTY WILLIE — George. Sit down, George.

DO-DADDY — Oh massa, massa, massa!

The group laughs at their role play.

FREEMAN You have just played out the American dream.

STUD Yeah.

FREEMAN And now we're gonna turn it into a nightmare.

EXT. FENCED–IN ARMY COMPOUND—NIGHT
Guard patrols back and forth in front of the entrance to the compound. One of the Black Freedom Fighters hunches down low by a car parked on the street outside of the compound watching the guard. He covers the barbed-wire fence with a blanket and helps two others climb over the fence. Another Freedom Fighter appears and helps another four men climb over the fence in the same spot.

The men maneuver their way through the compound, take out the guard, and open the gate. A city bus drives through and other members exit the bus. The Freedom Fighters load the bus and an army vehicle with weapons. Both the bus and the army vehicle exit the compound. The bus drives along a city street and then stops at the red light of an intersection. A woman slaps on the door of the bus to be let in.

WOMAN Open the door.

Do-Daddy is driving the bus and ignores her request.

WOMAN Please open the door. Please open the door.

A police car drives up alongside the bus.

STUD Pigs!

WOMAN Please open the door.

COP This one's off duty, lady. Can't you read? Take the next one.

The woman relents and walks to the curb, and the traffic light turns green. Bus, cop car, and army vehicle all drive on.

EXT. STORAGE LOCKER/HANGAR—NIGHT
The Freedom Fighters unload the bus and army vehicle.

FREEMAN Now, let's see what we've got.

Freeman opens the first crate and pulls out a rifle.

DO-DADDY	Oh, wow. Man what a rip-off!

Freeman tosses the weapon to Daddy.

PRETTY WILLIE	You know this gonna make the headlines.
FREEMAN	No. This won't hit the papers at all. It might give some other people ideas. But this place will be swarming with CIA and FBI.
PRETTY WILLIE	Do we go underground?
FREEMAN	No. They'll be looking for everybody except us. You see, this took brains and guts, which we don't have, right?
COBRAS	Right!
FREEMAN	Move it out.

INT. POOL HALL
Do-Daddy and Freeman playing pool.

DO-DADDY	Some of the boys is wanted for the draft, man. Now what we gonna do if they get caught? Go underground?
FREEMAN	Yeah. If they can beat it, they should. But we recruit every non-vet we can get. Right now I'm trying to recruit Dawson as a double agent.
DO-DADDY	Turk, you really think we can win?
FREEMAN	In guerilla warfare, winning is in not losing. When you sleep on the floor, you can't fall out of bed.
DO-DADDY	Then what we trying to do, man?
FREEMAN	Fight whitey to a standstill. Force him to make a choice between the two things which he seems to dig most of all. There is no way that the United

States can police the world and keep us on our ass, too, unless we cooperate. When we revolt, we reduce it to a simple choice. Whitey finds out he can't make either.

DO-DADDY — The Cobras is ready. What about the other brothers and sisters out there on the streets?

FREEMAN — Their choice is when we start. If they don't follow our program and turn us in to the cops, we lose in a week. But if they support us . . .

DO-DADDY — Yeah.

FREEMAN — . . . then it's hit and run, harass and hound, and we can paralyze this country.

DO-DADDY — Yeah, right. Training has started already in nine cities. Five groups is combat ready. Plus us.

FREEMAN — Right, and by next summer we should be able to hit the ten largest urban complexes in the United States.

DO-DADDY — Shit.

EXT. ALLEYWAY—NIGHT

Shorty Duncan runs down an alley with two cops in pursuit. The cops pull out their guns and shoot Shorty in the back. They run over to him, and it is clear that he's dead.

INT. FREEMAN'S BEDROOM—LATER THAT SAME NIGHT

Freeman is asleep with Joy when the phone rings.

FREEMAN — Yeah.

DO-DADDY — Turk, it's Daddy.

FREEMAN — Yeah.

DO-DADDY — Looks like a riot's gonna start, man. Pigs burned a cat.

FREEMAN	Who?
DO-DADDY	Shorty Duncan. Yeah, after all the training, it looks like this shit is gonna start over a jive-ass pusher.

EXT. PAY PHONE

FREEMAN	Where?
DO-DADDY	Alley behind the pool hall.

INT. FREEMAN'S BEDROOM

FREEMAN	Nothing moves till I give the word, right?
DO-DADDY	Right.
FREEMAN	Okay.

Freeman hangs up the phone, gets out of bed, and flips on the light.

JOY	Where you going?
FREEMAN	Cops shot a kid. Looks like it could be trouble.
JOY	Don't get involved.
FREEMAN	Gotta go. Don't worry about it.

EXT. ALLEY BEHIND POOL HALL—LATER THAT NIGHT

An increasingly restless and noisy crowd is gathered at the scene of Shorty Duncan's shooting. Freeman and another man walk through the crowd to find Dawson.

FREEMAN	How do things look?
DAWSON	Not good. Could blow any time.
FREEMAN	Anything we can do to help?
DAWSON	Just what you've been doing. Talk to the kids; tell them to cool it. They'll listen to you and Perk.
FREEMAN	What about the kids?
PERKINS	Everybody is pretty uptight, Dan.

FREEMAN Hey, look, Perk, go down to the drugstore, call up the office, tell the night girl to round up all of the street workers and get them down here quick. Then join me, right?

PERKINS You got it, Dan.

Freeman walks away through the crowd. A fight ensues, and Freeman steps in to break it up.

FREEMAN Hold it. Hold it. Wait a minute. Wait a minute. Listen to me. Listen to me. What is this gonna do, man? You've got a wife who is worried about you; you got a new job, and if you get busted, you gonna lose it, and you're one of the few people round here with a job to lose!

MAN Man, this has got to stop sometime and somewhere. We ain't animals!

FREEMAN Come on, y'all, just break it on up, break it on up.

POLICEMAN (*Speaking through a loudhailer*) All right now, come on! Let's start moving on out of here!

FREEMAN Come on, just go home. Come on, go on home.

The crowd begins to move, and Freeman pushes his way through until he reaches Dawson.

FREEMAN Looks like it's cooling down.

DAWSON Yeah, I think you're right. I should be able to pull my men out in another hour.

As a police car tries to move through the crowd, we suddenly hear dogs barking.

FREEMAN Dogs!

Freeman, Dawson, and the crowd start running toward the policemen. Dawson comes through the crowd toward one policeman in particular who has a barking, snarling German Shephard on a leash.

DAWSON Get those dogs outta here!

POLICEMAN The captain sent me up here.

DAWSON I'm telling you to get them out. I'm in charge. You know how these people feel about dogs.

POLICEMAN But I got my orders.

Dawson draws his gun and points it at the dog.

DAWSON Just move him. Or I'll kill him.

Policemen leave the crowd with the dogs.

DAWSON Okay, the dogs are leaving! Let's cool it! Let's go home! Come on, let's go, let's go!

Crowd is still riled up and starts running off in one direction. Dawson, Freeman, and Fred congregate together.

DAWSON It's no good anymore. We're gonna have to move back as soon as I can pull all my men out.

PERKINS Oh, man, it was gonna be all right.

Dawson shoots off a flare.

DAWSON Okay, let's pull it back.

The crowd becomes even more unruly as the police, along with Dawson, Freeman, and Perkins, back up to their cars. A lot of screaming and protesting. Crowd starts to violence. Freeman wants to join in, but Dawson pulls him out.

DAWSON Come on, Dan. Don't be a fool. You know we did the best we could!

FREEMAN But shit!

DAWSON Yeah, I know. They were on their way home. Why did they have to bring those goddamn dogs in here?

The crowd becomes more violent and fighting breaks out everywhere, as the police do battle with the protestors and make numerous arrests. A squad car is set alight. More police cars show up on the scene and start shooting. An explosion goes off on a building. The crowd and the police continue to fight as a fire truck appears on the scene. It has become a full-scale riot.

EXT. STREET CORNER—THE FOLLOWING MORNING

Stud is standing on the street outside a Mexican restaurant. Freeman pulls up in a car and gets out.

STUD	When we hit, Turk?
FREEMAN	The boys ready?
STUD	Been ready.
FREEMAN	And mood?
STUD	Mellow.
FREEMAN	Primary and secondary targets?
STUD	Check 'em twice a day.
FREEMAN	Weapons?
STUD	Oiled and ready. Everything ready.
FREEMAN	We have to wait.
STUD	What for?
FREEMAN	Stud, who is the Man?
STUD	Well, you the Man!
FREEMAN	And if they get me?
STUD	Do-Daddy.
FREEMAN	Then?
STUD	Me. Pretty Willie and so on down the line.
FREEMAN	So?
STUD	Oh, man. We go when you say go.
FREEMAN	Yeah. I'll check you tonight.
STUD	Right.

EXT. SHOT FROM HELICOPTER, FLYING LOW ALONG CITY STREETS, SOME DAYS AFTER THE RIOT

Helicopter spans the scene from the riot with burned out cars, empty streets, damaged buildings, and members of the National Guard patrolling the streets.

EXT. STREET IN FRONT OF LAUNDRY BUSINESS

A group of five young men are throwing bricks and cans at police officers. An old man stands to one side in a shop doorway. As the police run in, the young men all run away. The police arrest the old man and take him away.

EXT. CAR—DAY—CONTINUOUS

Dawson sitting in a car. Freeman taps on the window and gets in.

FREEMAN	Hey. How long since you've been in bed?
DAWSON	Not since the riot started.
FREEMAN	That was three nights ago, man.
DAWSON	Yeah, I know, catnap when I can.
FREEMAN	When did the National Guard come in?
DAWSON	Late last night. All white.
FREEMAN	I noticed.
DAWSON	Yeah, the people didn't dig it when they woke up this morning and, uh, found the troops were here.
FREEMAN	What do you think they'll do?
DAWSON	I can't see them trying to fight the army.
FREEMAN	They didn't mind fighting the police.
DAWSON	Yeah. I've never seen them like that.
FREEMAN	Maybe that badge has put distance between you and them.
DAWSON	Oh yeah! Yeah, I forgot. The pigs over here and the people over there. And never the twain shall meet, huh? Hey, man, I grew up down here, too. And I

know these people. And there were some good people out there on the streets the last few nights. Not just hoodlums like they say in the newspapers.

FREEMAN — At a scene like this, anybody can get involved.

DAWSON — But that's only gonna make it worse. We have to maintain law and order or we might as well be back in the jungle.

Freeman laughs.

FREEMAN — Daws, the ghetto is a jungle. Always has been. Understand? You cannot cage people like animals and not expect them to fight back some day. It has always been an army of occupation here, but police badges and uniforms. Huh? You and me, a cop and social worker. We are keepers of this goddamn zoo.

DAWSON — The streets have to be safe.

FREEMAN — Safe for who? You're here to protect property, not lives.

DAWSON — Well, that's what it is all about, isn't it? You worked hard to get what you got, didn't you? And you want to keep it, just like I do?

FREEMAN — Bullshit! Listen, you think because you got a badge and I got a couple of degrees that makes a difference? Do you know what white folks call people like you and me in private? Niggers, Daws! Niggers.

Dawson whistles.

DAWSON — Hey, hey, hey. I haven't heard you talk like that since we were in college.

FREEMAN — Well, I'm sorry, man. Maybe the last three nights been a little bit much. I gotta a board meeting, I gotta go reassure the white folks. Let's go get something to eat, okay?

DAWSON — Okay.

Dawson starts his car and they drive away from the scene. As the camera pans back we see the street with cops, National Guard, and hear the sound of a helicopter. A young man is arrested and taken away.

INT. RADIO STUDIO
A DJ sets a track to play on the record deck. The Freedom Fighters enter with guns. Uncle Tom—wearing a full-face balaclava—sits at the studio microphone and broadcasts an announcement.

FREEMAN	Hey, hey, ol' bean and you too, baby. This is Uncle Tom, commander-in-chief of your Black Freedom Fighters of North America . . .

EXT. CHICAGO SKYLINE—CONTINUOUS—NIGHT
Screen shows a couple shots of the Chicago skyline.

FREEMAN (V.O.)	. . . bringing you the latest news from your fighting black underground. Hang on brothers and sisters, liberation is near.

INT. MAYOR'S OFFICE—CONTINUOUS—NIGHT
Cobras, now called the Black Freedom Fighters, break into the mayor's office and plant a bomb underneath the desk.

FREEMAN (V.O.)	In just a few minutes, at precisely three o'clock, we will demolish the lavish offices of the mayor of white Chicago. Of course, we don't have a mayor, even if they do count our vote several times to elect him every four years. Remember brothers, in spite of the lies about an assassination attempt on the mayor, which will appear in the white press, this time we blew the mayor's office at night when he was at home to announce the beginning of our war of liberation. I'd dedicate this program to the National Guard, but we're fresh out of hillbilly music. And according to the press and television, the guard spends all his time playing basketball with the kids and helping old ladies cross the street. But we know better, don't we?

EXT. EXTERIOR OF MAYOR'S OFFICE BUILDING—CONTINUOUS—NIGHT

FREEMAN (V.O.) We know about the fourteen-year old girl . . .

INT. MAYOR'S OFFICE—CONTINUOUS—NIGHT

FREEMAN (V.O) . . . the trigger-happy guardsman shot last night and the people they beat up and the black businesses they destroyed, don't we?

The two Cobras finish planting the bomb and move out.

INT. RADIO STUDIO—CONTINUOUS—NIGHT

Freeman, masked, sits at the microphone making the announcement.

FREEMAN It's almost time. Ten seconds . . . nine . . . eight . . . seven . . . six . . . five . . . four . . .

EXT. CITY BUILDING—CONTINUOUS—NIGHT

FREEMAN (V.O.) . . . three . . . two . . .

INT. RECORDING STUDIO—CONTINUOUS—NIGHT

FREEMAN . . . one . . . Blast off!

EXT. CITY BUILDING—CONTINUOUS—NIGHT

City building blows up.

FREEMAN (V.O.) And the mayor's office is now air-conditioned, courtesy of the Black Freedom Fighters of Chicago. And the message is this . . .

EXT. CITY STREETS—CONTINUOUS—NIGHT

Police and firetrucks drive toward the exploded scene.

FREEMAN (V.O.) . . . pigs and the National Guard have to go . . .

INT. RADIO STUDIO—CONTINUOUS

Cops show up at the radio studio and find the workers tied up on the floor and to a chair.

FREEMAN (V.O.) . . . immediately if not sooner. If they have not left by midnight Sunday, we will kick them out.

Whitey, go home. We don't want you in our neighborhood either, and we will control our nation.

INT. POLICE STATION—A COUPLE DAYS LATER

Colonel Evans of the National Guard is holding a press conference.

COLONEL EVANS — We will leave when things are back to normal. With them at the bottom and us at the top.

REPORTER 1 — Colonel Evans would you care to comment on charges of brutality by the guard?

COLONEL EVANS — If they obeyed the law, we wouldn't be here. They'll get what they asked for, but there has been no brutality by the guard.

REPORTER 2 — Colonel, what about the threats by the Freedom Fighters to kick the guard out of the neighborhood?

COLONEL EVANS — They said midnight tonight. It is now twelve-thirty, which tells us exactly what we think of their threats. It's also time to put an end to this conference. I have a report to work on. Goodnight and thank you, gentlemen and ladies.

EXT. PARK—NIGHT

The Freedom Fighters are moving covertly through the park toward a National Guard building.

EXT. NATIONAL GUARD HQ—CONTINUOUS

The Freedom Fighters take out two guards and then proceed to enter the building.

INT. NATIOANL GUARD HQ HALLWAY—CONTINUOUS

Three Freedom Fighters are moving along a hallway when they hear voices from a nearby office.

VOICE 1 — Hold it right there. All right, you just killed your last white man.

VOICE 2 Did he die? My people attack.

VOICE 1 You don't scare me none, you snakey Indian.

INT. GUARDROOM—CONTINUOUS

The hallway opens into a guardroom where a guard sits at a desk watching an old cowboy movie on television. The three Freedom Fighters appear from the hallway and all pull out a gun at the guard.

INT. NATIONAL GUARD HQ—POOL ROOM—A FEW MINUTES LATER

Four Freedom Fighters hold down the guard down with his mouth taped shut. Do-Daddy is painting the guard's face black. Four other Freedom Fighters look on chuckling and sniggering.

DO-DADDY Li'l Black Sambo. Yeah, how you like that? Like that, don't you? Always wanted to be like that, didn't you?

Pretty Willie enters the room, and Daddy rips off the tape from the guard's mouth.

PRETTY WILLIE Coffee? Tea?

GUARD Poison? You're gonna kill me?

PRETTY WILLIE No, soul brother, just a little acid. You're going on a little trip. Hold him! Hold him!

Two Freedom Fighters hold down the guard and force open his mouth. Willie forces the drugged coffee into the guard's mouth.

EXT. STREET—THE FOLLOWING MORNING

The now blackfaced guard has been stripped of his clothes down to his undershirt and boxers and is riding a bicycle down the street. His face is still painted black and he is singing. Two National Guard soldiers confront him.

BLACKFACED GUARD Men? How are you? I just met the most marvelous bunch of niggers! The most marvelous bunch . . .

The blackfaced guard is shot by a sniper.

EXT. ROOFTOP—CONTINUOUS

We see that Stud and Do-Daddy are the rooftop snipers.

DO-DADDY	You get him?
STUD	(*Laughing*) Shiitt!

EXT. GHETTO NEIGHBORHOOD—NIGHT

Freedom Fighters throw an explosive device at a National Guard armored car. National Guardsmen line up and move out to search the area. Freedom Fighters hide in an abandoned housing building and open fire on the National Guard. Freedom Fighters then rush out of the building away from scene.

EXT. GHETTO NEIGHBORHOOD—NIGHT—CONTINUOUS

Officials and medics on scene of attack to attend to the wounded and deceased.

Two medics pick up a stretcher and carry the wounded man to the ambulance.

MEGAPHONE VOICE-OVER	We need two people over in this area. Please hurry.
NEWS REPORTER	Due to increased fighting in Chicago, the president has ordered a brigade from the 82nd Airborne into the war-torn South Side to reinforce the beleaguered National Guard . . .

INT. HOTEL ROOM TELEVISION SET—NEXT MORNING

Carstairs and the General are watching the television report.

NEWS REPORTER	. . . under heavy attack by black guerillas since late last week. This is Pat Bennell, Chicago.
GENERAL	You've been here from the beginning, Carstairs. How does it look to you?
CARSTAIRS	General, it couldn't be worse.
GENERAL	We have elite troops out here now against untrained black fanatics. The whole thing should be over before the weekend.

CARSTAIRS — Those troops are facing a highly trained underground guerilla army. They have military weapons, and they know how to use them. The commander of those elite troops insists he can put this thing down within a few days.

GENERAL — You disagree?

CARSTAIRS — Yes, sir, I do. They're a first class fighting unit.

GENERAL — You've prepared an options booklet?

CARSTAIRS — Yes, sir.

GENERAL — And?

CARSTAIRS — We have three. Root them out one-by-one. Starve them out by a siege. Total evacuation of the black population.

GENERAL — Evacuation?

CARSTAIRS — Now the first is too costly in lives and equipment. Neither evacuation or siege would work.

GENERAL — Why not?

CARSTAIRS — General, we sealed off the ghetto for three days last week. It paralyzed the city.

GENERAL — Paralyzed Chicago?

CARSTAIRS — Chicago is more dependent on black labor than one would think. Ninety percent of the garbage collectors are colored. Sixty percent of the hospital workers are colored. Sixty percent of the bus drivers and eighty percent of the postal workers. So although the concentration . . . the detention camps occurring under the 1950 Subversion Act are ready, we can't put them to immediate use.

GENERAL — Your recommendation?

CARSTAIRS We can end it alone, sir.

GENERAL Yes?

CARSTAIRS The Russians obviously have a top agitprop man here. Find him, destroy him, and you have disorganized ignorant Negroes to deal with.

GENERAL Cut off the head and the snake dies?

CARSTAIRS Exactly.

GENERAL All right, Carstairs. Get right on it. I'm going back to Washington. Get back to me by tomorrow noon.

INT. HOTEL ROOM

The General opens the door to an adjoining room.

GENERAL Honey, I'm going back to Washington. Why don't you amuse yourself here for a few days? Do a little shopping. Be back Sunday, huh?

General gets out his wallet to pull out a few dollar bills. The woman is revealed to be Dahomey Queen.

DAHOMEY QUEEN Sure, baby. I'll find something to do in Chicago.

INT. FREEMAN'S HOME

Freeman and Dahomey Queen stand at his door talking.

FREEMAN But how did you know how to find me?

DAHOMEY QUEEN I looked in the phone book.

FREEMAN Yeah, well, uh, you look great. So what are you doing in Chicago?

DAHOMEY QUEEN I'm here with my sponsor.

FREEMAN Oh.

DAHOMEY QUEEN I'm not hustling anymore. Got me a steady scene. He a little bit, um, freakish, like black skin. But the money is good. Got me some property. You know him.

FREEMAN	I do?
DAHOMEY QUEEN	Yeah. You used to work for him. You know, you his nigger. All the time he be saying if all of us niggers was like you, wouldn't be no trouble. First, I thought he was talking about somebody else.
FREEMAN	So?
DAHOMEY QUEEN	So they out to get Uncle Tom.
FREEMAN	What makes you think I know anything about Uncle Tom?
DAHOMEY QUEEN	I'm not saying you do, but you know Chicago, and I don't.
FREEMAN	Yeah, but what am I supposed to do?
DAHOMEY QUEEN	Warn him. Tell him they out to kick ass, and they ain't playin'.
FREEMAN	One thing. Why are you sticking your neck out?
DAHOMEY QUEEN	I'm black, ain't I?
FREEMAN	Yeah. Yeah, you are, baby. Who's in charge?
DAHOMEY QUEEN	Carstairs.
FREEMAN	What are they up to?
DAHOMEY QUEEN	They plan to get inside, find out who this Uncle Tom is, and kill him.
FREEMAN	Cut off the head and the snake dies. Do they know who Uncle Tom is?
DAHOMEY QUEEN	They think he's some guy from Russia.
FREEMAN	They would.
DAHOMEY QUEEN	You want me to see what else I can find out?

FREEMAN No . . . wait a minute. Two can play at this infiltration game. Find out all you can but don't pry. I'll have somebody contact you in Washington. Baby, be very careful. And don't contact me again unless I get to Washington.

EXT. GHETTO STREET—NIGHT

As National Guard jeeps drive down the street, Freedom Fighters attack them with explosives and gunfire. A fallen guard has his utility belt stripped from him by Pretty Willie.

GUARD Why me? Why me?

PRETTY WILLIE Cuz it's war, honky!.

Police sirens can be heard approaching in the background.

PRETTY WILLIE Split!

INT. FREEMAN'S APARTMENT—DAY

FREEMAN And why should you feel threatened by the Freedom Fighters?

JOY Because I am, and you are, too.

FREEMAN How?

JOY You know how. Look, all the progress we've made over the last few years will be wiped out if this thing isn't stopped soon. I heard even your foundation is on its way out.

FREEMAN Well, no. They decided to increase the budget and the staff.

JOY Yeah?

FREEMAN Uh-uh.

JOY Well, my husband was dismissed from the hospital. And he was the first and only Negro in a white hospital staff in the city.

FREEMAN	What is the connection between your husband and the Freedom Fighters?
JOY	Dan, that is the whole point! Innocent and decent people are suffering because of niggers who know nothing but hate and revenge.
FREEMAN	And it's all the niggers' fault right?
JOY	Look, don't romanticize those people, Dan. They're not beautiful!
FREEMAN	Only by contrast.
JOY	Dan, those Freedom Fighters are murderers.
FREEMAN	Hey listen, it didn't figure to be long before those niggers realized that you don't have no win throwing a brick at somebody with a gun.
JOY	Dan, whose side are you on?
FREEMAN	Your side. We're in the same bag, making the best of a bad scene.

INT. RESTAURANT—A FEW DAYS LATER
Joy and Dawson meet for lunch.

JOY	I think he's messed with those Black Freedom Fighters.
DAWSON	Yeah? You gotta be kiddin'.
JOY	I am sure of it. We were talking and—and he just—for a minute it was like he used to be.
DAWSON	Yeah? He was something else when he was in college. And that was before all this became fashionable.
JOY	He was defending those animals, then he caught himself. He said all the right things, but it just wasn't him. It just wasn't the man I know.

DAWSON — Perfect source of intelligence. Gig takes him all over the ghetto. I'll check it out.

JOY — Pete, I am doing the right thing?

INT. FREEMAN'S APARTMENT—LATER THAT NIGHT

Freeman enters the apartment and Dawson swings around in a chair pointing his gun.

DAWSON — Come on. Just put your coat down right there. Come on.

Freeman puts his coat down and laughs.

FREEMAN — (*Laughing*) What is this, Daws?

DAWSON — Come on, Uncle Tom. Come on!

FREEMAN — Uncle what?

DAWSON — Uncle Tom. Up against the wall. Come on. Against the wall.

Dawson shoves Freeman against the wall.

DAWSON — Spread your feet out. Come on.

Dawson pats down Freeman.

FREEMAN — Hey, easy now. What is this? Some kind of joke man?

DAWSON — Yeah. It's a joke. The joke is on me. I've been looking all over for Uncle Tom, but here you are under my nose. Cool Dan Freeman. Only digging sports cars and bread, good clothes, and chicks. Beautiful cover, man!

FREEMAN — Hey, man, now think about it. I mean really think about it. Would I, uh, risk all of this for that?

DAWSON — Well, I don't have to worry about that now. I got enough evidence to take you in, and that's what I'm gonna do.

FREEMAN — What evidence?

DAWSON — Oh, them tapes man. Them Uncle Tom propaganda tapes that you cats spread around the ghetto. Well, I listened to them over and over again, and it's you Dan. It's your voice.

FREEMAN — You gotta be crazy.

DAWSON — We'll see if a voice print proves whether I'm crazy or not.

FREEMAN — Now what?

DAWSON — Now what? Well, the scene is over. But one thing. One thing. Are you working for the Commies like they say? Who's behind you?

FREEMAN — How come there's gotta be someone behind me?

DAWSON — Oh, come on, man, don't put me on. No, no. The FBI says it's the most sophisticated underground movement in the Western hemisphere. The work of an expert!

FREEMAN — Uh-uh? And expertise is white man's monopoly right, Daws? Well, I am an expert! I spent five years flunkying to become an expert!

DAWSON — This gun makes me an expert.

FREEMAN — You're a big man with that gun and that badge. You know Daws, you want to have it both ways. You want a pat on your head from whitey and you want to love and respect your people. But you can't be with your people without betraying that badge. And you can't be a copper without betraying your people, you hypocrite.

DAWSON — You think nobody else feels the way you do? You think you're the only nigger with a sense of outrage?

FREEMAN — Well, then hit back! Join us! We can use you. We got undercover people on the force.

DAWSON On the force?

FREEMAN That's right.

DAWSON Who?

FREEMAN Nobody with your rank. Come on join us, Daws.

DAWSON You were using kids!

FREEMAN Who else am I gonna involve? People like you and me? Na-huh. The kids are our only hope, and I got to them before they got jailed or killed or turned into Dawsons. And now they'd do anything to be free.

DAWSON Who said you were free, man?

FREEMAN Well, Daws, even on the wrong end of your gun, I'm a lot freer than you are.

Freeman attacks Dawson and they fight. Freeman grabs the ice picker from the drink station and stabs Dawson while simultaneously Dawson shoots Freeman in the abdomen. Dawson dies instantly. Freeman struggles to his feet and reaches for the phone to dial a number.

INT. FREEMAN'S APARTMENT—LATER THAT NIGHT

Do-Daddy, Stud, and Pretty Willie enter the apartment. Freeman has changed his clothes and holds his wound. Do-Daddy goes directly to Dawson's body.

DO-DADDY (*incredulously*) It's Dawson!

STUD Hey, man. Dawson's your main man. You know that'd be like me killing Daddy.

FREEMAN Yeah. And maybe one day you'll have to kill Daddy. Or him you. You think we're playing games, killing white strangers? There are a lot of Dawsons out there, and some of them will try to stop us. But anybody who gets between us and freedom has got to go. Now that's anybody. You got the Airborne out there now, and forty percent of those troops are black. Maybe they'll help us, and maybe they won't.

But in the meantime, if you hesitate with any one of them because he's black—just once—you'll be one dead Cobra. Now if you ain't ready to pay them kind of dues, now you get out and go back to doing nothing. But don't tell me who I killed and what it cost me to do it. Now get him out of here. Get him out!

PRETTY WILLIE Right, Turk.

Stud, Pretty Willie, and Do-Daddy carry the body across the room to the front door of the apartment.

FREEMAN It is now condition red. All fighters in the field. Alert our groups everywhere. And remember: don't quit until you either win or you die.

Stud, Pretty Willie, and Do-Daddy exit with the body. Freeman closes the door.

SCENE ON SCENE.
As Freeman moves around his apartment, it begins to fade to show the continued fighting of the Freedom Fighters against the National Guard.

NEWS REPORTER (V.O.) The newest outbreak in the black section of Oakland brings to a total of eight the number of uprisings by black guerrillas in cities across the nation. The president has declared a state of national emergency.

INT. FREEMAN'S APARTMENT
Freeman salutes with his drink. The camera turns to show the statues from the opening scene.

End Credits

DAN FREEMAN	*LAWRENCE COOK*
JOY	*JANET LEAGUE*
DAHOMEY QUEEN	*PAULA KELLY*
DAWSON	*J.A. PRESTON*
DO-DADDY DEAN	*PAUL BUTLER*
STUD DAVIS	*DON BLAKELY*

PRETTY WILLIE	*DAVID LEMIEUX*
GENERAL	*BYRON MORROW*
CARSTAIRS	*JACK AARON*
SENATOR HENNINGTON	*JOSEPH MASCOLO*
MRS. HENNINGTON	*ELAINE AIKEN*
WILLA	*BEVERLY DILL*
CALHOUN	*BOB HILL*
PERKINS	*MARTIN GOLAR*
POLICEMAN	*JEFF HAMILTON*
OLD WOMAN	*MARGARET KROMGOLS*
SECURITY OFFICER	*TOM ALDERMAN*
COLONEL	*STEPHEN FERRY*
DORIS	*KATHY BERK*
BOY GUARDSMAN	*STEPHEN FERRY II*
TV COMMENTATOR	*FRANK LESLEY*
JACKSON	*HAROLD JOHNSON*
SHORTY	*ANTHONY RAY*
MRS. DUNCAN	*AUDREY STEVENSON*
STEW	*JOHN CHARLES*
MR. SOO	*PONCIANO OLAYTA JR.*
INSTRUCTOR II	*SIDNEY EDEN*
DANCER	*COLOSTINE BOATWRIGHT*
WAITER	*JOHNNY WILLIAMS*
WOMAN I	*CORA WILLIAMS*
WOMAN II	*BOBBIE DENE WILLIAMS*
STUNT GAFFER	*ERNIE ROBINSON*
TRAINEES 1–9	*DOUG JOHNSON*
	LENARD NORRIS
	MARK WILLIAMS

	WALTER LOWE
	ROBERT FRANKLIN
	HAROLD HARRIS
	JIM HEARD
	KENNETH LEE ORME
	DON GREENLEE
COBRAS	*JOHNNIE JOHNSON III*
	FRANK E. FORD
	MAURICE WICKS
	PERRY THOMAS
	CLINTON MALCOME
	ORLANDERS THOMAS
	LARRY LAWRENCE
	RODNEY MCGRADER
	TYRONE R. LIVINGSTON
	RAMON LIVINGSTON
	JAMES MITCHELL
	VIRGIE JOHNSON
DIRECTOR	*IVAN DIXON*
SCREENPLAY	*SAM GREENLEE*
	MELVIN CLAY

FROM THE NOVEL "THE SPOOK WHO SAT BY THE DOOR" BY SAM GREENLEE

PRODUCED BY	*IVAN DIXON*
	SAM GREENLEE
	THOMAS G. NEUSOM (ASSOCIATE PRODUCER)
MUSIC	*HERBIE HANCOCK*
CINEMATOGRAPHY	*MICHEL HUGO*

FILM EDITING	*MICHAEL KAHN*
	THOMAS PENICK
ART DIRECTION	*A. LESLIE THOMAS*
SET DECORATION	*CHERYAL KEARNEY*
SOUND MIXER	*JOHN SPEAK*
SPECIAL EFFECTS	*LOGAN FRAZEE*
STUNTS	*HARRY ABDUL MOORE*
STUNT COORDINATOR	*CHARLIE PICERNI*
STUNT GAFFER	*ERNEST ROBINSON*
CAMERA OPERATOR	*ANGELO DELLUTRI*
KEY GRIP	*LLOYD ISBELL*
GAFFER	*RALPH MCCARTHY*
BEST BOY	*EUGENE SIMPSON*
DOLLY GRIP	*EDDIE WILLIS*
CASTING ASSISTANT	*CASSIUS WEATHERSBY*
WARDROBE	*HENRY SALLEY*
PRODUCTION COORDINATOR	*R.J. LOUIS*
LOCATION PROJECTIONIST: DAILIES	*JERRY WHITTINGTON*

APPENDIX A

PRESS KIT

From the Hatch-Billops Collection. Courtesy Black Film Center/Archive, Indiana University, Bloomington, Indiana.

United Artists Pressbook

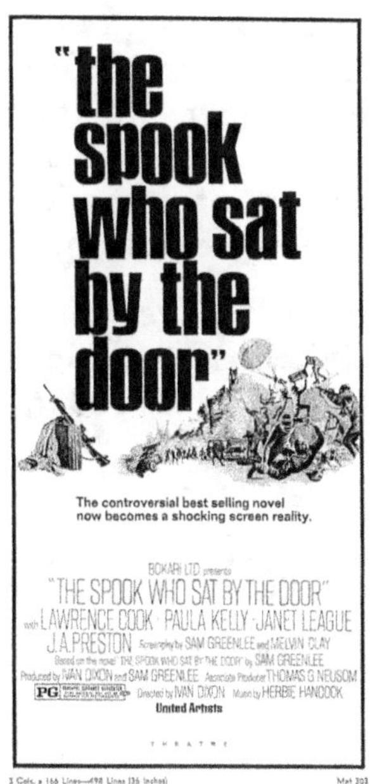

3 Cols. x 166 Lines—498 Lines (36 Inches) Mat 303

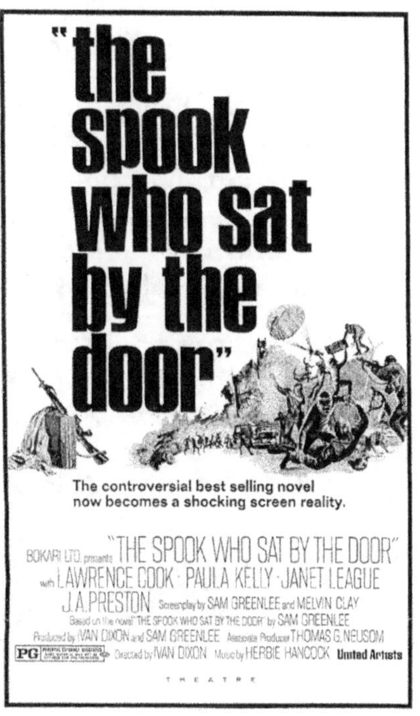

3 Cols. x 133 Lines—400 Lines (28 Inches) Mat 302

SPECIAL MAT No. 1

The following ads and scenes are available on a composite mat at a special low price at National Screen:

Ads: 101, 102, 201, 202, 203, 204
Scenes: 1A and 2A

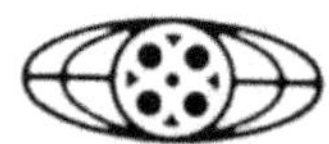

APPROVED

All advertising in this pressbook, as well as all other advertising and publicity materials referred to herein, has been approved under the standards for Advertising of the Code of Self-Regulation of the Motion Picture Association of America. All inquiries on this procedure may be addressed to:

Director of the Code of Advertising
Motion Picture Association of America
522 Fifth Avenue, N. Y., N. Y. 10036

This picture was rated:

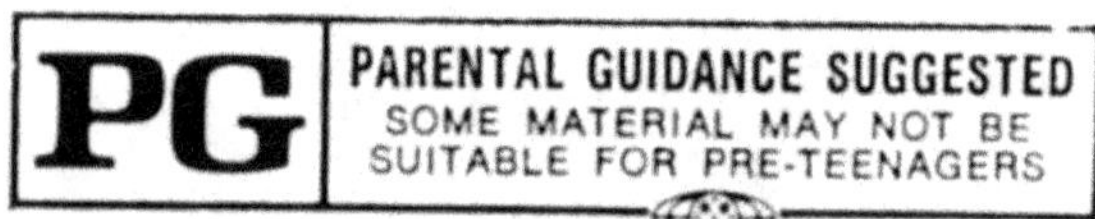

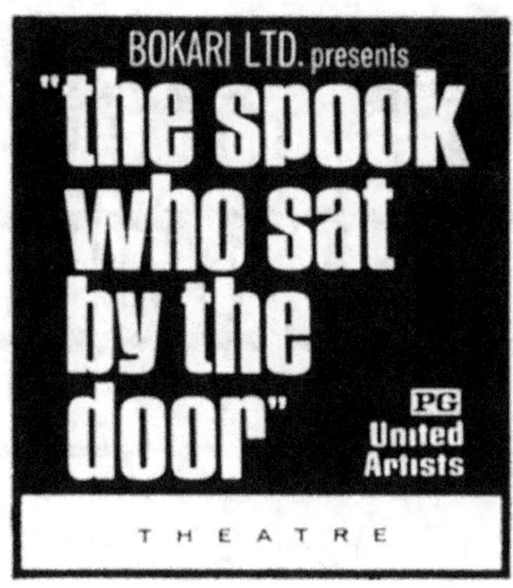

1 Col. x 28 Lines (2 Inches)
Mat 102

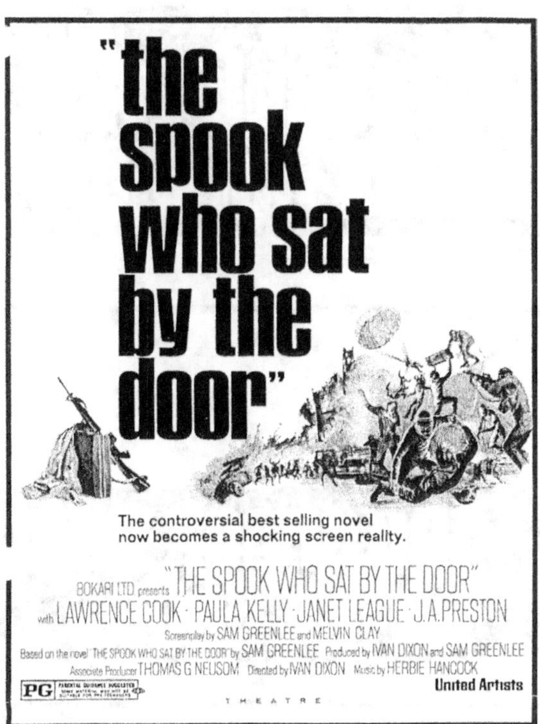

3 Cols. x 105 Lines—315 Lines (22 Inches) Mat 301

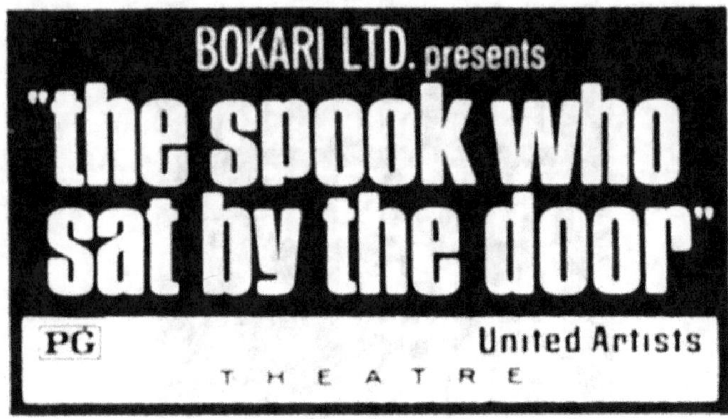

1 Col. x 14 Lines (1 Inch)
Mat 101

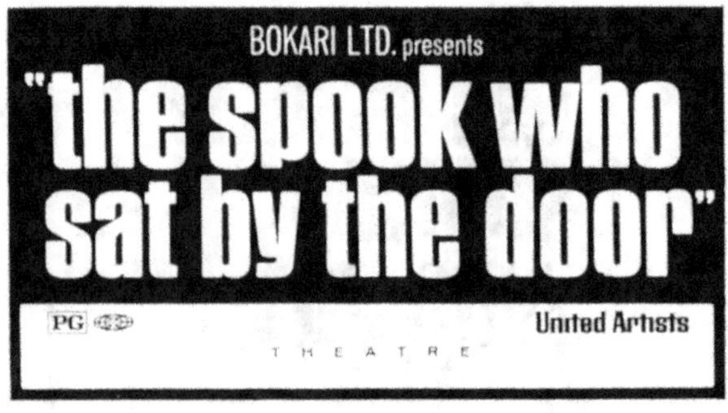

2 Cols. x 28 Lines—56 Lines (4 Inches) Mat 202

PAGE 3

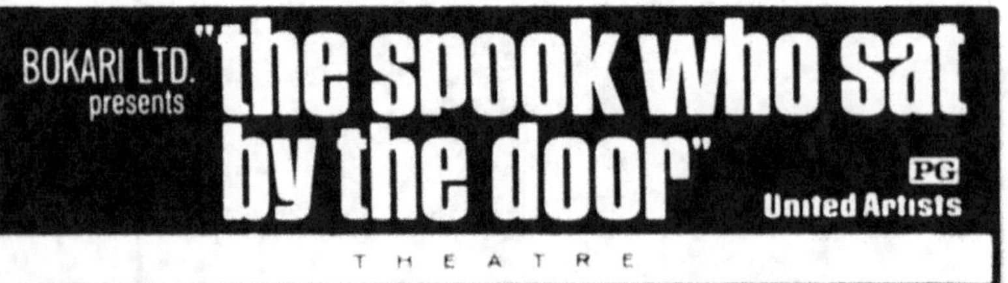

2 Cols. x 14 Lines—28 Lines (2 Inches) Mat 201

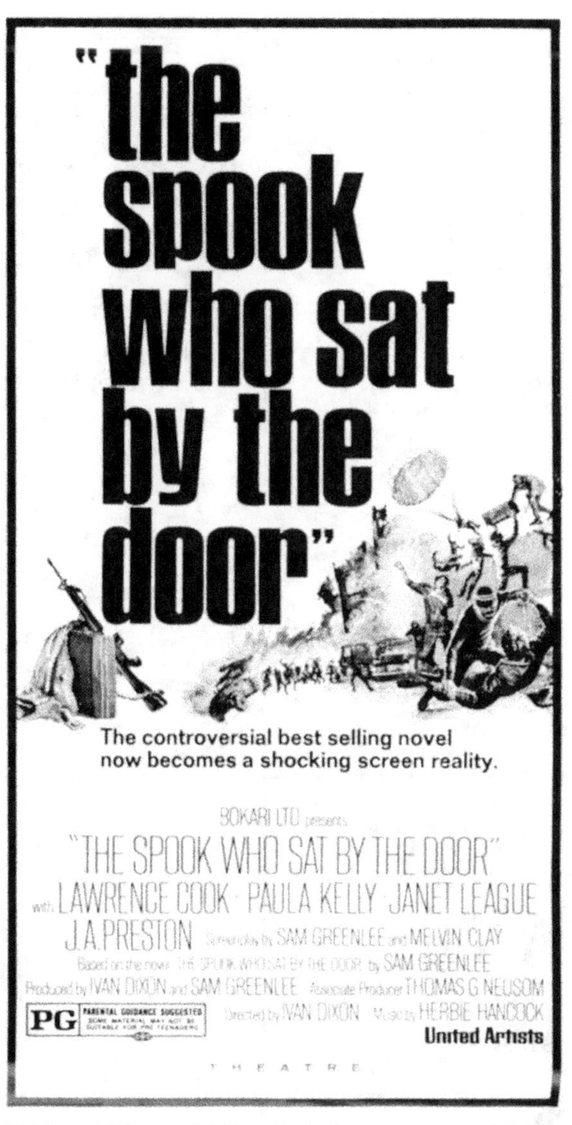

2 Cols. x 100 Lines—200 Lines (14 Inches) Mat 204

Order Ad Mats From

National Screen

Official Billing

BOKARI LTD. PRESENTS	35%
"THE SPOOK WHO SAT BY THE DOOR"	100%
With	
LAWRENCE COOK	75%
PAULA KELLY	75%
JANET LEAGUE	75%
J. A. PRESTON	75%
Screenplay by	
SAM GREENLEE and MELVIN CLAY	35%
Based on the novel "The SPOOK WHO SAT BY THE DOOR" By SAM GREENLEE	
Produced by	
IVAN DIXON and SAM GREENLEE	35%
Associate Producer	
THOMAS G. NEUSOM	35%
Directed by	
IVAN DIXON	35%
Music by	
HERBIE HANCOCK	35%
UNITED ARTISTS	35%

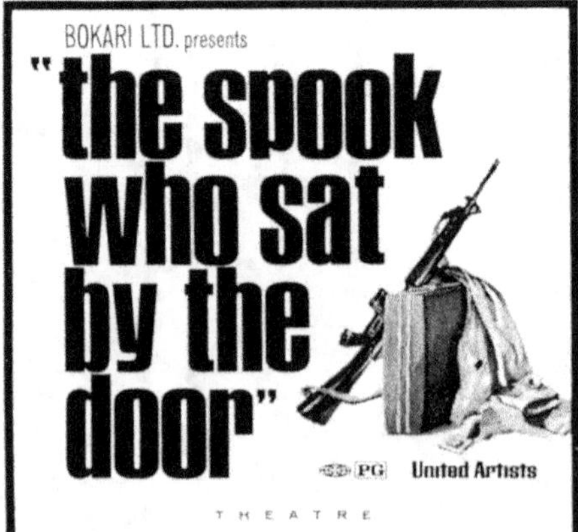

2 Cols. x 49 Lines—98 Lines (7 Inches) Mat 203

PUBLICITY MATERIAL

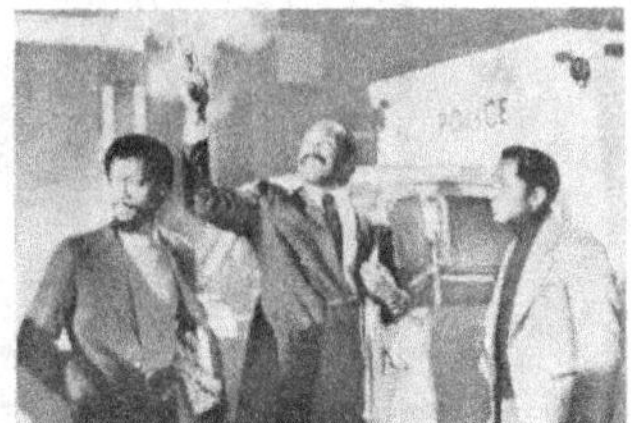

Still SD-1 *Mat 2A*

Lawrence Cook and Martin Golar look on as J. A. Preston, playing a police official, fires his flare pistol in an attempt to control a riot in "The Spook Who Sat By The Door," which will be shown starting...... at the...... Theatre through United Artists release.

'The Spook Who Sat By Door' Story About Black CIA Agent

(Advance Production Feature)

"The Spook Who Sat By The Door," a film based on Sam Greenlee's best selling novel, was produced by Ivan Dixon and Greenlee. It is the story of the first Black CIA agent who uses his training in undercover guerrilla tactics to organize a Black Revolution in major American cities. The picture will open .... at the .... Theatre through release by United Artists.

Lawrence Cook is starred as Dan Freeman, the Black CIA agent; Paula Kelly and Janet League provide the romantic interest, and J. A. Preston portrays Dawson, a Black detective, an old friend of Freeman whose loyalties are tested by race and duty.

'Spook' Picture From Greenlee's Best-Seller

Soon after the publication of "The Spook Who Sat By The Door," novelist Sam Greenlee began thinking in terms of a motion picture based on the book, which by then had become a best-seller. The film project officially got rolling when Greenlee formed a partnership with actor-director Ivan Dixon.

Dixon and Greenlee became co-producers; Greenlee wrote a screenplay in collaboration with Melvin Clay, and Dixon took over the directorial reins. The film will open ...... at the ...... Theatre through United Artists release.

Sam Greenlee soon discovered that being a motion picture producer exposed him to a new and complex world of film financing as well as a host of logistical and personnel problems far removed from his familiar arena as a writer and teacher.

Greenlee was born in Chicago, educated at the University of Wisconsin, where he received a degree in Political Science; did graduate work in International Relations at the University of Chicago, and then served with the United States Information Agency in Iraq, East Pakistan, Indonesia and Greece. He resigned in 1965 to devote full time to writing. He has written three novels, a play, published five short stories and a book of poetry.

Greenlee had difficulty finding a publisher for "The Spook Who Sat By The Door" because of its brutal frankness about the CIA and Black revolution. Two young British publishers accepted the challenge and the book became a best-seller in England and prizewinner (Book of the Year Award) from the London Times and London Telegraph.

When the novel was finally published in the United States, the American critics and public acclaimed it "as one of the most compelling books in the country today." It has since been translated into Swedish, Finnish, Dutch, Italian, German, Japanese and French and is a popular topic for discussion in college courses in contemporary American literature.

Now A Movie

Author Sam Greenlee was not content to sit back and enjoy the success of his controversial, best-selling novel, "The Spook Who Sat By The Door." He believed it had powerful potential as a motion picture and set out to prove it. The result is the new film, "The Spook Who Sat By The Door," which

Lawrence Cook, the handsome Black actor who heads the professional cast, was born in New York. He attended New York University where he majored in Dramatic Arts, and subsequently appeared on the stage in "The Blacks," "Mac Bird," "The Great White Hope" and "Wrong Way Light Bulb."

His principal film credits include three United Artists releases: "Cotton Comes to Harlem," "The Angel Levine" and "The Landlord." He also was in "The Man" and "Trouble Man."

Television audiences have seen Cook in "Mod Squad," "Dan August," "Search," "Cannon" and in the teleplay, "Caught In The Middle."

In the film, Freeman, a social worker, is recruited for the CIA by Carstairs, a white man and one of the top officers of the intelligence agency. For the role of Carstairs, director Dixon signed Jack Aaron, a New York actor, who won instant recognition from the Gary spectators the moment he stepped onto the set. They remembered him as the man who said, "Try It, You'll Like It," in the Alka Seltzer commercial.

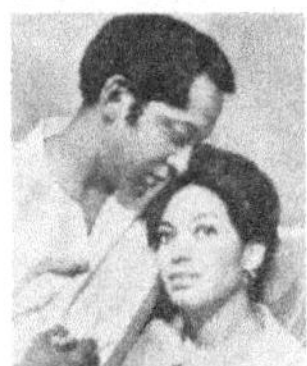

SD-19 *Mat 1A*

Lawrence Cook plays the first Black to be admitted to the ranks of the CIA, and Janet League is his girlfriend in "The Spook Who Set By The Door," a United Artists release now playing at the ...... Theatre.

Greenlee co-produced with Ivan Dixon and scripted in collaboration with Melvin Clay. Dixon also directed the movie, and Herbie Hancock composed the music.

Lawrence Cook, Paula Kelly, Janet League and J. A. Preston head the cast, and Bakari Ltd. presents the United Artists release.

POSTERS AND ACCESSORIES

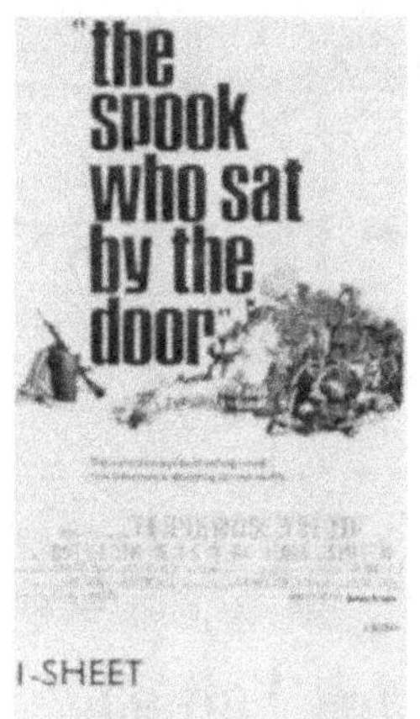

1-SHEET

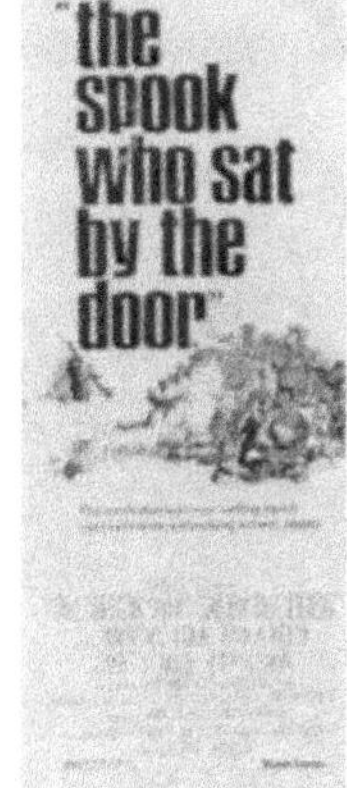

14 x 36
INSERT
CARD

Also
Available:

•

Set of Eight
8 x 10 Color Stills

•

Set of Eight
11 x 14's
Lobby Cards

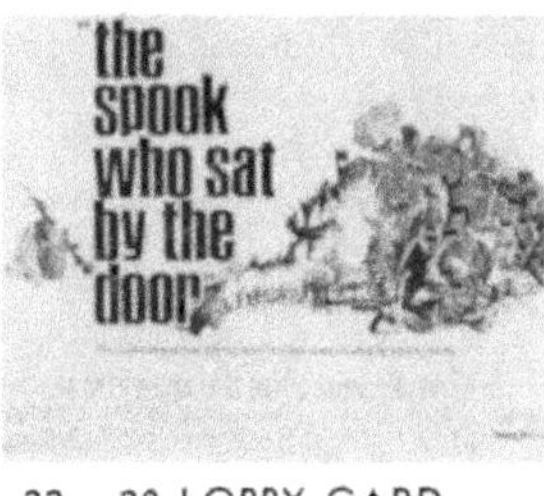

22 x 28 LOBBY CARD

Order From
National Screen

FREE TV/Radio Spots!

There are a set of Television and Radio Spot announcements available for a full advertising campaign on the air. Order your sets right away. They are available from:

Domestic Distribution Advertising Dept.
United Artists Corp.
729 Seventh Avenue, N. Y. 10019

ART STILL

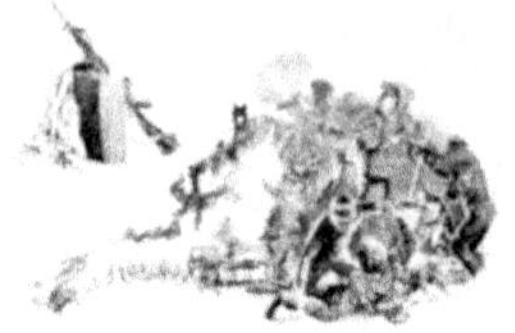

SD-ART I

Order By Number
From National Screen

Bantam Paperback Edition

Sam Greenlee's best-selling novel, upon which he based his screenplay, has been issued in a motion picture paperback edition by Bantam Books and is on sale wherever paperbacks are sold. Contact local outlets and supply them with posters and stills for counter and window displays. Perhaps you can get a bookshop to devote a window or counter to a complete display of the hardcover and paperback with ribbons connecting stills to corresponding pages of the books.

Also print a quantity of the one-column ads to be distributed as book-marks at bookstores, libraries and your theatre in advance of playdate.

The Cast

Dan Freeman ... Lawrence Cook
Dahomey Queen ... Paula Kelly
Joy ... Janet League
Dawson ... J. A. Preston
Do-Daddy Dean ... Paul Butler
Stud Davis ... Don Blakely
Pretty Willie ... David Lemieux
General ... Byron Morrow
Carstairs ... Jack Aaron
Senator Hennington ... Joseph Mascolo
Willa ... Beverly Gill
Calhoun ... Bob Hill
Perkins ... Martin Golar

Production Staff

Produced by ... Ivan Dixon and Sam Greenlee
Directed by ... Ivan Dixon
Screenplay by ... Sam Greenlee and Melvin Clay
Music by ... Herbie Hancock
Director of Photography ... Michel Hugo
Camera Operators ... Joseph Wilcots and Angelo De LLutri
Film Editor ... Michael Kahn
Sound ... John Speak

UNITED ARTISTS

Running Time: 102 Minutes

PRINTED IN U. S. A.

APPENDIX B

NATIONAL FILM REGISTRY ENTRY, *THE SPOOK WHO SAT BY THE DOOR*

Michael T. Martin and David C. Wall

Based on Sam Greenlee's provocative 1969 novel and, some say, urban revolutionary primer of the same name, Ivan Dixon's *The Spook Who Sat by the Door* (1973) tells the story of Dan Freeman, erstwhile CIA operative and consummate revolutionary organizer. Aware of his status as the CIA's token affirmative-action trainee, recruited in order to demonstrate the agency's commitment to racial integration, Freeman's carefully considered strategy is to maintain a low profile even while excelling at all of the agency's tests for both intellectual and physical prowess. Thus, unfailingly polite and apparently always eager to please, he is the living embodiment of Ellison's invisible man, "yessing whitey to death" while discreetly learning everything he possibly can about urban guerrilla warfare. Finishing his apprenticeship with the CIA, he returns to Chicago and proceeds to organize the Freedom Fighters, a clandestine militia, out of the disparate and ill-disciplined Cobras street gang of his former neighborhood.

In many ways, *The Spook Who Sat by the Door* is very much a product in correspondence with its historical moment. Greenlee, who himself had worked as a Foreign Service Officer for the United States Information Agency in Iraq, East Pakistan, and Indonesia during the 1950s to mid-1960s, conceived of his novel while living in Mykonos, Greece, in the summer of 1965. In response to decolonization struggles throughout Africa and Asia, as well as the increasingly fraught and fractious trajectories of the civil rights movement in the United States, Greenlee "determined to write the story of a Third World colonial revolution as it might happen in the United States."[1] By the time the novel was published in the United States in 1969, the rhetoric of nonviolent protest as embodied in Martin Luther King Jr.'s SCLC (Southern Christian Leadership Conference) had been rivaled by more militant voices of "black power," most notably those of SNCC (Student Nonviolent Coordinating Committee) and the Black Panthers. This in turn reflected a broader radicalization of social protest manifest increasingly by such disparate revolutionary organizations as the White Panthers, the Black Liberation Army, the Symbionese Liberation Army, Weather Underground, and the broad anti-Vietnam war coalition in solidarity with other anticolonial struggles in the global south. Further, events such as the police riot in Chicago at the 1968 Democratic Convention and subsequent show trials of the Chicago Seven, the 1968 assassinations of Martin Luther King Jr. and Robert F. Kennedy, the 1969 assassination of Chicago Black Panther Fred Hampton, and the murder of students at Kent State and Jackson State, all attest to the volatility and indeterminacy of American society in the years leading up to the release of *The Spook Who Sat by the Door* in 1973. Reflecting and refracting the tumult of these febrile political and racial contexts and events, the film itself was no less incendiary in its uncompromising vision of an American society on the brink of revolution. The screenplay, written by Greenlee and Melvin Clay, offers a broadly nonorthodox Marxist social analysis rooted in Third World independence movements and combined with the radical racial discourses of thinkers such as Franz Fanon and Stokely Carmichael. Indeed, like Gillo Pontecorvo's *The Battle of Algiers* (1966) and *Burn!* [*Queimada!*] (1969) that foreground the peasantry and lumpenproletariat as vanguard in revolutionary formations, in *Spook* the urban underclass and other marginal groups practice agential authority, constituting the vanguard for revolutionary change rather than proletariat.

The film's director Ivan Dixon, who had first found fame as an actor in Michael Roemer's *Nothing but a Man* (1964) followed by his role as Sergeant James Kinchloe in the CBS sitcom *Hogan's Heroes* (1965–1971), shared with Greenlee a determination to present black agency, black heroes, and powerful black characters who refuse to comply with the dominant tropes and stereotypes of Hollywood's representations of race. But they were also concerned to lay an economic critique across the vectors of race. This conjoining of determinant categories of both race and class are most clearly enunciated by Dan Freeman, instructing gang members that they understand themselves as a lumpenproletariat (read underclass), no less oppressed by the structural enclosures of class than by those of race. For example, at one critical point in the film, Freeman declares that the uprising is not about hating white people but in loving and longing for freedom for everyone. In this regard, the film is, arguably, most challenging by positing America's ghettoes as internal colonies and class struggle led by a black revolutionary vanguard but whose efficacy and success depends on solidarity across racial lines. (Consider, too, that when King conjoined racial discrimination and economic inequality as both symptoms of capitalism, his threat to ruling class interests was most amplified, sealing his fate.) Indeed, some of the film's most excoriating critique is reserved for the "black bourgeoisie" cast in the character of Joy (played by Janet League) who, as the wife of a prominent black doctor, articulates an unexamined investment in the social, economic, and racial status quo. Admonishing Dan, she defensively says, "Don't romanticize those people, Dan. They're not beautiful . . . those Freedom Fighters are murderers!" However, a corresponding female character, The Dahomey Queen (Paula Kelly), labors on behalf of the revolutionaries by spying on the CIA directorate's plans to quell the rebellion, thus speaking just as powerfully to black women's role in the struggle forward. In presenting the Dahomey Queen in this way, *Spook* proffers a conception of black women as freedom fighters no less important than their male counterparts. And, too, *Spook* conceives of a revolutionary practice that simultaneously engages the state security apparatus from within (by infiltrators, disaffected police and military personnel, and professionals) as it does from without by armed combatants.

As may be apparent from the description above, *Spook* is highly unusual for an American film in that its radical left-wing politics are so overt and explicit. In a general sense, any dominant cultural apparatus will always appropriate and transform initiatives that threaten to destabilize it. Consequently, any narrative and visual possibilities under hegemonic conditions of representation are perhaps inevitably compromised. And, indeed, the ideological and anti-systemic concerns in *Spook* did not trump economic ones in Hollywood's distribution of the film. Of some significance in this context, is the 1971 release of Melvin Van Peebles's independently financed *Sweet Sweetback's Baadasssss Song*. The film's massive success saw the major

Hollywood studios rush to replicate its themes and tropes and, in doing so, the emergence of what came to be termed blaxploitation cinema. But the political possibilities of blaxploitation in terms of its presentation of powerful black heroes, standing up to "the Man," and living entirely self-determined lives became rapidly compromised as the genre veered increasingly toward celebration of drugs and violence and the propagation of highly sexually charged black stereotypes.

United Artists response to this problematic film was to initially market *Spook* as a blaxploitation film, but it quickly became apparent that this was no ordinary blaxploitation flick. It is at this point that the historical and political contexts of the film collide and where the singular place that *The Spook Who Sat by the Door* occupies in the history of American political cinema becomes apparent. First, the production itself was subject to multiple obstacles. Though set in Chicago, the filmmakers (at the behest of then Mayor Richard Daley) were refused permission to film anywhere in the city. As a consequence, *Spook* was shot almost entirely just across state lines in Gary, Indiana, where the filmmakers were welcomed with an entire array of institutional support and resources (even being allowed the use of a Gary Police Department helicopter in order to get some overhead footage of the riot scenes.) Though in hindsight *Spook*'s assertion of the immediate possibility of armed revolution might seem a somewhat naive fantasy of resistance that could never have played out in an American context, at the time it was a theorized and commanding vision enough for the *LA Times*' Kevin Thomas to call the film "one of the most terrifying movies ever made."[2]

Many of those involved in the film's production believe that it was certainly subversive enough for the FBI to become involved with the quiet removal of the film from exhibition. In Christine Achem's documentary, "Infiltrating Hollywood: The Rise and Fall of *The Spook Who Sat by the Door*" (2011), Greenlee claims that movie theaters in Chicago were subject to visits from representatives of the FBI, advising that it would be in everybody's best interests if the film were pulled from display. Though there is no direct evidence for this, it is certainly a view widely held by all those involved in the film's production, and considering the dizzying array of disruptive tactics employed by Hoover's FBI and the COINTELPRO program from the late 1960s onward, it is certainly by no means far-fetched to consider this plausible. All original copies of the film disappeared except for one that the film's director, Ivan Dixon, secured in a storage facility under an assumed name. Having made the underground rounds on VHS throughout the 1980s and 1990s, Spook was finally rereleased on DVD in 2004, after which it has begun to receive the kind of critical and historical attention it demands.

NOTES

1. Sam Greenlee, "The Making of *The Spook Who Sat by the Door*" (unpublished email correspondence with authors, July 9, 2012).

2. Kevin Thomas, "Melodrama with Powerful Message," *The Los Angeles Times*, December 17, 1973.

The views expressed in these essays are those of the author and do not necessarily represent the views of the Library of Congress.

Michael T. Martin is Professor of Cinema and Media Studies in the Media School, Indiana University, Bloomington.

David Wall is Associate Professor of Visual and Media Studies in the Department of Art & Design, Utah State University in Logan, UT.

APPENDIX C

SAM GREENLEE: BIOGRAPHY AND SELECT BIBLIOGRAPHY

Biography

Sam Greenlee (1930–2014) was born in Chicago, Illinois. Growing up on the south side of the city, he was immersed from an early age in both politics and the arts. His mother performed on the stage as a singer and a dancer, while his father, who worked for the railroad company, was an active union member and organizer. Greenlee was both a gifted student and politically astute from an early age. As a teenager he became active in the National Association for the Advancement of Colored People when white students protested having to attend high school with black students. After his time at James McCosh grammar school and Englewood High, he attended the University of Wisconsin and subsequently the University of Chicago, where he studied international relations. Having spent two years as a lieutenant in the US Army's 31st Infantry "Dixie" Division, Greenlee then joined the US Information Agency (USIA) becoming one of their first African American recruits. He subsequently spent time with the USIA working in a number of countries, including Pakistan, Indonesia, Greece, and Iraq (where he received a meritorious service award for activities during the 1958 Qasim revolution.) He would later draw on these experiences widely for his second novel *Baghdad Blues*.

However, it was his first novel, *The Spook Who Sat by the Door*, for which he became most well-known. Greenlee began writing *Spook* in 1965 after visiting Chicago from his then home on the Greek island of Mykonos. The febrile atmosphere of racial tension in the United States, embodied most evocatively in the Watts rebellion in the summer of 1965, caused Greenlee to consider not only the possibility but also what he saw as the inevitability of armed revolution. Combining this with his own experiences working with the propaganda arm of the US government, he created the figure of Dan Freeman—erstwhile CIA operative and full-fledged revolutionary—and thus the novel's central premise that a Third World revolution might just as easily take place in the United States of America was born. Greenlee completed the manuscript in 1966 and spent the next three years trying to find a publisher. Rejected over forty times, *Spook* was eventually accepted by the newly formed Allison & Busby and published in the United Kingdom in 1969. A US publication followed from Bantam Books and then multiple editions in various countries around the world, with translations into German, Dutch, Finnish, Swedish, Italian, and Japanese. The film adaptation of the novel directed by Ivan Dixon and starring Lawrence Cook appeared in 1973. Plagued as it was by innumerable difficulties and hurdles, it was Sam Greenlee's belief that the movie suffered not only from the reluctance of Hollywood studios to finance the production because of its provocative subject matter but also from the active efforts of the FBI to get the film withdrawn from circulation shortly after its release. However, it is also the case that it is upon *The Spook Who Sat by the Door* that Greenlee's critical reputation rests.

A poet and playwright as well as novelist, Greenlee published three collections of verse, *Blues for an African Princess* (1971), *Ammunition: Poetry and Other Raps* (1975), and *Be-bop Man/Be-bop Woman 1968–1993: Poetry and Other Raps* (1995), as well as numerous short stories and plays. His second novel, *Baghdad Blues* (1976) picked up on, and continued, some of the themes that appeared in *Spook*. The main character Dave Burrell is an African American stationed at the American Embassy in Baghdad at the moment of the July 1958 revolution in Iraq that saw Abd al-Karim Qasim seize power in a coup d'état. The novel demonstrates the fundamental racism of the white American diplomatic corps in their treatment of Arab nationals, while painting a compelling picture of the Cold War paranoia that shaped US foreign policy in the region for decades. It is also a clear expression of the need for political solidarity among the dispossessed of both the first and third worlds. Though nowhere nearly as well known or as widely read as *Spook*, *Baghdad Blues* has had an increasing resonance in light of the history of US involvement in Iraq in the intervening forty years since the novel's publication.

Though a minor figure in the pantheon of African American letters, Greenlee is nevertheless assured a significant place not least as a consequence of the release of *Spook* on DVD in 2004. Though he worked on a handful of short films and wrote a screenplay treatment for a feature length movie version of his play *Lyssa Trotter*, his foray into filmmaking was brief. Seeing himself first and foremost as a writer, he was always deeply critical of the American film industry and reserved particular criticism for those African American filmmakers who he saw as too concerned with appealing to white audiences and critics. All this notwithstanding, he was always acutely aware of the cinematic and cultural importance of *The Spook Who Sat by the Door*. As he himself said, "If I never made another film, look at the film I made."[1]

Select Bibliography

Novels

The Spook Who Sat by the Door (London: Allison & Busby, 1969).
Baghdad Blues (New York: Bantam Books, 1976).

Poetry

Blues for an African Princess (Chicago: Third World Press, 1971).
Ammunition!: Poetry and Other Raps (London: Bogle-L'Ouverture, 1975).
Be-Bop Man/Be-Bop Woman, 1968–1993: Poetry and Other Raps (Cambrea Heights, NY: Natiki, 1995).

Short Stories

"Yes, We Can Sing," *Negro Digest* (December 1965).
"The Sign," *Negro Digest* (February 1966).
"Summer Sunday," *Negro Digest* (September 1966).
"Autumn Leaves," *Negro Digest* (January 1967).
"The D.C. Blues," *Negro Digest* (June 1969).
"Sonny's Seasons," *Black World* (October 1970).
"Sonny's Not Blue," in Woodie King, ed., *Black Short Story Anthology* (New York: Signet, 1972).
"Blues for Little Prez," *Black World* (August 1973), reprinted in Sascha Feinstein and David Rife, eds., *The Jazz Fiction Anthology* (Indiana University Press, 2009).

NOTE

1. *New York Times*, May 31, 2014, B8.

APPENDIX D

IVAN DIXON: BIOGRAPHY AND SELECT FILMOGRAPHY

Biography

Born April 6, 1931, in Harlem and died March 16, 2008, in Charlotte, North Carolina, at age seventy-six, Ivan Nathaniel Dixon III grew up in the South and graduated in drama from North Carolina Central University in 1954. Soon after, he appeared on Broadway in *Cave Dwellers* (1957) by William Saroyan followed by a role as a Nigerian student visiting America in Lorraine Hansberry's *A Raisin in the Sun* (1959).

A director, producer, and actor of extraordinary range and depth, Dixon's contribution to American cinema and television is as diverse as it is compelling. While best known for his memorable role as the radio technician, Sgt. Kinchloe, on the popular 1960s sitcom *Hogan's Heroes*, Dixon, however, according to his daughter Doris Nomahande Dixon, was most proud of his starring role in the character driven drama, *Nothing But a Man* (1964) by Michael Roemer and Robert Young; a seminal film evoking racial as well as class divides that resonates to this day among audiences and continues to be the subject of study, teaching, and critical and popular acclaim.

Along such lines as acting, until he took to directing in 1970, Dixon appeared largely in television series, among them *Perry Mason, The Twilight Zone, Laramie, The Fugitive,* and *I Spy*; he was cast with Sidney Poitier in the film *A Patch of Blue* (1965). Later, he performed the title role of a World War

II and Korean War veteran in *The Final War of Olly Winter* (1967), for which he was nominated for an Emmy Award.

Dixon's transition to director was for the most part in television. His directorial credits include episodes in the TV series and movies *The Rockford Files, The Bionic Woman, Magnum, P.I., The A-Team, The Waltons, Starsky & Hutch,* and *In the Heat of the Night,* and in film, the blaxploitation action thriller *Trouble Man* (1972). Arguably, Dixon's directorial prowess is most evident in the screen adaptation of Sam Greenlee's novel of the same title, *The Spook Who Sat by the Door* (1973), to which this volume calls attention. Here, too, his daughter claims, *Spook* was the film for which Dixon was most proud, together with his acting role in *Nothing But a Man.*

Filmography

The following filmography is not intended to be exhaustive in either content or detail. It is however a good reflection on the range, extent, and length of Ivan Dixon's life in film and television. Hopefully it will also serve as a productive starting point for any reader who might wish to conduct further research into Ivan Dixon's career.

Director – Television

The Bill Cosby Show	NBC 1970–71 [3 episodes]
Room 222	ABC 1970–71 [4 episodes]
Nichols	NBC 1971–72 [4 episodes]
The Sty of the Blind Pig	PBS 1973 [TV movie]
The Waltons	NBC 1972–81 [7 episodes]
The Rockford Files	NBC 1974–80 [9 episodes]
Palms Precinct	NBC 1982 [TV movie]
Bret Maverick	NBC 1981–82 [3 episodes]
The Greatest American Hero	ABC 1981–83 [6 episodes]
Magnum, P.I.	CBS 1980–88 [13 episodes]
In the Heat of the Night	NBC 1988–92 [1 episode]
Brewster Place	ABC 1990 [3 episodes]
Percy & Thunder	TNT 1990 [TV movie]

Director – Film

The Spook Who Sat by the Door	Los Angeles: United Artists, 1973.

Actor – Television

Have Gun—Will Travel	CBS 1961 [1 episode]
Laramie	NBC 1962 [1 episode]
The New Breed	ABC 1962 [2 episodes]
Perry Mason	CBS 1962–63 [2 episodes]
Dr. Kildare	NBC 1962–64 [2 episodes]
The Outer Limits	ABC 1963–64 [3 episodes]
The Twilight Zone	CBS 1964 [2 episodes]
The Fugitive	ABC 1963–67 [2 episodes]
Hogan's Heroes	CBS 1965–70 [145 episodes]
Ironside	NBC 1967–75 [1 episode]
The Final War of Olly Winter	CBS 1967 [TV play]
The Name of the Game	NBC 1968–71 [2 episodes]
The Mod Squad	ABC 1968–73 [1 episode]
Love, American Style	ABC 1969–74 [2 episodes]
Perry Mason: The Case of the Shooting Star	NBC 1986 [TV movie]

Actor – Film

Something of Value, directed by Richard Brooks (Los Angeles: MGM, 1957).
Porgy and Bess, directed by Otto Preminger (Los Angeles: Columbia Pictures, 1959).
A Raisin in the Sun, directed by Daniel Petrie (Los Angeles: Columbia Pictures, 1961).
Nothing But a Man, directed by Michael Roemer (New York: Du Art Film, 1964).
A Patch of Blue, directed by Guy Green (Los Angeles: MGM, 1965).
Suppose They Gave a War and Nobody Came?, directed by Hy Averbeck (ABC, 1970).
Clay Pigeon, directed by Lane Slate, Tom Stern (Los Angeles: MGM, 1971).
Car Wash, directed by Michael Schultz (Los Angeles: Universal, 1976).

Christine Acham is Associate Professor of the Practice of Cinematic Arts Program Coordinator at University of Southern California School of Cinematic Arts. She is author of *Revolution Televised: Prime Time and the Struggle for Black Power*. She also codirected and edited the award-winning documentary *Infiltrating Hollywood: The Rise and Fall of the Spook Who Sat by the Door*, which has screened at over twenty national and international film festivals and universities.

Michael T. Martin is Professor of Cinema and Media Studies in the Media School at Indiana University, Bloomington. He is the editor or coeditor of six anthologies, including *Redress for Historical Injustices in the United States: On Reparations for Slavery, Jim Crow, and Their Legacies* and *The Politics and Poetics of Black Film: "Nothing But a Man"* (IUP). He also directed and coproduced the award-winning feature documentary on Nicaragua *In the Absence of Peace*, distributed by Third World Newsreel.

Samantha N. Sheppard is Assistant Professor of Cinema and Media Studies at Cornell University. She worked on UCLA Film & Television Archive's LA Rebellion Preservation Project, and her ongoing scholarship explores how race plays a central role in sports films' generic representations.

David C. Wall is Associate Professor of Visual and Media Studies at Utah State University. He coedited *The Politics and Poetics of Black Film: "Nothing But a Man"* (IUP). Other recent work can be found in *Nineteenth-Century Studies* and *A Companion to the Historical Film*.

Marilyn Yaquinto is Associate Professor of Communication and Interdisciplinary Studies at Truman State University in Missouri. She is author of *Pump 'Em Full of Lead: A Look at Gangsters on Film* and coeditor of *Redress for Historical Injustices in the United States: On Reparations for Slavery, Jim Crow, and Their Legacies*. Dr. Yaquinto is a former journalist for the *Los Angeles Time* and shares in its Pulitzer Prize for spot news coverage of the 1992 LA riots linked to the Rodney King incident.

INDEX

www.ingramcontent.com/pod-product-compliance
Lightning Source LLC
LaVergne TN
LVHW020432080826
844660LV00034B/1403

* 9 7 8 0 2 5 3 0 3 1 7 9 2 *